Praise for *Artificial Intelligence Marketing and Predicting Consumer Choice*

'Full of hard-won practical wisdom, this is ... the complexity of market forecasting. Fore... characterizes discussions of artificial intell... ...thoroughly explains a wide range of methods, where their difficulties lie and how to get the best insights from each.' **Peter Goldstein, Software Engineer, Google**

'Dr Struhl's new book is a rare jewel among marketing science tomes – informative, easy to understand and, dare I say, even entertaining. Dr Struhl surveys several major analytic techniques in plain English, introducing the novice to foundational concepts while at the same time reminding the seasoned analyst of best practices often forgotten, all while sprinkling his wry humour like a spoonful of sugar to help the medicine go down. For techniques already familiar, it's an enjoyable refresher; for techniques unfamiliar, an excellent introduction. A valuable resource for beginner and expert alike.' **Dr Richard McCullough, President, Macro Consulting Inc**

'This book covers lucidly a number of research methodologies that commonly support very important new product development and marketing strategy decisions. Dr Struhl should be commended for making the materials accessible to a wide range of audiences by emphasizing the practicality, appropriateness, and pros and cons of the various methodologies.' **Jehoshua Eliashberg, Sebastian S Kresge Professor of Marketing, and Professor of Operations, Information and Decisions, The Wharton School**

'Dr Struhl has written another highly informative book. It offers an easy-to-understand way of thinking about how to best use data to answer bigger marketing questions. His explanations are clear and relatable, making this book an invaluable tool for anyone involved in commercial decision making, especially marketers and researchers.' **Katie Szelc, Manager, Customer Insights, Global Business Insights, Johnson & Johnson Medical Devices**

'An excellent all-in-one primer for today's marketer and researcher. This is clear, to the point and a comprehensive guide to this complex field.' **Louis A Tucci PhD, Associate Professor of Marketing, The College of New Jersey**

'Dr Struhl does an excellent job of explaining the strengths and weaknesses of methods of predicting consumer behaviour. This book is thoughtful, well-written, and also a practical book for marketers, marketing researchers and business consultants. If you help organizations make decisions, the best decision you can make right now is to read this book.' **David F Harris, author of *The Complete Guide to Writing Questionnaires: How to get better information for better decisions***

'*Artificial Intelligence Marketing and Predicting Consumer Choice* clearly explains the tools that drive sophisticated market research. I heartily recommend this book for anyone looking for greater insight and success with cutting-edge techniques.' **Robert Kaminsky, President, MedSpan Research**

'For researchers who want to tackle the complex tasks of predicting consumer choices and creating market simulations, this book is a great one-stop reference. In easy-to-read style with plenty of useful examples, the author covers conventional multivariate data analysis techniques (conjoint, discrete choice, CHAID, regression) as well as the latest ones (Hierarchical Bayesian analysis). The book also includes many key concepts and definitions useful for any quantitative researcher, such as statistical significance, sampling, and more.' **Kathryn Korostoff, Lead Instructor and Founder, Research Rockstar LLC**

'This book covers an extensive set of methods for predicting consumer choices, including conjoint analysis, discrete choice modelling, neural networks, classification trees, Bayesian methods, and so much more. Dr Struhl has written a genuinely practical guide to predictive analytics that is so easy, it reads like a bedtime reader. Having been a practitioner in this area for over 20 years, I found this book to not only be informative for a pertinent 21st century topic, but also a fun read.' **Don Meyer, Client Director, Analytics, AC Nielsen**

'I've been working with Dr Struhl for the past two and a half years and am truly impressed by his expertise. His book covers a truly expansive range of methods for predicting consumer choices. These include neural networks, ensembles, Bayesian Networks and classification trees. He also talks about how more established methods such as conjoint analysis and discrete choice modelling have benefited from machine learning methods. Here you will find the best applications of each approach, with plenty of examples from real life, showing what works and what does not. The online, downloadable simulator programs are incredibly impressive and show you the amazing things that can be done in the realm of predictions.' **Sung Lee, President, The Research Associates**

'This book covers a truly expansive range of methods for predicting consumer choices. Some of these include conjoint analysis, discrete choice modelling, neural networks, classification trees, and Bayesian networks. With practical tips and examples, and a welcome use of humour, this is a clear, easy-to-read and definitive guide for experts and novices alike.' **Paul Nisbet PhD, President, One Research**

'Steven Struhl's decades of experience as an analytics guru in real-world marketing applications shine through in this highly readable guide to modern analyses and models of consumer choices. In engaging and entertaining style, brimming with practical examples, without abstruse theory or sales hype, his book is a down-to-earth and much-needed guide that clears up the mysteries of these methods.' **Dave Lyon, Principal, Aurora Market Modeling**

'Dr Struhl has done it again! He's taken a cutting-edge topic and grounded it in very accessible prose, using real-life situations so that marketing and market research practitioners can immediately act upon Artificial Intelligence and its ability to predict consumer choice. I strongly recommend this book for anyone wanting to better understand how to use the growing presence of Artificial Intelligence and machine learning in our day-to-day responsibilities.' **Darrin Helsel, Past Research Chair, American Marketing Association, Portland**

'Dr Struhl's latest book, *Artificial Intelligence Marketing and Predicting Consumer Choice*, provides concrete and easy-to-understand information about a set of analyses that can be intimidating for researchers and clients alike. His examples are clear and applicable to the concepts being discussed and provide excellent insights into how these valuable analytical techniques can be used to answer real-life business questions. In addition, Dr Struhl also writes with a sense of humour which helps to make readers comfortable and the material even more readily understandable. This book is an excellent resource for both market research suppliers and clients!' **Julie Worwa MBA, Research and Marketing Consultant**

'Steven Struhl has a gift for taking complex methodological issues and explaining them in accessible, meaningful language. His writing is thought-provoking and entertaining. *Artificial Intelligence Marketing and Predicting Consumer Choice* tackles many of the contemporary challenges of turning an abundance of data into crucial insights. It is a must-read for anyone who is exploring the use of artificial intelligence methods to inform marketing tactics and strategies.' **Larry Durkin, Senior Consultant, MSP Analytics**

Artificial Intelligence Marketing and Predicting Consumer Choice

An overview of tools and techniques

Steven Struhl

KoganPage

Publisher's note
Every possible effort has been made to ensure that the information contained in this book is accurate at the time of going to press, and the publisher and author cannot accept responsibility for any errors or omissions, however caused. No responsibility for loss or damage occasioned to any person acting, or refraining from action, as a result of the material in this publication can be accepted by the editor, the publisher or the author.

First published in Great Britain and the United States in 2017 by Kogan Page Limited

Apart from any fair dealing for the purposes of research or private study, or criticism or review, as permitted under the Copyright, Designs and Patents Act 1988, this publication may only be reproduced, stored or transmitted, in any form or by any means, with the prior permission in writing of the publishers, or in the case of reprographic reproduction in accordance with the terms and licences issued by the CLA. Enquiries concerning reproduction outside these terms should be sent to the publishers at the undermentioned addresses:

2nd Floor, 45 Gee Street	c/o Martin P Hill Consulting	4737/23 Ansari Road
London	122 W 27th St, 10th Floor	Daryaganj
EC1V 3RS	New York, NY 10001	New Delhi 110002
United Kingdom	USA	India

www.koganpage.com

All the Figures/diagrams in this book are original work by the author; where photographic and other elements have been incorporated from third-party sources, these have been acknowledged in source lines.

© Steven Struhl, 2017

The right of Steven Struhl to be identified as the author of this work has been asserted by him in accordance with the Copyright, Designs and Patents Act 1988.

ISBN   978 0 7494 7955 8
E-ISBN 978 0 7494 7956 5

British Library Cataloguing-in-Publication Data

A CIP record for this book is available from the British Library.

Library of Congress Cataloging-in-Publication Data

Names: Struhl, Steven M., author.
Title: Artificial intelligence marketing and predicting consumer choice : an overview of tools and techniques / Steven Struhl.
Description: 1st Edition. | New York : Kogan Page Ltd, [2017] | Includes bibliographical references and index.
Identifiers: LCCN 2016055015 (print) | LCCN 2017009070 (ebook) | ISBN 9780749479558 (alk. paper) | ISBN 9780749479565 (eISBN)
Subjects: LCSH: Marketing research. | Consumer behavior. | Artificial intelligence.
Classification: LCC HF5415.2 .S787 2017 (print) | LCC HF5415.2 (ebook) | DDC 658.800285/63–dc23

Typeset by Integra Software Services, Pondicherry
Print production managed by Jellyfish
Printed and bound by CPI Group (UK) Ltd, Croydon, CR0 4YY

CONTENTS

Preface xi

01 Who should read this book and why? 1
What we cover in this book 1
What can you expect in this book? 3
Data versus information 6
What is important? 8
The methods we will be discussing 10
Implicit views of people and biases 11
One way of comparing these methods 13
Sense and sensibility with predictions 15
Where we will not be going 20
Summary of key points 21

02 Getting the project going 27
At the beginning 27
Know who you are talking about or talking to 28
What is the most you can expect from each method? 31
How do you judge the result? 35
What is significant? 36
On to correlations 43
How do I plan to evaluate the results? 45
Know what sensible goals might look like 50
Summary of key points 51

03 Conjoint, discrete choice and other trade-offs: let's do an experiment 55
The reasons we need these methods 55
The basic thinking behind the experimentally designed methods 59
What the methods ask – and get 60
What is a designed experiment? 66
The great measurement power of experiments 70
Getting more from experiments: HB to the rescue 71

A brief talk about origins 74
Applications in brief 78
Summary of key points 80

04 Creating the best, newest thing: discrete choice modelling 85
Key features 85
Thinking through and setting up the problem 90
How many people you need 103
Utility and share 105
Market simulations 107
Making more than one choice: allocating purchases 114
Using the simulator program in the online resources 114
Rounding out the picture 118
Summary of key points 120

05 Conjoint analysis and its uses 127
Thinking in conjoint versus thinking in choices 127
Conjoint analysis for single-product optimization 132
Using the single product simulator in the online resources 133
Conjoint remains an excellent method for messages 136
Conjoint analysis for the best service delivery 147
Using the message optimization simulator in the online resources 152
Conjoint analysis and interactions 154
Variants of conjoint analysis 156
Summary of key points 159

06 Predictive models: via classifications that grow on trees 165
Classification trees: understanding an amazing analytical method 165
Seeing how trees work, step by step 166
Strong, yet weak 173
A case study: let's take a cruise 174
CHAID and CART (and CRT, C&RT, QUEST, J48 and others) 191
Summary: applications and cautions 194

07   Remarkable predictive models with Bayes Nets 197

What are Bayes Nets and how do they compare with other methods? 197
Let's make a deal 205
Our first example: Bayes Nets linking survey questions and behaviour 213
Bayes Nets confirm a theoretical model, mostly 218
What is important to buyers of children's apparel 223
Summary and conclusions 226

08   Putting it together: what to use when 229

The tasks the methods do 230
Thinking about thinking 235

Bibliography 237
Index 249

Bonus online-only materials are available at the following url:

www.koganpage.com/AI-Marketing

- Bonus online-only Chapter 1: Finishing experiments and on to the non-experimental world
- Bonus online-only Chapter 2: Artificial intelligence, ensembles and neural nets
- Online-only Simulators: three different simulators in Excel format, one in PowerPoint format and one in PDF (Adobe Acrobat) format, allowing you to interactively optimize products and messages. (You will need Flash Player installed on your computer for the PowerPoint format and PDF (Adobe Acrobat) format simulators to work.)

PREFACE

News and articles on **artificial intelligence** seem to be everywhere. At least they do if you are writing a book with the words 'artificial intelligence' in the title. But what is artificial intelligence?

Critical as this field is, it appears that there is no clear definition. A reporter went to Alphabet (formerly Google), the epicentre of artificial intelligence, and asked people working there for an explanation. Here are some of the answers:

'I would definitely interview someone else.'

'No thanks. Sorry. Good luck.'

'I don't know. I'll pass.'

'It's machine learning.'

'I work at Yahoo…'

Still, this topic is vitally important for you and for answering the increasingly difficult questions you are likely to encounter. This book will give you the practical information and pointers on applications that you need to know to succeed. But this is vital for your future campaigns, and this book will tell you what you need to know to get ahead.

In Chapter 1, we propose a working definition. There is no question that **artificial intelligence** and **machine learning**, if not in fact the same, overlap substantially. This of course raises the question of what machine learning means.

This definition also varies depending on who you ask, just like asking about the height of PT Barnum's elephant, Jumbo. (Jumbo was twelve foot six inches high if you asked Mr Barnum, and ten foot nine if you asked someone with a tape measure.)

An online article purporting to teach about machine learning included **regression** and **clustering** among advanced machine learning methods. These are two of the most august and long-standing of analytical approaches. Regression was widely used well before computers existed.

Even taking a less expansive definition, machine learning has been with us for decades. It has been working in the background as often as in the foreground, solving problems that would have been impossible to approach without it. This is worth noting separately.

> ### Hiding in plain sight
>
> We have been using machine artificial intelligence/learning methods for years. It has been an essential part of many methods used to predict consumer choices. We will be laying out some key applications and how they relate to artificial intelligence throughout this book.

Now that we have established that, or at least said it, we should give you some basic information so you know if you are about to sit down in the movie you wanted to see. We would like to give you some sense of who this author is anyhow, who is asking you to soldier through territories that are fraught with complexity, and often described with obscurity and obfuscation.

If you are peeking inside an online preview, or (rarity of rarities) looking at this in a book store, this could be your spot to decide if you want to continue to the next glance. If you looked here by mistake, then now could be the time to realize this was a lucky stroke after all.

This book aims to cut through much of the murky language, the jargon, recondite formulations, and even utter nonsense surrounding this field. We will have to go over vocabulary. But we will do this only so you will be prepared when you encounter such terms as **orthogonal design** and know that they are nothing to fear.

We will steer around equations, subscripted notation and Greek letters whenever possible. If you were hoping to see all of those, then this could be your cue to investigate elsewhere.

This book is not a guide to the types of services that vendors supply. Rather, we aim to describe enough about each method so that you get an idea of how it works – and, more importantly, how you best apply it. Reading this book will help you to deal with sellers as they approach you with their newest, latest things. The information you get here will enable you to evaluate their claims in an informed and suitably inquiring way.

Looking at other prefaces, this seems to be the place where I take a turn to the first person, and tell you a little about myself. You may be questioning how and why I came to write a book like this in the first place. Here's what I can come up with. I have been working in applying data analysis to practical problems for over 30 years. My clients have included many Fortune 100 companies, but also a host of mid-size and smaller entities, along with charitable, educational and non-profit organizations. I run a consulting company, Converge Analytic, specializing in advanced analytics.

I have written over 25 articles and two other books, one of which has been in print for over 20 years. You can see both on Amazon (and even buy them, not that I am hinting at anything). You can even order the newer one, *Practical Text Analytics*, directly from the Kogan Page website.

I have taught advanced statistics to bored graduate students who had to take it to get their degrees, given numerous other courses and seminars, and continue to teach certification courses online.

About my own education, I started as an undergraduate in the sciences. Beyond this, I have an MBA (University of Chicago), a doctorate in psychology (Chicago School of Professional Psychology) and an MA in language and linguistics (Boston University). This combination does at least seem congruous with the topic of the book. It also gives rise to the question of why, when I was younger, I didn't just get a job.

Concerning the methods that we will review, I have been working with most for at least 20 years and some for over 30. Everything I write about has worked in real applications for at least several years. Therefore, everything you see here will have a solid track record in real applications.

Many thanks are in order here. We should start with Jenny Volich and Anna Moss at Kogan Page for making this book possible. My particular thanks to Charlotte Owen and Rajveer Ro'isin Singh for their helpful editing and encouraging comments.

I also would like to give a heartfelt 'thank you' to my wife Debra, for again tolerating late nights and working weekends. Especially, my thanks to her for stepping far outside her field and acting as a kind of royal food taster for you, the readers. She tried out various sections of the book to find out whether they were particularly indigestible.

Two quotes about expertise help define the aims of this book. One often attributed to Edward de Bono says, 'An expert is someone who has succeeded in making decisions and judgements simpler through knowing what to pay attention to and what to ignore.' Another, reportedly said by Niels Bohr, defines an expert as a person 'who has found out by his own painful experience all the mistakes that one can make in a very narrow field'. To the extent that this book can make decisions simpler and help you to avoid some harrowing slipups, it will have served its purpose.

To my wife Debra and my mother Lydia

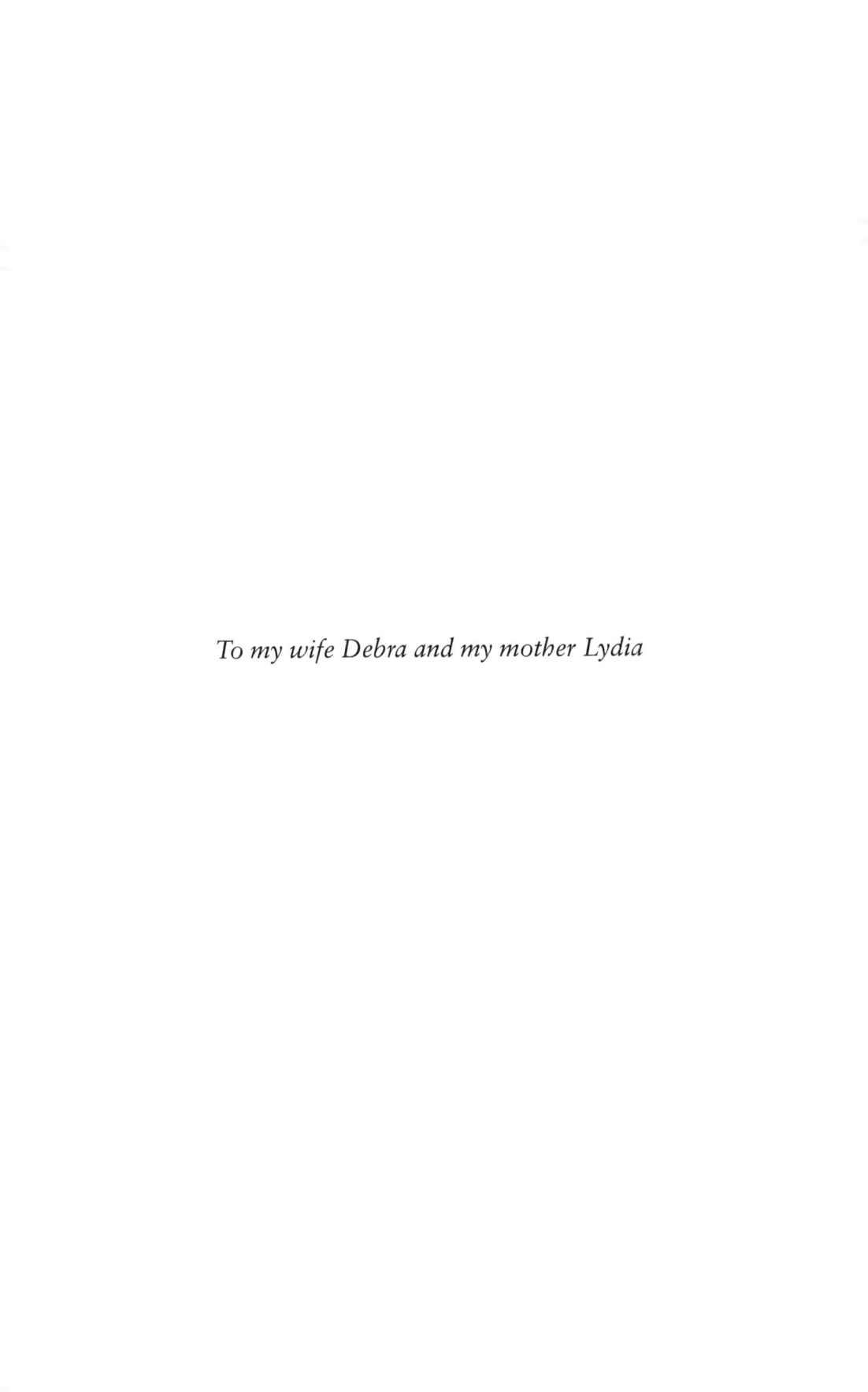

Who should read this book and why? 01

This chapter explains who should read this book, practitioners who need to deal with predicting consumer choices, and students who want to understand what is involved. It discusses the issues involved in trying to predict these choices. Here we also explain what makes up data itself and what makes up information, introduce the types of analyses and their natures, and outline what you can expect to get once all the work has been done.

In this chapter, we also introduce a critical guideline we seek to follow throughout our discussion, as delineated by Lewis Carroll: 'Begin at the beginning… and go on till you come to the end: then stop.' We also need first to consider exactly what we want to analyse, what we hope to get from it and why. This chapter starts us on this process.

What we cover in this book

We give you practical pointers and successful strategies to deal with many situations involving the prediction of consumer choices. Thinking about the following should clarify where we are going. If faced with any of the following, what would you do?

- ✓ Making the best possible new device or service, including the best features and setting the best price.
- ✓ Understanding how much to charge for the fine product or service you already offer.
- ✓ Countering a competitor coming into the marketplace with a new offering by revamping your product or your claims.

✓ Fine tuning your product offerings in the best way.
✓ Getting the best message conveying the benefits of your fine product or service.
✓ Or perhaps just selling much, much more of the goods or services you have.

Which of these strategies would you follow? Would you...

- Ask people directly what they really want?
- Look at what people have been choosing and try to figure out what they would buy next?
- Try to build a model that explains self-reported attitudes and behaviours in relation to buying or buying intent?
- Do an experiment, like a scientific experiment, to get to an answer?
- Put your trust in a theoretical model that sounds attractive?
- Talk to a few likely customers?
- Look at social media for clues?
- Throw darts or trust the faint rumblings in your gut?

All of these and more have been tried. Our goal is to give you the best approaches for predicting consumer choices in different situations – and to tell you which ones to avoid at all costs.

So is this a book about predictive analytics?

The short, but infuriating, answer is yes – but no. Using data to figure out what people will choose is the human side of advanced analytics. There are many other analytical approaches that keep tabs on what is happening in sales or transactions, or that aim to predict events not involving decisions, such as disease progression or mechanical failures, or that predict the likely outcomes of sporting events – and indeed that try to predict the outcomes of many other events and processes.

We will be discussing the parts of the field that concentrate on understanding the choices that people make, whether these are in buying a product or service, enrolling in a programme or school, subscribing to a service, choosing something on a web page, donating to a charity or volunteering their time. We also provide guidance on which methods work extremely well in the right situations and those that do not offer good guidance.

We address these questions:

- Which method is right in which situation?
- What are the salient strengths of each?
- What are the implicit views of the world and biases in each?
- What are the cautions and limitations?

While many books address the subjects we cover, only a few have a scattered chapter or two touching even briefly on multiple approaches. This book will put them all into perspective, and so provide a useful guide for:

- the person who must plan the project;
- those who must understand the results and apply them;
- the student trying to learn what works.

What can you expect in this book?

We will focus on the **planning, execution** and **application** of the widely diverse methods used to predict what people will choose. We will talk about several primary areas, including:

- the basics, such as reasons for doing the analyses and core tasks such as selecting data or selecting a sample, framing the right question and focusing on what matters most;
- the different types of models and what they really predict about choices;
- different kinds of output and how they best can be used.

We will be explaining some advanced topics, but you will need little more than a passing acquaintance with statistics or analytical methods to grapple with these ideas. Any time we introduce a new term (and given the nature of practitioners in the field, these are not in short supply) there will be an explanation. Those of you hoping for subscripts, Greek letters and multi-tiered equations have definitely sat down in the wrong theatre.

Look for ordinary English, not equations

Everyone can breathe a sigh of relief. We will not be resorting to equations filled with recondite symbols and do not expect you to have mastered advanced statistics or maths. We will be addressing complex topics, but everything will be explained in plain English.

Some definitions we need

Prediction versus forecasting

Prediction is a concept grounding all our discussions. This term is just convenient shorthand, following the common usage that we see in such terms as **predictive analytics**. Actually, no one can **predict** anything. If that were true, your author would now be sitting on the deck of his J-Class yacht with a cool drink. Writing this book, of course, but still on the yacht.

The more correct term is **forecasting**, something like forecasting the weather. Some of our forecasts can be incredibly accurate – and indeed can look like predicting. Some other approaches are not as fortunate – and we will talk about those. Sadly, though, we do not have the advantage of weather forecasters, who can stick their hands out of the window and solemnly 'forecast' that it is now raining. Everything we discuss will go beyond just taking the current temperature and reporting it.

Artificial intelligence

Moving to another key topic, let's talk about **artificial intelligence**. One often-seen definition: anything done by a machine that responds to its environment and takes actions that maximize its success. The machines we will discuss are computers. Their environment is data. Their success criterion lies in finding patterns in the data that we cannot perceive – and that help us to take more effective actions.

We are not talking about robots that can do our work for us (sorry if you were expecting this). As penetrating as a machine's analysis may be, you must make the final decisions, and you must decide how to put the information garnered into action.

Practical artificial intelligence

Artificial intelligence broadly means anything a machine does to respond to its environment to maximize its chances of success. The machines we use are computers and we set their goal as detecting complex patterns that we cannot in order to aid in our making better decisions. For those expecting robots to do our work for us – sorry, not yet. Some systems with low-level intelligence are automated. Otherwise you are the one who needs to decide how to use the information that the machines provide.

Even if we are not treading in the realm of science fiction, we will see how remarkably machines can parse and understand data in ways that we cannot, and see patterns that we never could. There is much that is amazing in this arena – as we will discuss throughout this book. Also, some systems do make autonomous, low-level decisions based on rules that we devise. And we will talk about those.

Who is a consumer?

This is our last major definition. Of course, the term **consumer** includes ordinary shoppers dealing with the often bewildering array of choices we encounter in modern life. However, a consumer could also be any of these:

- a doctor choosing medications for patients;
- a purchasing agent choosing which type of rubber bushings will fill the stockroom;
- a donor choosing where to pledge;
- a student choosing where to matriculate;
- an executive trying to choose which manufacturer of mobile phone towers will get the bid.

By the way, mobile phone towers are those tall and often unsightly objects that allow us to enjoy the wonderful world of smartphones everywhere we go. They are very expensive, and very few people on the entire earth decide about buying them. These towers (and their buyers) appear in one of our examples about pricing.

And, finally, what is a mathematical model?

We will be discussing these throughout. By this, we simply mean any type of regular manipulation of a set of variables to forecast or predict the values of some target variable. This could be as simple as adding or multiplication, or as complex as some of the mind-bendingly difficult approaches that we discuss later in the book. These variables can be any quantity or quality that varies from one person to the next, and can include personal characteristics, ratings, consumption patterns, choices made, stated beliefs and so on.

Moving forward

Stay tuned as we discuss, and try to make sense of, work from communities that rarely make much mention of each other. This will be an interesting journey and throughout we will try to follow the advice put forth by Lewis Carroll: 'Begin at the beginning… and go on till you come to the end: then stop.'

Data versus information

We hear a lot about **data** and even have entire careers named after it, such as data scientist. One of the first things we need to settle is the difference between **data** and **information**.

Data simply means anything that can be measured in any way:

- Measurements of the hum given off by neon lights are data.
- Exaggerations, conflations, misrepresentations and downright lies are data.
- Collections of videos recording inactivity on empty streets at night are data.

Information is data that has been gathered and processed to give you insights so that you can deal with a situation – in particular an unexpected one:

- Reports that a truck is stalled on the highway and your expected route has been delayed are information.
- Analyses of factors influencing trends in enrolment at your school are information.
- Analyses of what people have bought so that you can sell them more of the right items are information.
- Linking consumer interest in specific product features to levels of purchasing provides information.

> **A critical difference: data is not information**
>
> **Data** is anything that can be measured in any way. **Information** is data that has been gathered and processed so that you can use it to deal with a situation – in particular one you do not expect. Data does not do anything by itself. You must find how to turn it into information, then knowledge, and finally actions.

Authors Clifford Stoll and Gary Schubert take this a few steps further when they say that data is not information, information is not knowledge, knowledge is not understanding, understanding is not wisdom. The methods we describe here can get you all the way to knowledge. The rest is up to you.

Fallacies about having lots of data

A belief that still lingers is that having more data might just solve all problems. If we recall that data is just basically bits and pieces, we can see that this is wrong. Yet we encounter this erroneous idea in many places on the web, and even in some (bad) books. We should know better. The author of one such book made such a claim while speaking at a conference (and right before your author spoke, which did not start things off very well). This person even said that more data is **always** better, even if you are adding bad data.

The audience, mostly people with long experience in direct marketing, sat with either amused or annoyed expressions. On the way out, one person said, 'Well, he's an academic. He must not have practical experience.' This comment captures an important point. Many ideas about data seem attractive but do not survive exposure to reality.

More data of the wrong type actually is bad for you. If you are looking for a needle in a haystack it does not help to have a larger haystack.

While it is a worthwhile goal to collect as much data as possible, **data quality**, and **knowing which data will address your needs**, remain paramount. Some frustration with having huge repositories, and yet finding no useful purpose in them, can be seen in the relatively new term **data swamp**. This is a **data lake** that has gone bad (or was never good).

A **data lake** is also a new idea, basically a gathering of various data sources that are kept in their native formats with little to no upfront attempt to integrate them (the earlier **data warehouses** attempted to do at least some integration). The hope with a data lake is that some newer software, such as the often-mentioned **Hadoop**, will do the magic that allows the data to get called up, aligned, cleaned and integrated – all of which then just might lead to an analysis that provides something useful. Cleaning up data and getting it to match with data in other formats in themselves are formidable tasks. Too often, even getting this far can consume great amounts of time and effort.

> **Try to avoid this misconception**
>
> Data, and especially great masses of data, get played up as **the answer** in the press, on the web and even in some books. Simply having a lot of data does not help solve problems. Data that has not been collected for the purposes of a specific set of analyses may never yield an answer, regardless of how much data you have. Adding more data unconnected to your questions will make your task harder, not easier. The larger the haystack, the more difficult it becomes to find the needle.

What is important?

If we could count everything that people chose, then any event that caused a change in our count would be important. Suppose you are running a non-profit radio station, and you start a so-called pledge drive asking for donations, and after days of begging, you raise money. You can, therefore, say that this endless wheedling had an important effect. Similarly, if you want to see if a product will sell, you may put it out on shelves and watch what happens.

However, in neither case can you say you have done the best you could. With the radio station, you cannot answer the question of how much money you could have raised by other means. For instance, you might simply remind people that you need donations to continue (this has been called a 'silent donation drive').

With the product, you cannot tell how much you might have sold if you configured it differently or charged some other price. By simply putting the product on the shelf you also have incurred numerous expenses. These include distribution and presumably promotion (so that people know it is on the shelf waiting for them). Failing this way costs a great deal.

Measurement is not insight

While direct measurements of behaviour have the advantage of being real data, they do not give us any insights into alternatives we might have tried, or into the reasons for people making a decision.

Direct measurements also can prove to be surprisingly difficult. Suppose you run a bank. Clearly, you would like to attract more deposits, more loan business and perhaps more financial-advising business. However, while you could see some immediate returns to your promotional efforts, some consumer decisions in these areas take more consideration and might happen over weeks or months.

Waiting this long to see if your promotion has had the desired effect has numerous disadvantages. First and most obvious is the span of time itself. We also encounter the problem of events that could intervene during that time. What if something in the external conditions changes, as a result making your product more or less attractive? What if a competitor draws business away by copying – or worse, outdoing – your promotion?

If we can sum up, if you rely just on what you can observe in behaviour, you may sell more of your fine product, enrol more students, get more charitable pledges – and so on. But you will not know how much better you could have done by altering your approach.

> **The limitations of direct measurement**
>
> Measuring behaviour directly gives you real data. However, it does not allow you to determine if you could have done something better. It also does not give you any insight into consumers' impressions or motivations. Even if you measure responses to several alternatives simultaneously, you still are severely limited in what you can test compared with the experimental methods that we will discuss, and do not have information about why people are responding as they do.

Using precursors or surrogates for behaviour

All these factors lead to the use of other methods, including interviewing and measuring variables that are supposed to be precursors to or surrogates for behaviour. Some of the surrogates widely regarded as suggesting what might happen when people choose are:

- awareness of the product or service;
- ratings, for instance satisfaction ratings on a 1 to 10 scale;
- associations with desired characteristics for the product;
- buying intentions;
- preference.

There are numerous others, but these will give us a start. In some cases, these measures are treated as **outcomes** – for instance, measuring awareness, liking and/or ratings of a product (or service) marks the end of the exercise. Again, the presumption here is that these measures are precursors to behaviour. In some instances, these measures have real consequences in themselves, for instance, where employee compensation gets tied to scores in satisfaction.

Very often these measures, and others such as demographics or past purchases, get rolled into mathematical models of various sorts. And indeed, we will be discussing how models like these work and showing examples throughout this book.

The methods we will be discussing

The methods we will be discussing fall into four broad classes:

- experimental or trade-off methods;
- questions and answers;
- models based on stored or historic data, machine learning, artificial intelligence;
- various theoretical models.

Some of these may sound mysterious now. We aim to clear up any uncertainty as we discuss each. Let's talk about each briefly.

Experimental methods

These were designed to develop new products, service offerings or communications. They involve interviewing people. These include extremely powerful approaches, in that they can estimate responses to many thousands of product/service configurations or messages in **market simulations** – including the **market simulator** programs that we will show you. If done well, their predictions can be highly precise. These methods have track records of over 30 years and extensive academic support. Work developing one of these methods – discrete choice modelling – won a Nobel Prize in economics in 2000. These methods have been extended and strengthened by the use of machine learning approaches.

Questions and answers

The name itself explains the next set of approaches. People get interviewed and asked a variety of questions. Methods available for analysing these answers have advanced considerably. In fact, here we will also encounter artificial intelligence, in at least one unexpected place.

Many types of output come from questions and answers, ranging from simple descriptions to powerful models that show the effects of different variables on some outcome (or even multiple outcomes). Some outcomes that you can see predicted include levels of satisfaction, degree of preference, and even (with some newer methods) market share. We will bring you up to date on what experts are talking about and doing.

Models based on stored or historic data

These can go deeply into machine learning and artificial intelligence, and appear to make up much of marketing science. Many times, data that has been collected for purposes other than a specific analysis get assembled, probed and examined. Outputs include models for scoring customers and prospects, and even algorithms for quick decisions such as whether to show a particular person an advertisement on a given web page.

This is the arena that gains the most attention and causes the most concern about breaches of privacy. Perhaps surprisingly, all the methods that get used here (excepting computer-based ones that assemble sources of data) also get used in analysing questions and answers.

Theoretical models

These are important because they influence so much of the work that gets done in investigating data. These models attempt to explain which factors lead to behaviour, and which often unseen underlying causes can change what a person chooses.

Implicit views of people and biases

Models based on stored or historic data

These have at least these two implicit views of people. First is the logical-seeming idea that we can forecast what a person is likely to do by observing what they have done. So, for instance, if you have bought a box of the wonderful breakfast-like substance Kardboard Krunchies every week, it seems reasonable to assume you will buy one next week.

Another implicit view is that you as a consumer are likely to buy what people somehow similar to you have bought. So if women in the last trimester of pregnancy buy a lot of cotton balls, then we might assume that Thisbe, who also is in the last trimester of her pregnancy, is likely to buy cotton balls.

These assumptions can work effectively, but also can lead to problems, as we will discuss. A great deal of effort in marketing sciences goes into finding cohorts and observing what they are most likely to do. This type of alignment of individual with a group is one basis for certain systems that show low-level artificial intelligence, including the **recommendation engines** we will discuss later.

Analysis of questions and answers

The obvious but critical assumption here is that if you ask fairly direct questions, whatever people tell you will provide valuable information. Direct questions asking for ratings of importance in particular have numerous problems, including people giving overly positive ratings (**acquiescence bias**), people giving the same answer repeatedly (**straight lining**), cultural and personal differences in how scales are used, and inaccurate responses due to the common desire to give **socially desirable answers**.

Trying to minimize these problems, methods of more indirect questioning have been devised. It is the **experimental methods**, though, that go furthest to overcome these pitfalls of direct questioning.

The experimental methods

This set of approaches arose due to the realization that people cannot or will not tell you directly by ratings what they most value in a product or service. These methods ask people to make choices in various ways and so reveal the true hierarchies in what they value.

Powerful as these **experimental methods** can be, they have their own implicit assumptions. They are based on the belief that a product, service or message can be broken down into discrete features that can be tested and compared. It is true that nearly everything we encounter has at least one measurable feature. However, with some products, services or messages, the features we can measure may not be the most important ones.

There also have been some objections to these methods based on various notions about how people think and process information, and whether these methods truly capture that. As we will discuss, these cavils are largely beside the point.

And finally, the theoretical models

These obviously are **ideas** about how people think, feel and behave – and often came into existence without any firm empirical evidence. Still, these inform a great deal of what marketers and even marketing science types do, so it is important to know about them.

One way of comparing these methods

We can arrange these methods comparatively in a number of ways. Figure 1.1 shows one of these, based on how much effort of different types each requires. The two axes represent:

- how much is required in planning to interact with consumers to get the needed information;
- how much analytical complexity could be involved.

Let's review Figure 1.1. The first axis is inviolable – there is no way around the effort required in interacting with consumers if the methods are to work. The second axis is more discretionary, as it may be possible to get by with less analytical complexity using some methods some of the time:

Figure 1.1 One way to categorize the methods we will discuss

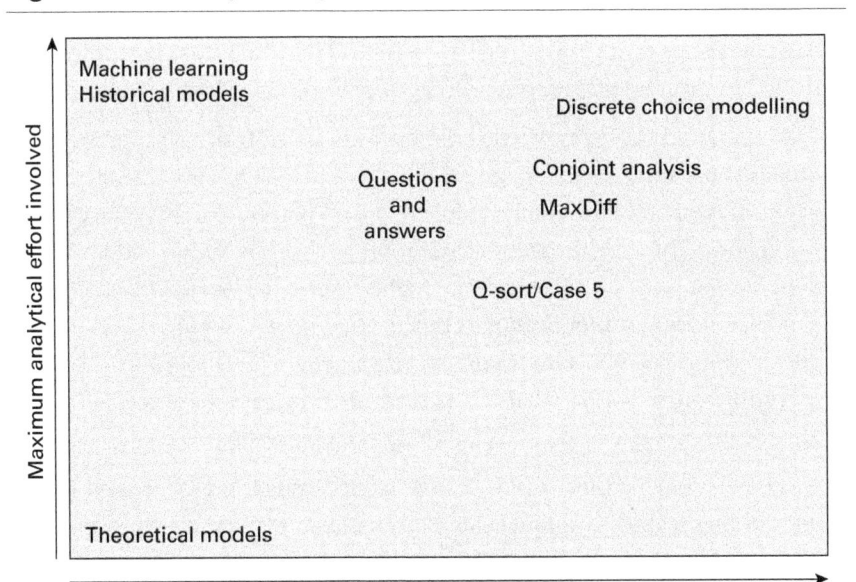

```
Maximum analytical effort involved ↑
│
│  Machine learning
│  Historical models
│                                   Discrete choice modelling
│
│                    Questions       Conjoint analysis
│                    and             MaxDiff
│                    answers
│
│                              Q-sort/Case 5
│
│
│
│  Theoretical models
└─────────────────────────────────────────────→
         Amount of planning to interact with consumers
```

- The **theoretical approaches** reside in the bottom-left corner, since as ideas, they need involve neither interacting with actual people nor any analysis. We need at least to mention them, as they often underlie other approaches.

- We find **discrete choice modelling** methods at the opposite extreme, as they have both high requirements for planning to interact with consumers, and typically high levels of analytical complexity. The requirements of these methods, both in theory and execution, can seem daunting. We hope to clear up the difficulties here.

- **Approaches based on historical or transaction data** typically involve great analytical complexity but little or no interaction with consumers. These methods rely on data that has been stored by an organization, often overlaid with other information gathered from various secondary sources. In the United States, vast amounts of data can be appended to nearly any person, some of it at the individual level, some household, and some at the block or neighbourhood level.

  The amount of data that has been ferreted out about nearly everyone is staggering – one service, for instance, offers to get a name, address, age, ethnicity and gender from a simple e-mail address – and for over 90 per cent of US households. Then, once the address is in hand, other services can provide literally hundreds of items.

  As follows, privacy concerns have been most strongly voiced about **data mining** investigations. After all, much of this information was gleaned without the person's knowledge of consent. This also is far more information than most people realize any organization could have about them.

- **Questions and answers** preceded the more analytically driven approaches – and in some form probably go all the way back in human history. Their pre-tech roots remain highly visible in many places. You may encounter rudimentary or even no analysis in reports about questions and answers. Simple counting is a staple on the nightly news, where for instance you can hear solemn announcements to the effect that, '14 per cent less Brits are drinking tea this year than six years ago.' This should lead to the inevitable question 'So what?' – as we have a factoid disconnected from any idea that it is causative of anything else.

  Nonetheless, scaled measures, selections of appropriate items and rankings all **might** lead to sophisticated models that help guide decisions and actions – if set up and analysed reasonably well. We will show you how this can work later in this book. Even verbatim comments collected in interviews can show considerable predictive power. This is discussed in another volume (*Practical Text Analytics*).

Sense and sensibility with predictions

First, it is worth restating that we do not **predict** – popular as this word may be – we more accurately **forecast**. The methods we discuss have greater and lesser degrees of accuracy in making forecasts. With each, endless possibilities exist to make serious mistakes. Experience with these methods in the marketplace can help us to overcome many of these. Sadly, these are often learned by actually making the mistakes.

Forecasts are not **projections** to the marketplace. This is a critical difference. In fact, going from a forecast to a projection often proves to be far more difficult than imagined, and so becomes a very humbling experience.

Some of the difficulties in projections

Suppose you generate a model based on your customers' transactions that says that you will attain a 15 per cent likelihood of them buying your fine product if you run a coupon. This does not mean that 15 per cent of the marketplace will buy it, or that your sales will go up by 15 per cent – or in fact that 15 per cent of customers will finally make the purchase.

Your customers cannot make up the entire market, and determining what percentage of the marketplace your customers make up can be terrifically difficult. You must answer these questions, just to get started:

- What percentage of the total marketplace do your customers represent?
- What percentage of your customers are actually aware of your fine product?
- Of those who are aware, what percentage understand what it actually is and does?
- How well is the product distributed? What percentage of your customers can actually find your product? If you are on the web, can people find your product and succeed in buying it?
- Can your production keep up with new demand? If you are on a website, can it keep up with traffic?
- And how many non-customers are going to join in and purchase whatever you have to offer?

Finally, to get to figures for the total marketplace, you have to know its true size. This may seem obvious but can prove highly difficult. With any conceivable product or service, this is not just a count of the general population. You need to start with people who might possibly have a use for your product (even if a faint possibility). This will be more than your customer base. And while you may have a count of your customers, this also could be less accurate than you imagine. Unfortunately, it is a rare organization of any type that has an exact customer list.

> ## A cautionary tale about customer lists
>
> A large bank set up a massive computerized database to keep track of its commercial customers. Because they had many thousands of customers and prospects, and were constantly updating this information, they had a large computer and a large staff busily at work. This was a number of years ago, so the computer system was still a hulking and intimidating presence on one floor of the bank.
>
> Their salespeople (who they called account executives) were supposed to supply information on their customers to the staff. That is, they were supposed to hand over sheets with customer names, locations and facts.
>
> In time, the bank decided to do a survey testing interest in a new product for commercial customers. It seemed entirely logical to use this customer database as one source of companies to contact. Other contacts would come from outside lists of companies in the area.
>
> Much to everyone's consternation, the survey found that **60 per cent of the customer names contacted were not good** – that is, they had no working relationship with the bank, or were out of business entirely. Some 25 per cent of the names listed as contacts actually were dead. These facts upset everyone involved, and particularly the person heading the computer database operation.
>
> How could such a thing happen? Two factors contributed strongly:
>
> - The input given by the salespeople was simply entered into the database and not completely verified. The task of just keeping up with what the salespeople provided already took eight staff. The bank baulked at the prospect of adding yet more staff to validate more than the company's name and location being correct. No one from the bank called up the purported contact just to check on whatever was entered.

- The salespeople had a strong motivation not to enter all the names of their best clients, and to make up any quotas for calls that they missed with spurious information. If they kept some names to themselves, and the time came for them to go and work elsewhere, they could take a base of valuable customers. Bank rules would prevent them from taking active customers known to the bank. However, if these customers' names never made it into the central database, then the salespeople could do as they pleased. And in many cases, that is precisely what they did.

There are several important lessons in this story. The one we need to take away here is that customer databases often are not as good as we would like. They typically do not fail in as spectacular a way as this, but their lack of reliability can be quite surprising. Customer surveys based on these databases frequently turn up rafts of incorrect names, addresses, company affiliations and postal or ZIP codes. An error in any one of these, of course, could make the listing useless.

Difficulties in projecting from surveys

Survey-based forecasts encounter all the problems of starting from inaccurate databases, and add more. We encounter the problem of whether the sample used had usable names but names that still misrepresented the entire population sought. We also run into problems when study participants are **screened** (allowed into the survey or not) based on many criteria.

Projecting after study participants have gone through this type of screening is one bane of all survey-based research. We do this screening because we at least want to find people with some possible use for or interest in the product in question. But then, once, we have them, just how many people do they actually represent? Even if we apply the best survey-related method for forecasting, **discrete choice modelling**, we can run into significant problems making marketplace projections.

Surveys also may have problems with not finding enough of the right people, with people who do not answer thoughtfully, with survey participants not following directions, with people typing answers such as 'asdhfakjdhgajghad' when asked for their opinions, and so on. These may happen even with surveys that are put together well.

Artificial Intelligence Marketing and Predicting Consumer Choice

> ### Case: problems projecting due to overly specific screening
>
> A major software maker wanted to test responses to various configurations of its new product, and do so considering various likely competitive responses. To determine the likely outcomes, they correctly chose discrete choice modelling, which has an outstanding track record for addressing this type of problem.
>
> However (and against all objections of those working with them), they decided that their sample had to consist of software engineers with more than a certain amount of experience, who had at least five computers running their operating system, at least two computers running another operating system, and at least one on a back bench somewhere running yet another operating system.
>
> They set so many conditions that there was no way to estimate how large this population might be in the marketplace. No sources existed where someone could look up the size of this tightly defined group. As they added each condition for including a person in the survey, errors in their estimates were compounded – and projections became less accurate. They also had no way of knowing how the broader population – people not exactly like those they surveyed – might act. Since their product was overwhelmingly prevalent, it was safe to assume that people outside the small cohort they interviewed were likely to buy this new product as well.
>
> In the end, the outcome was a mixture of success and failure. They managed to configure a product that sold terrifically well, since the discrete choice model was well executed and did indeed show them a highly desirable combination of features and pricing. However, they grossly underestimated demand, by a factor of about three. They could not keep production up with sales, resulting in product delays, angry customers, mockery in the press, and order cancellations.

Unfortunately, far too many surveys end up not asking the right questions or not analysing data correctly to get useful answers. Overall, it is not as easy to put together a survey providing the right information as it may seem. As a result of many subpar efforts, research in general has suffered a black eye, or maybe two.

Models often aim just to increase likelihoods of behaviour

In many cases, these methods do not **forecast** as much as suggest ways to **increase the odds** of something happening. An estimate like this could come from looking at similarities with people who have already bought, or could be an estimate of odds of buying based on a group's other purchasing behaviour.

Increasing your chances of getting a desired result, or reducing your chances of failure, are of course highly worthwhile endeavours. However, if the output shows increased odds of success, you have neither forecast nor projection. You may have a useful guidepost, but no real idea of how much better you will do once you reach your destination.

Forecasts are necessarily short term

No matter what the forecast, it becomes invalid with sufficient change in the marketplace. An unexpected new product or service entering the market can disrupt everything. When something new shakes up the market, methods based on stored data, such as customer transactions, can fail entirely.

One of the experimental methods, discrete choice modelling, can address the likely effects of new products or services, even disruptive ones, entering the market. One example involves an established cancer drug that was facing two new entrants, both of which were far more effective. Forecasts for what might happen to this drug as it faced this major change were borne out in the marketplace.

In fact, when using this method, it is always best to test possible competitive actions in response to changes in your product or service. This may be the point at which the marketing team tells you that you are giving them a headache. However, even after developing severe soreness around the temples from all that hard thinking, anticipating what competitors might do poses quite a challenge.

Also, any forecasts you have made likely will become invalid if your organization runs into problems with communications, distribution or production. Similarly, even the best forecasts can become worthless quickly if something unexpected happens that causes problems in public perceptions of your product or service.

Where we will not be going

Too many methods!

We will explain how a number of advanced methods work in practice and show their applications with actual marketplace data (which does have to be disguised, though). However, we have an overabundance of methods that could be discussed. For instance, the free analytical program Weka lists over 100 methods, many of them using advanced machine learning – and more than a few with names likely to be highly unfamiliar, such as J48, LibSVM, HyperPipes, CLOPE, Tertius, etc. Anyhow, we might possibly not mention one of your favourites.

Not substantiated = not here

A plethora of unsubstantiated methods and systems now surround us. Any time on the web will turn up large numbers. We will not review any method supported just by a vendor's website, even if that vendor has put plenty of their own papers there. Everything we discuss will be backed by both a strong track record in practical applications and strong theoretical foundations, meaning methods that have passed academic scrutiny in peer-reviewed papers, and more than just one of those. Either one alone – either anecdotes based on practical experience or publication in a journal – is not sufficient. Proprietary systems that are largely 'black box' also are off our menu, as fascinating as some of these may seem.

No recommendations for specific software or solutions

Many fine software packages have been developed, so many that is has become impossible to review and test them all. Statistical analysis software almost invariably is complex, and even the relatively easiest requires some learning and adaptation by the user. The larger statistical packages, such as SPSS, SAS, Stat, Statistica, Systat and NCSS all make some implicit assumptions about users knowing what they are doing, more or less – and why they are doing it. The more complex analyses often involve programs that can be quite abstruse and require considerable learning.

All this means that if you have a favourite software application, it may not appear here. And while we discuss specific software programs, this should not be taken as giving recommendations or endorsements. Any program that appears here simply is something that the author has used and finds useful. This does not mean that whatever you see is the only way or the best way to get an analysis done. These are just products that have worked well, have strong academic credentials and seem highly reliable.

Prices range from astronomical (often called **enterprise class software**) to completely free. Free does not mean puny. No-cost options include the redoubtable **R** and the amazing **Weka**.

The program **R** actually is a vast collection of problem-solving and statistical routines that you download to your computer from online repositories. That is, if you get and start **R**, you can then load a dizzying assortment of analytical choices.

This program is made by and largely for academics. It runs based on computer syntax, meaning instructions that you write, and it is wholly unforgiving about mistakes. In its most usual incarnations, it poses fiendish difficulties for most users.

Weka comes with four different interfaces, three of them involving **graphical user interfaces** (**GUIs**) – the system of menus and visual displays we find in many familiar programs. It includes many routines that fall under the heading of **machine learning**. Its style favours visualizing data whenever possible. And it has quirks of its own – for example, a colleague who is a former rocket scientist finds it puzzling, but others have taken to it right away.

We will be talking more about software throughout this book. While we do not spell out the details of writing specific syntax or take you step-by-step through routines, we will keep you filled in about which applications seem particularly well-suited to a given task.

Summary of key points

This is a book for practitioners who need to deal with predicting consumer choices, and for students who want to understand what is involved. One key goal is to winnow through the many approaches to predicting these choices, giving you the best ones to apply in different situations – and telling you which ones to avoid.

We will talk about the human side of predictive analytics, the part that aims to forecast what people will choose – and in some cases, why they make those decisions. It is not about predictive analytics as a whole. For instance, we could otherwise try to predict when a pipe will burst, where a disease will progress, or which team will win at a sporting event – attempts to model such processes or outcomes fall outside our scope.

The term **consumers** can mean people dealing with the confusing array of everyday products and services that we find all around us, including small and large purchases, financial services, technology and telecommunications. But we also take consumers to mean doctors making decisions about which fine pharmaceutical to buy, purchasing agents looking at the wide array of industrial bushings to fill their warehouses, and so on.

This book takes the approach that we can discuss concepts, methods and results in plain English. While we will be going over some advanced topics, and talking about how methods work, we will be avoiding subscripted notation, matrix algebra, statistical proofs and Greek letters. There will be no multi-tiered equations. Anyone expecting any of those will be sorely disappointed. Our focus is on understanding, planning, execution and application.

We explain a wide array of methods that rarely get considered together, compare their applications and put them into context. Each approach has its best uses and limitations, and we began considering those in this chapter.

Some key definitions get covered before we get to the methods, as these are important for later discussions. First, and perhaps most important, is the understanding that data is (are) not information. **Data** rather means anything that can be measured in any way, whether or not it has any meaning or use. Information is data that has been processed and analysed so that it can be used to deal with a situation, particularly a novel or unexpected one. Data does not do anything by itself. As several authorities have pointed out, data is not information, and information is not knowledge. Some take it further and remind us that knowledge in turn is not wisdom. We will show you how to get to information, but the rest will be up to you.

There are some prevalent fallacies about data that we hope to dispel. Foremost among these is the mistaken belief that more data is always better. There is a strong undercurrent in the literature and on the web saying that if you have enough data, perhaps at the magical point where it turns big, then you will solve your problems. More of the wrong kinds of data actually causes problems. You do not find a needle more easily by having a bigger haystack.

Data quality, and knowing what your data can be used to do, remain paramount. Anyone saying otherwise is probably trying to sell you something – and you do not want it.

If we could count everything that people chose, anything that caused a change in our count would be important. However, counting definitely is not predictive, as it of course only happens after you have done something – and even then the act of measuring can prove surprisingly difficult. Therefore, various precursors to behaviour have been proposed, with the theory being that seeing changes in these can be predictive of changes in behaviour. Some of these include measuring awareness of a product or service, ratings, associations, buying intentions and preferences. Sometimes, these are treated as outcomes in themselves, as in when measurements of customer satisfaction are tied directly to compensation.

Classifying the methods

The methods we will be discussing fall into four broad classes: 1) experimental or trade-off methods; 2) questions and answers; 3) models based on stored or historic data, machine learning, artificial intelligence; and 4) various theoretical models:

- **Experimental or trade-off methods** were designed to develop new products, service offerings or communications. They involve interviewing people. These include extremely powerful approaches in that they can estimate responses to many thousands of product/service configurations or messages in market simulations – including the market simulator programs. Machine learning methods have expanded the capabilities of these methods – as we will show.
- **Questions and answers**, as the name implies, involve people getting interviewed and asked a variety of questions. Methods available for analysing these answers have advanced considerably. In fact, here we will encounter artificial intelligence, in at least one unexpected place.
- **Models based on stored or historic data** can go deeply into machine learning and early uses of artificial intelligence, and appear to make up much of marketing science. Many times, data that has been collected for purposes other than a specific analysis gets assembled, probed and examined. Outputs include models for scoring customers and prospects, and even algorithms for quick decisions such as whether to show a particular person an advertisement on a given web page.
- **Theoretical models** are important because they influence so much of the work that gets done in investigating data. These models attempt to explain which factors lead to behaviour and which often unseen underlying causes can change what a person chooses.

Each of these methods has its own implicit views of people. Models based on stored or historic data have at least two implicit views of people. First is the logical-seeming idea that we can forecast what a person is likely to do by observing what they have done. Another implicit view is that you as a consumer are likely to buy what people somehow similar to you have bought. These assumptions can work effectively, but also can lead to problems – in particular, the second, if a person gets assigned to the wrong group. And these methods generally do not provide useful guidance when situations change or when you want to develop new products or services.

Analysis of **questions and answers** rests on the obvious but critical assumption that if you ask fairly direct questions, whatever people tell you will provide valuable information. This can work if the questions are asked in the right way. However, asking people directly about what they think is important has been shown to provide misleading answers.

The **experimental methods** in fact arose due to the realization that people cannot or will not tell you directly by ratings what they most value in a product or service. These methods ask people to make choices in various ways and so reveal the true hierarchies in what they value.

Powerful as these experimental methods can be, they have their own implicit assumptions. They are based on the belief that a product, service or message can be broken down into discrete features that can be tested and compared. It is true that nearly everything we encounter has at least one measurable feature.

And finally, **the theoretical models** are simply ideas about how people think, feel and behave – and often came into existence without any firm empirical evidence. Still, these inform a great deal of what marketers and even marketing science types do, so it is important to know about them.

One possible arrangement

We can arrange these methods comparatively in a number of ways. One useful way to do this is based on **how much effort of two different types** each requires. These are: 1) how much work is required in planning to interact with consumers to get the needed information; and 2) how much analytical complexity could be involved. Not all useful analyses need reach their maximum level of analytical complexity, but the amount of effort involved in planning to interact is inviolable.

The **experimental methods** require the most effort in planning to interact with consumers, and among these **discrete choice modelling** requires the most analytical effort.

Questions and answers preceded the more analytically driven approaches – and in some form probably go all the way back in human history. Their pre-tech roots remain highly visible in many places. You may encounter rudimentary or even no analysis in reports about questions and answers.

However, they can be used with more rigorous and involved analytics, as we will show.

Approaches based on historical or transaction data typically involve great analytical complexity but little or no interaction with consumers. These methods rely on data that has been stored by an organization, often overlaid with other information gathered from various secondary sources.

The **theoretical approaches,** as ideas, need involve neither interacting with actual people nor any analysis. We need to review them, as they often underlie other approaches.

Keeping sensible with predictions

We rounded out what we will cover by discussing sensible approaches to prediction, starting with the reminder that **we do not actually predict anything**. We make **forecasts,** like weather forecasts, rather than consulting our crystal ball and coming up with the winning number.

Forecasts are not **projections,** and in fact any projections are fraught with difficulties as we try to estimate how the data (or information) we have at hand relates to the entire marketplace. Even the best data gathering can leave us uncertain about how well we have captured everything in the outside world. And too often, data that we have on hand turns out to be lower in quality than we had suspected.

Finally, even the best of forecasts should not be expected to hold up indefinitely. Changes in the marketplace or the external environment will lead to a need for new analyses and new estimates.

Getting the project going

02

Here we discuss the key first steps in planning for a project that you want to conclude with a prediction of what people will choose. As with any in-depth analysis, you need both to plan carefully and get the right data. Here are some of the steps that need to be taken. This chapter also introduces some of the key concepts and language that we must learn (alas) to plan the analysis and understand what is happening in it.

At the beginning

You can find a great many articles and books that advise you about what to do when starting a project. While we hesitate to pile into this particular fray, there are just a few key issues that could stand a review, and a few questions to consider.

These are several questions to keep in mind before any project:

- What can **change**, based on doing this analysis?
- What do I really need to know to help that change happen?
- What data do I need to analyse and/or which people do I need to interview so I get the answer?
- What is the **most** I can expect to get based on doing this?
- How will I know if I reached a good answer?
- And do the people who need to use this understand what they will get from this?

Know who you are talking about or talking to

Let's give everyone the benefit of the doubt and assume that the first key first question has been answered. All work should start with some understanding of what can change as a result. Still, in planning for some kinds of analyses, deciding what you want to know can take up as much time as everything else you do. For instance, if you want to optimize a new product or service with one of the experimental methods (conjoint or discrete choice, in particular), getting to the final list of features to vary and measure typically takes considerable thought and effort.

You also must figure out where you will get your basic data and what limitations you have in your sources. In Chapter 1, we described a few possible pitfalls in dealing with internal data. What about data that you gather from the web or from interviews? In either realm, it is remarkably easy to gather data from the wrong places or about the wrong people – and so data that will not provide reliable guidance.

Unfortunately, errors persist

Sometimes it can be quite tempting to take a shortcut and run with data that does not quite match the question at hand. And, of course, this almost inevitably will sabotage your results no matter how much of the incorrect data you have. Thanks to the web, we now have access to more of the wrong data than was ever possible. So this caution has become critical.

Sadly, when you get the basic data incorrect, your conclusions might be nearly right, more or less right, or terribly wrong – and you will have no way of knowing unless you can check with another source. In many cases, there is no other source.

> **Poor results from overconfidence in data**
>
> Predictions of what a group will do are fraught with difficulties. No place are mistakes in predictions more clearly revealed than in elections. These prognostications are highly publicized and easily compared to the outcomes.
>
> One of the most colossal mistakes in prediction happened with an enormous sample, perhaps the largest ever used to predict who would win

an election. (This story also appears in *Practical Text Analytics*, but it is important – and so bears another telling.)

A magazine called *Literary Digest* went to the huge expense of mailing out **10 million** letters asking likely US voters who they would pick for president. The year was **1936**, and the candidates were one Alf Landon and a slightly better known person, Franklin Delano Roosevelt.

This mailing covered one-quarter of all US voters registered that year. The magazine got back some **2.4 million** responses. They crowed that they would be able to get the results right to within a fraction of a point. Their prediction: Landon would win 53 per cent to 47 per cent. However, we never did have a president Landon. Instead, Roosevelt won by a crushing 62 per cent to 38 per cent.

The magazine missed by **over 15 percentage points**. How could they have got things so wrong, especially with so many people? The simple answer, which you may have suspected: they got back a great many responses, but from the wrong people for making a projection.

They had used names from telephone directories, magazine subscription lists and club memberships. However, telephones were still a relative luxury in 1936, with only about 40 per cent of US households owning one, and in the midst of the cash-strapped Great Depression, relatively few could afford a magazine subscription or a club membership. As a result, they missed the vast cohort of less privileged voters, among whom Roosevelt had an overwhelming majority.

Meanwhile, George Gallup (of the eponymous Gallup poll) used a much smaller, more scientifically selected sample, and got the election results right. Where the millions led to a wrong answer, the carefully chosen thousands led to a much more accurate prediction.

We have had 80 years to absorb this lesson. Yet too often, people still make the same mistake.

Some highly erroneous results based on starting in the wrong place have been reported, much to the humiliation of those making this mistake. But many other such errors get buried quietly – sometimes only after the organization suffers from the poor decisions that result.

Sample frames

Any place where you gather data is more technically called a **sample frame**. Whether you gather data by interviewing, by collecting data online or from

Figure 2.1 Getting the frame right is critical

data warehouses (or lakes) that your organization maintains, you likely will be dealing with a sampling of all possible data. Of course, doing interviews, the odds that you have a sample approaches 100 per cent.

Like the frame for a picture, if the sample frame does not fit, you will not see the picture correctly. Figure 2.1 first shows the right frame, and then what happens when frames are off in two different ways.

Let's suppose, for instance, you can gather all possible data about avowed beer drinkers on a large social media site, such as Facebook. This would be a huge number of beer drinkers, doubtless many thousands and perhaps millions. However, even this many users would represent a subset of all beer drinkers.

We cannot know whether people who indicate on a social media site that they like beer or drink beer are **representative** of all beer drinkers. 'Representative' means that they match the entire population in terms of which beers they like and drink, and how much of those beers they drink.

Therefore, based on patterns you see in the data you gathered from a social media site, you cannot say with any confidence that you have captured patterns in beer drinking in the general beer-drinking population. So you could not, for instance, crunch this massive amount of data and say that you have found who drinks the most of various beers in different cities. Again, it does not matter how many people you have if they are not the right people.

Care in getting data and more care in projections

Overall, we need to be very careful as to where we get our data. And if we want to make a **projection** from our data to the general population, we have to be even more careful. Using what you have at hand and trying to estimate what will happen in the marketplace is fraught with problems and pitfalls.

What is the most you can expect from each method?

We are optimistic that no one out there will be making up the goals of a project as they go along. In Chapter 1, we talked briefly about the key outputs you get from each broad class of methods. We will be talking more about the specifics in each section. Let's take a minute to talk about the most you can expect or, put another way, some of the limitations of each type of method.

The most from historical or transaction data

These methods obviously can give you the best possible fix on how well a given promotion or marketing effort influenced short-term sales. But without added questioning, these methods cannot tell you how efforts are influencing impressions, perceptions and reactions to a given brand, service or institution.

An example can be seen in what happens to a brand after running a great many coupons and promotions. These can boost sales in the short term. But they can also position a brand very firmly as not being worth full price.

Ignoring underlying perceptions and associations can have highly negative consequences. For instance, for many years the department-store chain JC Penney engaged in an intricate scheme of heavy discounting. Then the management decided to 'reposition' the store as an exclusive brand, brought in an executive from Apple computers (presumably for his expertise with higher-priced, heavily branded merchandise) and cut the discounts.

This effort failed miserably. It did not accord with what people saw as Penney's identity. The store even took to advertising an apology for turning its back on what it truly was. Many of the discounts returned. The store clearly had at last asked its customers some of the right questions, but too late. The damage has lingered.

Limited ability to experiment with transactional data

These methods cannot tell you anything about what else you might have tried. Ability to experiment and to anticipate new turns in the marketplace remains extremely limited no matter how penetrating the analysis. You cannot answer 'what if' questions with tactics you have not tried – as you can with the experimental methods.

Do not expect the unexpected

A stream of commentary running through the popular press keeps circulating the notion that insights can arrive almost spontaneously from 'patterns' in the data. This ties in with the belief that because you have a great deal of something, you must be able to do amazing things with it.

This storyline actually started gaining currency in the early 1990s, when data warehousing and mining were in their formative stages. (Data warehousing was the precursor to big data, differing in that it typically involves data that has been organized as well as stored.)

Belief in the mystic power of data

One widespread story supposedly supporting the near magical powers of data concerned a 'major store' that was said to have discovered you could increase beer sales by promoting this product along with diapers, and preferably leading up to the weekend. The supposed logic was that young fathers would be dispatched to the store to buy diapers for Saturday and Sunday, and of course, this made them think of beer.

This was in fact an urban legend about data mining. Its legend-like status was underlined by the way that the name of the store changed in different accounts, and by the way in which the purported sales increases from this joint promotion increased by differing but always very precise amounts, such as '224 per cent'.

After a number of years, the fellow who made up this story came forward and confessed. He had done it, he said, to show how ridiculous anecdotes about finding serendipitous 'patterns' in data could become.

By the time the truth emerged, this tall tale had been reprinted innumerable times in support of the mystical potential of data. It had even appeared in a textbook about data mining. This underscores the allure of getting a solution easily, but there really is no substitute for advance thinking about the problem you need to solve.

The most from questions and answers

We can do much more with survey-based questions involving scaled ratings and selections of answers than was possible even a few years ago. For instance, thanks to newer and more powerful methods of analysis, such as the Bayesian networks discussed in Chapter 7, we now can successfully link questions in surveys with external data, such as market share or share of wallet. (This kind of linkage was almost never possible with well-established methods based on various forms of regression.)

However, even with these powerful new methods, we rarely arrive at detailed prescriptions for action. For instance, an analysis of a survey may tell you that you could gain up to 10 share points from doing more to train people working in your inbound customer call centre – but it likely will not tell you just what you need to improve in that training. Therefore, you likely will reach only the first steps in understanding what needs to get more attention. However, you could turn to one of the experimental methods if you need much clearer direction. We give an example of finding specific actions to improve customer satisfaction in Chapter 5.

The most from the experimental methods

Among these approaches, **discrete choice** and **conjoint analysis** can give you very precise fixes on how much a given change in your product or service will increase **share of preference**. The correct term is **share of preference** because you must add more calculations to the basic output to determine the true share of sales in the marketplace.

Two important factors are missing from **share of preference**: how many are aware of the product or service and how well distributed the product is. Everyone involved in an experimental study becomes 100 per cent aware of all the choices they are evaluating – so responses can be overstated versus the actual marketplace. And, as should be apparent, the product cannot sell if people cannot find it.

Other factors that can cause share in the marketplace to differ from share in a survey are how effectively messages promoting the product perform, and how well the product is presented where it is available. Expect strong adverse effects on performance in the marketplace from either garbled messages, fostering the wrong associations with the product or its users, or poor presentation in stores.

An example of adjusting for awareness and distribution

In a study of pricing for men's casual slacks, a sponsoring company invested considerable time and effort in inviting hundreds of people to survey locations where their brand and competitors' brands were displayed and could be examined (but not tried on). These brands were shown at different prices, and then reshown with prices varied according to an experimental method – and this was repeated a number of times. People participating in the study were asked which brand they would choose, given that the brands were at the specific prices shown. (We will discuss the details of this method, discrete choice modelling, in Chapter 4.)

One brand that did not sell well in the marketplace performed strongly in this test. This apparently puzzling result was explained by the detailed figures the sponsoring company had about how aware shoppers were of the various brands and how extensively each brand was distributed. The one brand that strongly overperformed in the test was neither well known nor widely available.

When the figures for awareness and distribution of this brand were factored in along with its average in-market pricing, the study's estimates of its share fell into line with the best available marketplace sales figures. Current conditions could be matched in the **market simulation** because, of the several alternative prices that were tested for each brand, one price was the marketplace average. This gave strong confidence in projections of what would happen if prices were to change. These expected effects were shown by a special market simulator program created to run under Microsoft Excel, allowing prices to be changed and sales effects to be seen in real time. (This may seem somewhat abstract now, but will be shown in detailed examples in Chapters 4 and 5.) The sponsoring company was able to embark on a new pricing scheme that helped increase sales and profitability.

> **About share of preference**
>
> Some methods can deliver remarkably accurate results showing which features drive choices of products or services, and even provide estimates of shares and how changing features influence these. However, these are predictions of **share of preference**, not **market share**.
>
> Share of preference in a research study must be adjusted for how many are **aware** of the product, how many **comprehend** the product, and how widely the product is **distributed**, to match actual shares of sales. If figures for these critical factors can be found (not too often the case), then share of preference can be translated into actual marketplace values.

These methods show what will happen but not why

These methods can show what will happen in the short term under varying market conditions. But they do not explain what people are weighing aside from features, prices and/or messages when making a decision. For instance, there was a time when Sony could charge more than other brands for most consumer electronics products. This was observed in many experimental-based studies and confirmed in the marketplace. However, these studies did not provide insights into what people perceived about this brand that allowed it to charge higher prices. Research based on more traditional questions and answers was needed to start filling in this part of the picture.

How do you judge the result?

At the outset of any project, you need a plan for how the results will be evaluated. A question you may hear determining the goodness of an analysis goes something like this: 'Is that significant?' Another common question you may encounter is: 'Was there a correlation?' Sometimes these even get combined into: 'Was there a significant correlation?' These questions are asked for good reason, because of a basic need to evaluate whether the effect is real.

Still, these questions are shorthand at best, and often inaccurate or misleading. Let's see if some of the issues surrounding these can be clarified.

What is significant?

We need to talk briefly about **statistical significance**. Wait, come back! We promise not to drive around this in endless circles.

Those of us with more academic experience have heard a great deal about this topic. This gets frequent use in reporting about research, of the scientific and market varieties. Yet this term is not well understood. So let's get to the essentials.

Getting past some terminology

Perhaps you recall the term **null hypothesis**, with more or less dread. Less formally, this means **the belief that nothing is happening**. That is all.

We go from there to **rejecting the null hypothesis**. This means you are **not saying that nothing has happened**. That convoluted-seeming formulation is at the heart of significance testing. Statisticians want to be sure that they are **not falsely claiming something is happening** when it is not.

Making that kind of false claim is sometimes called a **Type I error**. As the name **Type I** implies, statisticians start from a position of extreme caution. The first rule is not saying something mistaken.

A convention has arisen that an effect is **significant** only if we are at least 95 per cent certain we are not making a false claim. (This is also called 95 per cent **confidence**.) Why is the threshold 95 per cent? The best answer that seems available is: just because. This is just a convention, if a long established one.

Based on the number of scientific papers that go through incredible contortions to reach this 95 per cent level, you might think there is some magic behind it. But there is not.

Power versus significance

Statistical power tests whether you are really seeing something happening. We should see frequent mentions of this, but that is not happening. The higher the level of statistical significance we demand – say going from 90 per cent confident to 95 per cent confident to 99 per cent confident – the more statistical power goes **down**.

That is, the more we want to be certain we are not making a false claim, the more likely we are to miss something real. Let's illustrate this. Suppose we are bird watching and we can see the birds fairly well, but we are not 100 per cent certain which birds we are seeing. For instance, if we wanted to identify a duck flying overhead, and we needed to be 95 per cent certain that a random bird we saw was a duck, some actual ducks would fly by and we would not be sure enough to call them correctly. If we needed to be 99 per cent certain, even more actual ducks would get by without us exclaiming, 'Duck!' Missing something that actually is happening is that other type of error mentioned in statistics class, **Type II error**.

> **Statistical significance** is often mentioned, but its meaning is not well understood. When a result is significant, it means you are highly confident that **you are not making a false claim**. Significance does not measure how likely you are to be missing something real, which is determined by the much less used **statistical power**.

Traditional **significance testing** also breaks down with very large samples. If you have enough data, every difference or effect starts seeming significant. This problem occurs well below today's threshold for big data. For instance, investigating opinions of about 12,000 people who answered the NORC General Social Survey, we found that people with the astrological sign Leo watched significantly more television than anyone else. However, don't go and chide your Leo friends. This is simply an artefact of testing for significance with a large sample – you can find random-seeming items passing the test.

> **Significance testing can break down** with huge samples or with hundreds or thousands or comparisons. Alternative methods of testing models are used by some procedures. These other methods involve finding how well the model works on new data, or on data put to one side before the model has been made. You need to use **the test of what is sensible** along with statistical significance testing.

Traditional significance testing also can stretch past its limits while doing dozens or hundreds of comparisons, trying to find which effects or values are larger. Some methods, such as the Bayesian Networks we discuss in Chapter 7, may use a **value of information** approach rather than traditional statistical testing to overcome this problem. (We will get to this definition in Chapter 7.) Other methods, such as the classification trees we discuss in Chapter 6, can deal with this issue by using highly sophisticated testing, advanced enough to be called artificial intelligence.

Some say forget significance testing entirely

A few authors have even advocated abandoning statistical significance in favour of what they call searching for 'repeatable patterns', which boils down to seeing how well the model holds up on other data, or perhaps some part of the data that you have set to one side before you made the model. Testing on other data, even data you have put to one side before making the model, is a sound idea – but it also is worth keeping the extra guidance that significance testing can give you on what definitely **should not** go into a model.

Significance testing needs to make sense

Statistical tests of any kind cannot determine if what you seem to be seeing makes sense. For instance, in Chapter 6, we use significance testing but do not automatically accept all the results the computer identifies as passing the test – because it did not make sense to use them. (This problem arose partly due to using a large sample.) Especially with huge swaths of data, you would be most prudent to use statistical significance testing as suggesting a threshold below which you do not want to go, rather than as forming the final decision.

Mistakes on the small side of sampling

Oddly, in this time when 'big' data gets so much attention, many decisions still get made using little or no data. While there is no way to count how many, often major organizational decisions involve no more than checking the rumblings of a gut. You even can find entire books giving advice about decision making that barely make any mention of how to analyse and interpret information.

Numerous other decisions appear to rest on interviewing small numbers of consumers. You will encounter this in two popular forms of research, **focus groups** and **in-depth interviews**. These methods have good uses, but using either to make a final determination rarely is one of them.

All samples have error

All samples, that is using anything less than 100 per cent of all possible data, introduces some error into our measurement. That is, we cannot be certain that our sample accurately reflects the entire population. This uncertainty somewhat more formally is called **sampling error**.

Using small groups of people (or small samples) we typically run into real problems due to this type of error. The smaller the sample you use, the less likely it is to match or represent the larger population accurately.

But how do you know how much error? Most statistics textbooks talk about this problem by discussing a giant barrel filled with different-coloured balls – which is fine, but a little boring. Let's instead suppose we had a large dumpster filled with boxes of two fine breakfast-like substances, Kardboard Krunchies and SoggyOs. Suppose it is a huge dumpster, say, about a city block long. How many boxes would you have to pull out to estimate the proportion of each of these in the dumpster accurately? And how accurately?

We can do advance estimates for some types of sample error

Fortunately, some exceedingly smart people determined exactly how much error you are likely to have in a sample where there are only two choices (that is, as in our example, Kardboard Krunchies versus SoggyOs, but also yes versus no, and blue versus white – where those are the only colours present, and so on). The chart in Figure 2.2 shows you the sizes of the errors for different samples if you are facing this type of problem.

First, let's clear up the 95 per cent confidence level. Dealing with a sample, you never are 100 per cent confident that the sample you take accurately reflects, or **represents**, the entire population. As you may recall, being **95 per cent confident** is the standard threshold set in statistics. (As another reminder, the reason for this requirement basically boils down to '**just because**'.)

Therefore, the lines on Figure 2.2 reflect how many percentage points around our sample value we must allow so we are 95 per cent confident that the actual percentage in the whole population falls into that range. This is points plus or minus, meaning above and below the measurement we took. This range is sometimes referred to as the **margin of error** – and may be familiar to those following elections where polling results are reported.

These ranges become increasingly large once the sample drops down below about 150. The size of the sample is the largest factor determining the margin of error. However, in determining error, we also need to consider the percentage itself that we have measured.

At a percentage of 50 per cent, or going down the middle, the error is largest. As we approach the extremes of zero and 100 per cent, the error gets smaller. The error around a percentage of 90 per cent is the same as the error around a sample of 10 per cent. The error around a sample of 80 per cent is the same as the error around a sample of 20 per cent, and so on.

Figure 2.2 Sample percentages' errors at different sample sizes

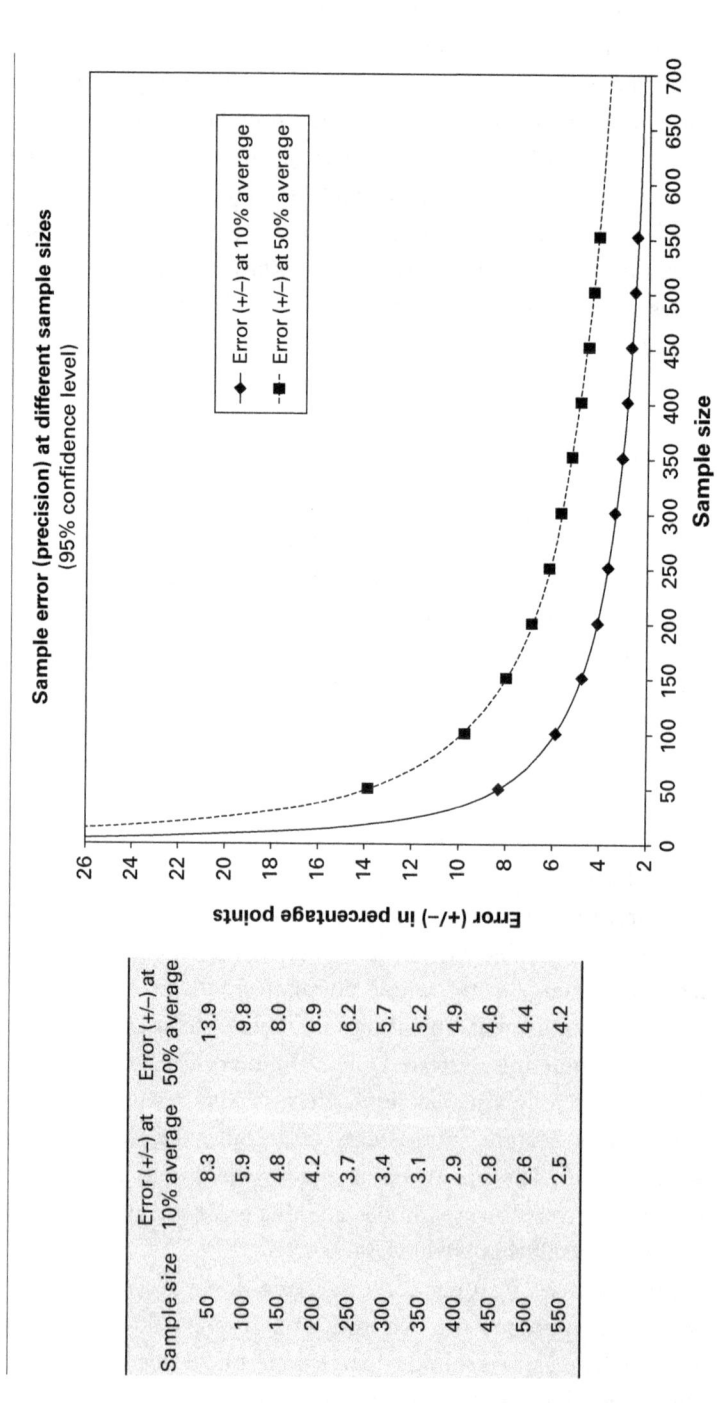

Sample error (precision) at different sample sizes
(95% confidence level)

Sample size	Error (+/−) at 10% average	Error (+/−) at 50% average
50	8.3	13.9
100	5.9	9.8
150	4.8	8.0
200	4.2	6.9
250	3.7	6.2
300	3.4	5.7
350	3.1	5.2
400	2.9	4.9
450	2.8	4.6
500	2.6	4.4
550	2.5	4.2

Back to our breakfast-like substances, if you pulled out 400 boxes and exactly half of them were Kardboard Krunchies, you would be 95 per cent certain that the entire bin contained somewhere between 45.1 per cent and 54.9 per cent of this fine product.

Why tiny samples do not work for estimation

If you think about what an error of +/- (plus or minus) 14 points means, you realize that the actual value for the whole population could be anywhere within a 28-point range of what was measured. For instance, when the sample's value is 50 per cent, the actual value could be anywhere between 36 per cent and 64 per cent, if the whole population could be measured. Few would argue that this wide a range forms an acceptable basis for making a decision. Yet, that is all you get with a sample of 50.

If the sample is below 30, this formula breaks down, and we actually need a somewhat different set of calculations. However, as Figure 2.2 shows, errors balloon with small samples.

The risks in estimating based on small groups

As mentioned, gatherings of small groups for interviewing, or **focus groups,** typically range between 5 and 15 people. In one or two of these, a total of anywhere between 5 and 30 or so people in total have offered their opinions. Unless the item being discussed is a complete and unmitigated disaster (as can happen) or an astronomical, unprecedented success (as we have yet to see), you need far more people to make a sound final decision.

So why do focus groups?

Aside from detecting disasters, these groups have several valuable applications. You learn about the language that people use in discussing the product, and in particular the terminology that they can understand. You can find out if what you are saying is hopelessly confusing from the perspective of people who actually use the product. You can open up unexpected avenues for further questioning. You can learn some humbling lessons about how much the people who use your fine product think about it (generally far less than one would imagine).

A tale of misleading small samples

This is a story about a decision that was made in entirely the wrong way. It appeared in a training video, and even briefly on television. This was quite a few years ago, and the tape seems to have vanished into the mists of time. Nonetheless, it has been documented and stands as a clear example of what not to do.

Those involved were a marketing team from a major manufacturer of men's jeans. They wanted to evaluate a new product, men's suits bearing their brand name. They started their investigation with a massive quantitative research study, almost sociological in nature. The questions delved deeply into basic needs for clothing, for social approval and so on. This part of the programme cost in excess of $800,000 in current dollars.

Following this, they concluded with a few focus groups to evaluate their new product idea. They had prototype suits made and asked a few small groups of men to give their reactions, in particular to the question, 'Would you buy these?'

Using these few responses as the basis of their decision, they put the suits into production, distributed them to stores and promoted them through national advertising. If you cannot think of a brand of men's suits made by a manufacturer of men's jeans, this is not because you missed something. This venture was an abject and expensive failure. They could not have made such a mistake had they used adequate numbers and methods to inform their decision.

A suggestion for small versus large numbers

Using small numbers, you can get an overview, something like looking at a general view of a landscape that you will traverse. Larger numbers are like the detailed directions about where exactly you will be going. Having both gives you the most assurance that you will get where you need to go as efficiently as possible.

Concluding our talk about significance

Figuring out how much error you find in a percentage is the simplest form of significance testing. The formulas get more complex for comparing more than two samples, for figuring out the error in a sample average (such as the average rating on a 10-point scale), for comparing scores in a group to other scores in the same group, and in a host of other statistical procedures.

By the way, all these formulas work correctly only for what is called a **random sample** – meaning that you do not have any linkages among the people or items you are sampling. If you are dealing with, say, doctors together in a given hospital, and even hospitals together in a given geography, more complex formulations for testing are needed to get accurate results.

That said, most statistical testing procedures involve determining how large the error in the measurement (or the effect) is and comparing that to the measurement itself. Getting the effect just 1.96 times as large as its calculated error is enough to pass in many procedures. (We will not be going into all the maths behind this number, fortunately.) This may seem like not much to demand, but this has been the standard for many years.

On to correlations

In casual conversation, **correlation** can stand for almost any relationship. In statistics, though, **correlation** only means a simple summary measure of how well two variables fit a straight line. Correlation can range from a high of +1, where the two variables rise and fall in a perfect straight-line relationship, down to −1, where the two variables have a perfect inverse relationship (one falls precisely as the other one rises).

The correlation statistic is called **R**. This should not be confused with **R**, the free statistical software package. (Apparently, those who invented **R** were thinking primarily of an earlier software program called **S**. This is really true.)

However, the **R statistic** is the underpinning of the **R-squared value** that may be familiar from regression. Regression in its ordinary version (also called ordinary least squares regression) does indeed look for straight-line relationships.

Correlation also is strictly for a pair of variables. If we hear talk about four variables being correlated, either we are listening to some slightly sloppy language, or someone has checked all the ways in which these four variables can be compared two at a time.

Not all the world falls into a line

Many regular, predictable relationships do not fall in a straight line, or are not **linear**. Figure 2.3 shows three examples. In each, we follow the standard practice of indicating the value of the first variable along the horizontal axis and the second along the vertical.

The first diagram (Typical Growth Curve) shows a standard growth curve. You might see this pattern in nature when a colony of mould grows in

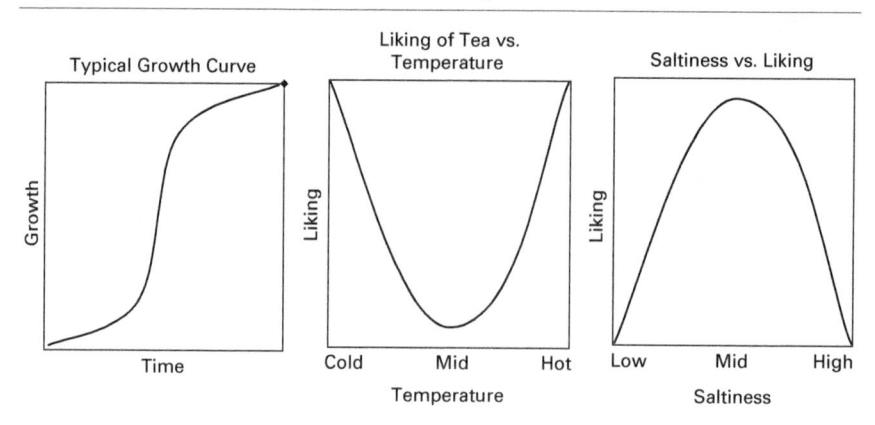

Figure 2.3 Not everything falls into a straight line

Typical Growth Curve (Growth vs. Time)

Liking of Tea vs. Temperature (Liking vs. Temperature: Cold, Mid, Hot)

Saltiness vs. Liking (Liking vs. Saltiness: Low, Mid, High)

a Petri dish. It takes a while for growth to become noticeable. Then growth takes off and stays at a fairly steady rate. In time, growth reaches a saturation level. It slows and then stops.

We also often see this curve with the adoption of products. A small brand has a great deal of trouble making itself visible, but once it reaches a certain threshold, growth comes much more rapidly. Finally, the brand reaches a point where it has saturated its market and further growth becomes very difficult.

Even though a straight line does not fit this growth curve pattern well, the correlation could still be deceptively strong, even as high as 0.9, misleadingly suggesting that the relationship is a straight line. Without looking at Figure 2.3, and looking just at the 0.9 correlation, it would be easy to make this mistake.

In the last two examples in Figure 2.3, the correlation actually is zero. If we paid attention only to this one statistic, we might be fooled into thinking that there was no relationship at all. We can in fact find that there is a perfect correspondence in the latter two relationships, but it is not linear.

We hope that there is no longer any question about needing to set sights on something other than a 'significant correlation'. We need something

> Correlation is a simple summary measure of how closely two variables fall compared to a perfect straight-line relationship. Correlation is known as R in statistics. R-squared is indeed the correlation value squared, and is the most widely used measure showing how well a regression model performs in fitting values to a straight line.

stronger and more focused. And, as a reminder, we typically cannot spend the time and money involved in simply putting a product or service out in the marketplace and seeing how it does. In some places, we can do a limited marketplace test (such as testing out a promotion on the web), but again, these do not give us much chance to experiment with alternatives. So when planning a project, what should we have in mind as our criteria for deciding if the approach we have chosen should succeed?

How do I plan to evaluate the results?

Some measures have been used for many years in judging the goodness of statistical models. **Correct classification** and **explained variance** are likely to be the most familiar. Newer measures include **information criteria** such as the Akaike Information Criterion (**AIC**) and Bayesian Information Criterion (**BIC**). You may come across many other measures if you spend time around statistical types, but these are a start.

Correct classification seems intuitively most approachable. This measure is used for **categorical** data and data that can take just a few values, such as ratings on a 1–5 scale. We need to use different types of testing for different types of data. Before we go much further, we should probably review the basic types of data.

The basic types of data

- Categorical data uses numbers as place holders for non-numerical values. For instance, you could use the numbers 1, 2, 3 and 4 to stand for four regions of the country, such as north, south, east and west. Clearly 'west' is not worth four times as much as 'north' (even though this might be disputed by people living in the west). Here we are simply putting the categories into a numeric form that is easier for the computer to manipulate and store than its text equivalent.
- **Ordinal data** shows which values are larger than which others, and so provides an **order** to the values. But it does not show how much larger one value is than another. For instance, if we have three contestants in first, second and third place, we know only the order in which they are placed, and not how much better first did than second or second did than third.
- **Interval-level data** gives us a set distance between the values, but does not allow us to say that one value is a certain multiple of another.

Temperature is an example of this kind of measure. For instance, if it is 40 degrees outside, we cannot say that it is twice as hot as 20 degrees. We can say that 40 degrees is 20 degrees more, and 60 is 20 more than 40, and so on.

- **Ratio-level data** gives us the most comparative information. Weight is an example of this type of measure. We can indeed say that if Hans has 20 kilos of sausages, he has **twice as many** sausages as Fritz, who has only 10. (We also can say Hans has 10 kilos more, the lucky fellow.)

Ratio-level data and interval-level data can be lumped together as **continuous** data, that is, data that can take any value, including fractional or decimal values. If you have a five-point scale, there is no value between (for instance) four and five. Similarly, there are no values between the '1' assigned to 'north' and the '2' assigned to 'south' in our nominal data example.

There have been, and probably continue to be, many arguments about whether the **scales** used in many surveys are just **ordinal-level** data or if they are **interval-level**. That is, you can argue that '5' on a five-point rating scale is the same distance from '4' as '4' is from '3'. That would make the scale **interval-level** if true. (However, this scale is definitely not ratio-level: you cannot say that a rating of '4' is twice as good as a rating of '2', and so on.)

At times you will see scaled ratings treated as if they were interval data or ratio data. For instance, you will see the average rating on a five-point rating scale shown as (say) 4.3, even though no one could possibly have given that exact response. In spite of the fact that treating scaled ratings in this way violates basic rules and guidelines, and there are better things you can do, we find that some methods hold up fairly well when scaled ratings are misused in this way.

Back to correct classification

If a person is **correctly classified** based on a mathematical model, this means that the model can apply some rules or manipulations to a set of predictor variables and correctly predict the score that person would have, or the group to which the person would belong. That is, we aim at a target value for each person by constructing a model, then check to see if prediction matches reality.

Some models will take multiple passes at the data, refining the model at each step. When the analysis can do no better, it then compares the number of correct and incorrect values, and gets a percentage.

Figure 2.4 Correct classification table – 63 per cent correct overall

		Actual response		
		No (n = 5,142)	Maybe (n = 2,902)	Yes (n = 9,651)
Prediction response	No	70.5%	20.8%	4.4%
	Maybe	6.8%	12.9%	12.8%
	Yes	22.7%	66.4%	82.8%

NOTE Cells highlighted show percentages correctly predicted

Figure 2.4 shows an example of a correct classification table. The 'yes' and 'no' responses are predicted by the model much better than 'maybe'. The dark squares in the figure show the percentages correctly predicted for each type of response. The 'yes' responses are predicted best – some 82.8 per cent of the 9,651 people who said 'yes' were correctly identified by the model. Conversely, 'maybe' responses are incorrectly predicted more often than not – some 66.4 per cent of these are misidentified as having said 'yes'.

When we multiply the percentages correctly predicted by the numbers in each group, we get to the overall correct prediction level. This is 63 per cent, brought down by the low level of correct predictions for the group saying 'maybe'.

Explained variance

You will see this measure used with many procedures, such as different types of regression models, but also with some kinds of classification tree analyses and in factor analysis – and you will see it cropping up in many other places. **Variance** is the pattern of scattering in the data, and **explained variance** then is how much of the pattern of scattering in the values of some target variable the model is able to capture.

With regression-based models, explained variance is the (perhaps familiar) **R-squared** statistic. As a reminder, **R-squared** is the correlation value squared, so with regression this is a measure of how well the prediction from the model and the actual values of the target variable fall into a straight line. Explained variance is always positive and can range from zero to one (or alternatively from 0 per cent to 100 per cent).

Information-based criteria

You may encounter these with some of the newer methods. For instance, the statistics program SPSS has a newer clustering method that they call TwoStep, and it shows the **AIC** and **BIC** statistics. These measures are good for comparing statistical models. A smaller score is better. How much smaller is open to interpretation, but an often-cited standard for the BIC is that a difference of two gives weak evidence that one model is better than another, and a difference of six gives strong evidence. There are no absolute standards for either of these tests, though. Also, many other information-based tests exist, but do not seem to get much use in the methods we usually encounter.

One more criterion: the RMSE

You also may see mentions of the **RMSE**, which stands for the root-mean-squared error. Like the information-based criteria, it is useful for comparing models. However, it is difficult to interpret directly as it does not fall into a fixed range, like explained variance. Rather it is in the units of the basic measurement you are making. For instance, an RMSE value of 0.7 is good if the basic measurement goes up to 1,000, but not good if it goes up to 1.

What are good results?

'All models are wrong but some are useful' – GEORGE E BOX

George Box was talking about the fact that any mathematical representation of the real world, even the best, leaves out some aspects. This is of course correct. Mr Box was an eminent statistician, and an excellent source of guidance on matters of interpreting data.

Knowing that we are shooting for a model that is 'good enough' and useful, we steer directly into some disagreement. No hard and fast rule exists for what makes for a 'good enough' score with the evaluative criteria we are discussing.

Few argue that anything less than 50 per cent correct could count as good. But beyond this, it becomes a matter of personal preference. Still, more than a few models have been accepted as useful, even with lower levels of being 'correct'. Sometimes one goal of an analysis is to determine just how well a specific question can be answered. In that case, a low level of performance is itself informational, showing that a specific approach or data set cannot provide strong guidance.

An example of a poor result being helpful

At a major pharmaceutical manufacturer, senior management decided that poor sales of a given drug had to be due to the sales force not adequately explaining the benefits of this fine product to the doctors who they regularly visited (pharmaceutical company salespeople, called representatives, are sent to doctors' offices, hospitals and clinics to describe the wonderful benefits of their particular brand of drugs). An elaborate study was set up, in which hundreds of doctors were contacted within 48 hours of a visit. No matter how the data was analysed, no more than 28 per cent of the variance in sales could be attributed to doctors correctly recalling the message about the drug. Management found this conclusion difficult to accept, but after enough attempts with different analyses, they reluctantly decided that the problems lay outside the sales force.

Be ready for strong preferences in testing

You may encounter guidelines or benchmarks – certain levels of test performance that must be met or a solution will get rejected. Some of these can be very strongly held, even if they seem arbitrary. For instance, one organization would not accept any solution that did not reach 70 per cent explained variance, and another insisted just as strongly on two-thirds (this latter threshold works out to roughly 66.67 per cent, which not only **is** arbitrary but transparently **looks** arbitrary). Understanding expectations about what passes as 'good' is a critical part of planning the project.

Results and validation

Results are considered stronger and more indicative of what the whole market would do when they are **validated**. We have not yet discussed **validation**. So perhaps this is the time. Validation is not a new idea, but the notion that you should use it regularly has gained support as data sets have become larger and models have grown more complex.

Validation involves first building the model on part of the data while holding aside the rest of it. You then try out the model on the part of the data that you held to one side. When you try the model on this so-called **hold-out sample**, predictive accuracy usually comes in at a lower level than when you simply look at the how the model performed where it was made.

Even the best predictive modelling technique will fit some random bumps and fluctuations that are found only in the data set on which a model was built. Trying out the model elsewhere, even on another part of the same data that you set aside, gives you some safeguards against **overfitting** to seeming patterns that you will not find in the outside world.

Validation typically comes built in by default only in newer statistical routines, such as those that do the Bayes Nets analyses we discuss in Chapter 7. More traditional methods, such as linear regression, often do not include validation methods, as they grew up in a time when computing power was not up to doing this type of testing as a matter of course.

> **Validation** means putting part of your data aside in a **hold-out sample**, building the model with the remainder, and then testing the model with the hold-out portion. This is supposed to safeguard against building a model that will work well just with your particular data set. Getting a model that fits the random fluctuations that appear in your data, but not elsewhere, is called **overfitting**. Validated results usually have lower predictive accuracy than a model built with all the data, and so are considered more realistic in judging the goodness of a model. Validating results is advisable where possible, and particularly so with larger data sets.

It is always sound practice to validate with larger data sets. In these, many effects may seem to be meaningful simply because you have so much data. You may recall that statistical tests start to break down with masses of data, because every effect or difference seems significant. When you have a huge data set, it is entirely feasible to put some of it to one side and have ample amounts left for building a complex model. So particularly if you have a lot of data, testing with a **hold-out** sample is worth including in the analysis.

Know what sensible goals might look like

Any analysis or project should be built around reaching the desired result, which may seem obvious but often is not easy to do. One common difficulty lies in aligning what people **want** with what they can **reasonably expect**.

Sometimes unreasonable expectations follow analyses that basically make sense. Too often, this happens because no one working on the project has discussed what the results are likely to show with the people who need to use them. (By the way, you may see these people called **stakeholders**.) For the people who will apply the results, you also need to remind them about what you have been doing along the way, if elapsed time to completion is more than a couple of weeks. It is surprising what very busy people can forget in just a short time.

There probably is no way to stop some people from going into projects with unrealistic expectations. When considering what might be reasonable, the first question is whether your source of data can address the question at hand. For instance, it is rational to look at customer transactions to estimate how many will respond to a new offer similar to a recent one. However, it is not sensible to turn to this data source and expect to glean ideas for developing a splendid new product. (In the following chapters we will go over subtler problems that can arise from starting with the wrong sources.)

Summary of key points

Starting considerations

This chapter talks about first steps in planning a project. Several considerations are key at the outset, and while some may seem apparent, it seems many a project has lurched into life without considering all of them. Key among the questions to ask are **what can change** based on the analysis. And, as follows, you must also determine what you really need to know to help that change happen. You also must understand who you are talking about or talking to – and avoid the trap of just running with whatever comes easily to hand. Thanks to the web, there is more data that will prove to be wrong for answering your question than ever – so this is a particularly key caution.

The place from which you draw your data more technically can be called a sample frame. As with the frame for a picture, if you pick one that is the wrong size or that obscures the picture in part, you will not be seeing what you should.

The most to expect

You need to consider the most you can expect from your data, or less positively put, the limitations of different kinds of analyses. With **historical** or **transaction data**, you can reasonably expect to forecast what will happen if you do something similar to what you have already been doing. You should not expect to make a fantastic new product with this, though.

With **standard questions and answers** from surveys, you can predict more than you might have suspected, particularly with some newer analytical methods (which we will discuss). However, you are more likely to get overall guidance about what you need to address, rather than specific direction. For instance, you may find that you can increase share by improving customer service, but not precisely in which ways or by how much. The experimental methods, particularly conjoint and discrete choice, can provide that specific level of information.

These latter methods, also called **trade-off methods,** are the best suited for determining the extent to which specific changes will lead to changes in marketplace behaviour. Even **discrete choice modelling,** the most realistic and powerful of these methods, still will only forecast **share of acceptance** (rather than actual market share) unless you can adjust at a minimum for how many are aware of the product in the marketplace and how widely the product is distributed.

The other trade-off methods, **MaxDiff** and **Q-Sort/Case 5,** provide clearly differentiated importances for lists of items such as claims, messages, or specific sets of product or service features. They cannot test the effects of changes in features on whole products or services. Both of them provide information at the ratio level, meaning you can say (for instance) that one feature is twice as important at the other. MaxDiff provides importances for every person, while Q-Sort does so only for groups. Q-Sort can prioritize many more items than MaxDiff, though, up to 100 (versus up to 35).

Setting up to judge the results

You will do the best, and gain widest acceptance of results, if you decide how the results will be judged at the outset of the project. People commonly ask about whether results are 'statistically significant' or 'correlated' or even 'significantly correlated', but these are usually not what they want for evaluation.

Look at significance and more

Statistical significance in fact is widely misunderstood. It is not the chances that something actually is happening. Rather, it is the chances that you are avoiding making a false claim. That is, the **null hypothesis,** other than being a term filling many of us with dread, means the belief that nothing is happening. When you are 95 per cent confident you can reject that belief, *voila*, that is significant. This is called avoiding a **Type I error.**

Seeing something that actually is happening is different. That is measured by **statistical power,** which we should be seeing discussed a great deal more than we do. Power goes down as you demand higher levels of statistical significance – the more certain you have to be that you are not making a false claim, the more likely you are to miss something that is really happening.

Significance testing starts to break down with very large numbers in a sample or with many tests being done. Some newer methods try to deal with this. Still, with large numbers, significance should be seen as a bottom floor – that is, if an effect or difference does not pass, you can be sure nothing is happening.

Significance testing always needs first to make sense. The main question is whether a statistically significant difference or effect you are finding is meaningful.

Sample size, sample error and the dangers of small samples

You often deal with a portion, or sample, of all the possible data you might use. All samples have some error. We can determine in advance what sample error will be if we have a sample percentage and know the sample size and the percentage we are measuring. Sample error goes up dramatically as samples fall below about 150.

A surprising number of decisions get made with little or no data, even in the face of this supposedly being an era of 'big data'. Too often, decisions get supported by talking to no more than a handful of consumers, often in the (likely familiar) setting of a focus group. These groups have many valuable uses, but making a final decision based on them is not one of those.

Using small numbers, you can get an overview, something like looking at a general view of a landscape that you will traverse. Larger numbers are like the detailed directions about where you will be going. Having both gives you the most assurance that you will get where you need to as efficiently as possible.

Better testing methods

Correct classification and explained variance are two measures commonly used to assess the goodness of results. Correct classification is applied in models that have categorical target or dependent variables. Explained variance is used in models that have a continuous target variable and in some other methods that do not have a target variable like factor analysis.

That said, we wander into considerable disagreement about how good is good enough. No model is a perfect representation of the outside world, so we have to decide how good an approximation we will accept. Strong biases may exist about what is good enough. You should find out about these before you start the project, so you have a threshold for what is acceptable.

You may also run into various information-based criteria for testing the goodness of models. Most common among these are the Bayesian

Information Criterion (BIC) and Akaike Information Criterion (AIC). These are always relative, used to compare two or more models to determine which is mathematically best.

Another relative measure you may encounter is the root-mean-squared error, or RMSE. Like the information-based criteria, it is useful for comparing models, but difficult to interpret directly.

The term correlation is often inaccurate shorthand

Correlations are taken to mean almost any relationship in casual conversations, but in statistics mean only how closely two variables fall into a straight line. Many regular relationships among factors in the real world do not fall into a straight line. Correlations also measure only straight-line relationships between a pair of variables. With more than two things at a time, we need to talk about other measures.

Results and validation

Results are considered stronger and more representative of what you will find in the real world if they are validated. This involves first putting aside part of the data and building the model on the rest. You then test out the model on the part of the data you did not use to build the model, the so-called hold-out sample. Results usually are not quite as strong in the hold-out sample and in the part of the data you used to build the model. Even the best possible models usually fit some irregularities, lumps and bumps that are peculiar just to the data set at hand – and that you will not find in the outside world.

Know what sensible results will look like

One common difficulty lies in aligning what people **want** with what they can **reasonably expect**.

Sometimes unreasonable expectations follow analyses that basically make sense. Too often, this happens because no one working on the project has discussed what the results are likely to show with the people who need to use them.

You may at times encounter unrealistic expectations. A good way to deal with these is considering carefully whether your source of data can address the question at hand. Then explain how reasonable outcomes might look.

Conjoint, discrete choice and other trade-offs

03

Let's do an experiment

This chapter addresses best methods for developing new products or services or combinations of messages – allowing you to predict responses to many hundreds or thousands of alternatives by testing a small, scientifically selected fraction of them. These are the experimentally designed approaches, also called the trade-off methods. At their simplest, they can provide clear differentiation in preferences. At their most complex, they can accurately simulate what will happen under new circumstances in the real world. These fall into three broad classes: discrete choice, conjoint analysis and other forced trade-off exercises. These all fall towards the end of the continuum of methods that require high planning for engagement with consumers and have high analytical requirements. We will discuss briefly how each method evolved and its relative strengths and weaknesses. These methods have been greatly expanded and strengthened by machine learning approaches. The next chapters will show how.

The reasons we need these methods

These methods were developed to address a salient problem with questions asking about what is important. We cannot get at the right answer by simply asking people to give us ratings such as 'How important is this to you on a scale of one to five?' When this type of direct question is posed, people cannot or will not give answers that reflect what they truly value the most.

For instance, suppose you wanted to develop a new floor-standing wine cooler, and your product team came up with a variety of possible features,

Figure 3.1 Rating the features of a floor-standing wine cooler

Features of your floor-standing wine cooler	How important to you is each feature?					
	Not at all important	Not too important	Somewhat important	Very important	Critical
Lowest price	☐	☐	☐	☐	☑
Thickest insulation	☐	☐	☐	☐	☑
Genuine gold plating	☐	☐	☐	☑	☐
Built-in icemaker	☐	☐	☐	☐	☑
Parking brake to prevent slippage	☐	☐	☐	☐	☑
UL listed	☐	☐	☐	☐	☑
Battery backup for power outages	☐	☐	☐	☐	☑
Extendable handle with umbrella	☐	☐	☐	☐	☑
Extra wide mag wheels	☐	☐	☐	☑	☐

including some that were just slightly far-fetched. If we asked an average consumer questions about how important these features were using a standard set of importance rating scales, we would get a pattern like the one shown in Figure 3.1.

Asking for ratings in a survey, everything becomes highly important. This is a real problem. Morwitz (in Scott Armstrong's *Principles of Forecasting*, 2002) did a very thorough review of 60+ years of research about trying to predict behaviour with scaled ratings, and found no consistently good way to use them.

There is one possible exception: if you have masses of historical sales data, a great deal of historical ratings data, the product category is not changing, and its buyers are not changing. As you might guess – this combination is not likely. However, if all these conditions could be met, then you would have **norms** and the question of interpreting the scaled ratings would come down to referring to historical patterns.

CASE STUDY The essential 3 am banker

A major bank entered the Chicago market once several Byzantine laws restricting banks from having many branches were nullified. It bought a whole portfolio of smaller banks, proudly emblazoned them with its logo, and put large signs in the windows saying, 'Talk to a live banker 24 hours a day!!!'

After a month or two, these signs were changed to say 'Talk to a live banker until 1 am!!' Not long afterwards they changed again – to read 'Talk to a live banker until midnight!' Before the seasons changed, the signs changed again – to read 'Talk to a live banker until 10 pm'.

After that, the signs came down, or perhaps fell down due to the weight of all the patches with revised times that had been placed on them. Clearly, not many people actually woke up at 3 am, slapped themselves on the forehead, and said, 'Oh my, I really need to talk to a banker!'

Yet the bank had behaved as if they expected people to do this. Why did this happen? Conversations with those involved revealed that they had asked people, **using scaled importance ratings**, what would be important in a shiny new bank bearing their corporate name. When people were given the chance to provide these direct ratings, they often ticked 'talking to a live banker' as critical. Yet it clearly was not crucial in their actual banking. It was just that they could not say 'no' to what looked like a free offer.

The people who framed the questions were rueful about this, referring to organizational pressures, not having enough time – and that, besides, someone else made the final decision about the survey. Excuses aside, they got useless answers and wasted a chance to enter a new market with a more valuable offer.

They would have done much better using one of the trade-off methods we are discussing. In future efforts they did, avoiding the mistake of acting as if bankers were essential at 3 am. Their later offerings were substantially better received.

Shortcomings in scaled importance ratings

In the typical situation, where you do not have a long and applicable history, scaled importance ratings suffer from numerous well-documented problems. Salient among them are these:

- acquiescence bias;
- straight-line and extreme responses;
- socially desirable responses;
- cultural skew.

Acquiescence bias means the tendency of people to respond to questions with positive responses. That is, most people are predisposed to avoid negatives and will choose a more flattering response if possible. For instance, the vast majority of responses on a five-point importance rating scale do indeed fall into the top two points of the scale (the ratings corresponding to the most importance).

Straight-line or extreme responses arise from limited cognitive effort being put into the interview task. Some individuals will agree to do the interview but then repeatedly check either end of the rating scale (highest or lowest), rather than thinking of more subtly differentiated responses. One alternative pattern of giving straight-line response that is fairly common is a person's repeatedly checking the second highest box on a rating scale, such as '4' on a five-point scale.

Socially desirable responses reflect what people believe should be said, rather than what they actually believe. For instance, if we were to ask for direct ratings of the importance of safety features in a new car, nearly all people would rate them as 'essential'. Yet many cars in the marketplace continue to sell well in spite of indifferent or even below-average safety ratings.

Cultural skew reflects the well-documented differences found in ratings among people with different cultural backgrounds. For instance, doctors in Japan are notoriously hard in ratings. They might rate their favourite product at '7' on a 10-point scale. Doctors in Latin America, conversely, might rate all products at '9' or '10', even products that they would never use. Sometimes, even finer geographic differences matter. For instance, people in large northern cities in the United States tend to give lower ratings than people in southern, less urban areas.

These problems led to adoption of new methods

The inherent unreliability of rating scales led to a search for, and common adoption of, new methods. These have been put under the broad heading of **trade-off methods** – most also are designed like **scientific experiments**. All of these methods ask respondents to weigh specific elements or features of a product, service, claim or message against each other.

> Problems with traditional scaled importance ratings are numerous, well known and thoroughly documented. All of these together lead to ratings of this type providing unreliable results for predicting behaviour. Salient among the factors that make these ratings non-useful include: **acquiescence bias** (tendency to rate positively); **straight-line or extreme responses** (from people who do not put in effort answering questions); **socially desirable responses** (or the common tendency to say what it seems should be said, rather than really answering); and **cultural skew** (different use of scaled ratings depending on social background).
>
> Practically speaking, nearly everything rated tends to become highly important or critical, because it costs nothing in a survey to say that everything is important. These problems led to the widespread adoption of various trade-off methods, in particular, the experimentally designed ones we discuss in this section of the book.

It is entirely possible that the severe problems with scaled importance ratings for use in prediction led to a devaluation of the entire field of survey-based research. Many practitioners still have not accepted the idea that these trade-off methods, if done reasonably well, can overcome these limitations.

The basic thinking behind the experimentally designed methods

These methods, as a reminder, also are called **trade-off studies**. They measure responses to distinct features or distinct variations of definite features. That is, products, services and messages are assumed to be collections of features that are measurable and comparable. These methods also assume that the value of each feature can be **traded** versus the value of other features.

This is as far into the psychology of decision making as these methods go. They do not address the underlying intricacies of decision making – it seems more accurate to consider that they are aiming to capture the outcome of the decisions rather than their inner workings.

Features can be broken into discrete variations or levels

Another implicit assumption is that features that vary continuously in the real world can be measured at specific fixed values. Each distinct variation of an attribute is called a **level**.

For instance, suppose a course of medical treatment could be priced anywhere between £2,000 and £9,000. Several distinct prices would be chosen to measure in this range, such as: £2,000, £4,500, £6,800 and £9,000. These and only these get measured directly. Other points in between are estimated by **interpolation**.

As we will see, in any of these methods, choosing the right points to measure is critical. You also need to keep to as few as possible that measure what you need to know. This all arises from the requirements of designed experiments.

The feature level with the most utility wins

The values of the various attributes and their variations or levels are measured in abstract units called **utilities**. These are used as a kind of bookkeeping, as a way of measuring everything on the same footing. This leads to another assumption of these methods: that the level of each attribute with the highest utility will **win** in a choice. This does not mean that people look at all the attributes, or choose carefully. It also does not mean that they cognitively follow a utility-based decision process.

These methods are more usefully seen as aiming to match the **outcome** of the decision process, rather than trying to decipher inner workings. They do assume, though, that decisions at least are generally consistent. Some methods provide measures of how consistent people are when answering. Answers will pass thresholds for being consistent in trade-off studies – if those involved understand what they need to do. Making these studies clear is critical.

What the methods ask – and get

Each of these methods gets a different type of information by using a specific form of questioning. The most complex, discrete choice modelling, shows a representation of the product or service choices in the context of competitive offerings – and asks for a decision. The least complex, the Q-Sort/Case 5 method, shows a list of features or claims and asks people to rank part of them. Let's briefly go over what each method presents during an interview, in the hope of making this more tangible.

Discrete choice modelling

Study participants in a typical online interview see a series of screens showing them **marketplaces** or **scenarios** (or **market scenarios**) representing the main choices that they have. The features of the alternative products or services shown in these scenarios vary from one screen to the next. For each scenario they evaluate, study participants are told to think only about that particular set and, given that the choices have the features and prices shown, to choose the best of them. Many of these exercises are set up so that people also have the option of saying 'none of these'.

Research has shown that people do better with these tasks if they are told to imagine that they really would like to buy something and to choose 'none' only if everything is truly unacceptable. Figure 3.2 shows an example of one screen from a discrete choice study done among computer hardware engineers.

Figure 3.2 A sample marketplace scenario for discrete choice modelling

Here is the next 'purchase scenario' for you to evaluate. Please look at the different options offered and review the characteristics of each. Please think of these and only these choices – not anything you may have seen in another scenario. Again, assume that you are in the market and really would like to buy something if any of the choices is at all acceptable. We realize that the features we have included may or may not be important to you. Just focus on the ones that matter to you. Then tell us which one, if any, you would buy.

Giant Blue	NP Hardware	Valley Computers	
Max # of users: 15	Max # of users: 75	Max # of users: 10	
Sharing data		Sharing data	
Desktop/server e-mail			
Integrated wireless access			
Remote Access			
Work with customers		Work with customers	
Anti-virus/Anti-spam			
Storage capacity: 400 GB	Storage capacity: 200 GB	Storage capacity: 100 GB	
Storage Expansion: Can add an external drive	Storage expansion: Can add an internal drive	Storage expansion: Not possible	
5 user licences included. User licence additions: $59 per user	5 user licences included. User licence additions: $489 per block of 5 users	5 user licences included. User licence additions: $99 per user	I would not buy any of the products shown here
Price: $499	Price: $1299	Price: $299	
○	○	○	○

Definitions   Continue

Conjoint analysis

The term **conjoint analysis** is used to cover several related forms of analysis, as mentioned in Chapter 2. Some consider conjoint to be a broader heading and will include discrete choice modelling as a part of it. However, because these two methods arose from different disciplines, and because some of their basic ideas differ, we will discuss them separately.

Full profile conjoint is the first form of conjoint analysis to have gained widespread use. It shows an entire product or service described as a set of attributes. In a typical study, people look at a series of these **product profiles** and give each of them a rating. (Before these studies were routinely done online, people also could get a set of cards and either rate them or sort them into order from most to least preferred. Sometimes one product profile is still referred to as one **card**.)

Figure 3.3 shows one screen used in a full profile conjoint study about service from a telecom company. This study diagnosed which levels of service in various areas would be associated with higher levels of overall customer satisfaction – and by how much.

By showing the entire service experience, this analysis overcame the problems inherent in asking for direct ratings of the importance of service features. Chapter 5 discusses this type of analysis and its outcomes in more detail.

Figure 3.3 A profile of a service for conjoint analysis

Please consider this package of services only. Try not to think of any other packages you may have seen. If these services could be delivered reliably as shown, how satisfied would you be with your service overall?

Feature	For this service:
Frequency of account reviews	Six months
Contract length and trial period	Three-month trial period
Time on hold to reach tech support	Call back option within five minutes
Frequency of status updates for critical issues	Daily
Wait time for mission critical repair	Within 24 hours
Repair appointment window	AM/PM (8–12 or 12–5)
Wait time for non-mission-critical repairs	Within four hours
Frequency of status updates for non-critical issues	Hourly
E-mail response time	Eight hours
Frequency of status updates	Weekly
Wait time for local telephone service	Two weeks
Wait time for high-speed internet	One week

Please put in your rating on a scale of 0 to 100 [ ]

Figure 3.4 A simple simulator for one product

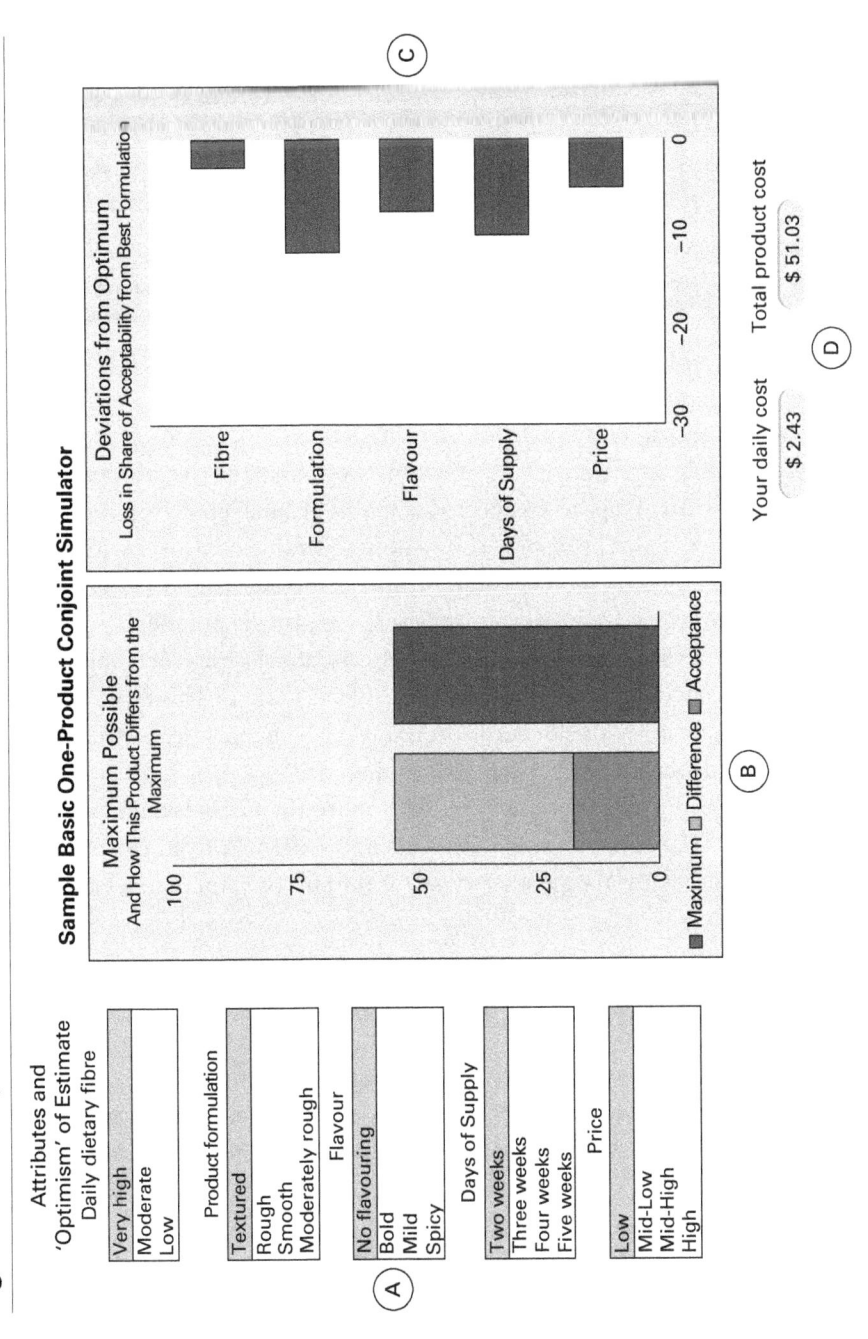

Market simulators

Conjoint analysis and discrete choice modelling both can lead to **market simulator programs**. We will talk more about **market simulators** in the next two chapters. To help this become more specific, we will show a simple one now and explain its general features.

In Figure 3.4, next to the letter **A**, you see a set of controls that a user can change. Each time a new variation is chosen for each feature, the expected **share of acceptance** value (above letter **B**) changes. (In Chapter 2, we laid out the difference between share of acceptance and market share. If this is feeling distant, please check back there.)

The shaded selection in each control corresponds to the way the product is now configured (very high fibre, textured formulation, no flavouring, two weeks' supply and low price for its formulation). This is one of 3 x 4 x 4 x 4 x 4 possible variations or **768 possible ways** to make this product.

The **share of acceptance** expected with this product configuration appears above the letter **B**. The display shows how this value compares with the best possible product. Sometimes these displays include charts of numbers as well as graphs, and sometimes you would see just the numbers.

Near letter **C**, you see the specific effects of selecting each variation of feature, when compared to the best possible variation. (This type of display does not appear in all simulator programs.) The figures near letter **D** show the price for the product (both daily and total).

Examples of market simulators with more than one product appear in Chapter 4. They contain more elements and so benefit from more explanation. More details about other types of output also appear in Chapters 4 and 5.

Maximum difference scaling (MaxDiff)

MaxDiff uses a list of features, attributes, messages or claims and provides a clear reading of relative importances. It breaks a list of about 8–35 attributes into sets, which can range from two to six at a time. For each set, it asks for the most important of the ones shown. With three or more in a set, it is also possible to ask for the least important. This is typically done in a web interview. A typical screen appears in Figure 3.5.

Unlike conjoint and discrete choice modelling, MaxDiff does not measure the relative importances of different **levels** or variations of attributes. Using its direct comparisons, it does not make sense to compare, for instance, 'shelf stable for three months' versus 'shelf stable for six months' – the longer time

Figure 3.5 A survey task for maximum difference scaling (MaxDiff)

When considering buying one of these products, which one is the **most** important and which one is the **least** important?

Most Important		Least Important
	Highest quality	
●	Best safety features	●
	Most comfortable grip	●

Next

would always win if these two were to be compared. You could, though, compare 'excellent shelf stability' to other attributes.

The attributes being compared should not make up an entire product or service. Therefore, this method loses the distinct advantage of conjoint or discrete choice, in which specific features appear in the context of all other features.

MaxDiff provides relative importances at the **ratio level**. We can, for instance, say 'Attribute N is four times as important as Attribute R' after doing a MaxDiff analysis.

Q-Sort/Case 5

This was the first method developed (back in the 1920s). It uses a partial guided ranking of items. We use only part of the **Q-Sort** method, namely ranking the few best and few worst items in a long list of items. This leaves the rest 'tied' as unranked items between the best set and the worst set. In a list of, for instance, 50 items, we might ask for the top 10, then ask for the first, second and third best to be ordered – and then do the same with the bottom 10.

The rest of Q-Sort, which we do not use, sounds somewhat mystical. It talks about typing people based on how they sorted the items.

The analysis is carried out by a method called **Thurstone's Case 5**, or 'The Law of Comparative Judgements'. Thurstone had the advantage of working in the 1920s, when it was still possible to call a statistical analysis a law.

Using Case 5, rankings get converted into ratio-level data like MaxDiff. However, unlike MaxDiff, this method provides information only at the group level. Therefore, while Q-Sort can process more items than MaxDiff (100 items in a list has been reported), it does not provide importances for the items for each individual.

Figure 3.6 A survey task for a Q-Sort/Case 5

Features you might have in your new grout cleaner: first pick your top five	
New easy-pour spigot	Buy three and the fourth is free
Delightful pine/ozone/blackberry smell	As advertised on TV
Six-pack comes with free cardboard carton	No longer sticks to clothes or hair
No rinse needed (on coloured grout)	Handy travel handle
Good for camping	USDA approved
Recommended by Chef Alfonso of TV's *Mighty Meals*	Cleans drains too
Asbestos free	Delightful cherry flavour
Safe for pets (over 45lb)	Sizes over three gallons come with free fire shovel
New non-leaking seams (not in 64oz size)	Guaranteed 99 per cent free of U 238
Turns blue when it is through	Easy open – no can-opener required
Designer container (not in six-gallon drum)	Non-GMO

Study participants would respond to something like the list in Figure 3.6. This method actually is **not** based on a designed experiment, although it is supposed to follow rules about how items are sorted and ranked.

Both MaxDiff and Q-Sort provide a listing and/or chart of relative importances for the attributes that were tested. These charts can apportion 100 per cent of importance among the attributes, or use an index. The index could show, for instance, how all attributes compare in importance to the average, with the average set to 100. (In this scheme, an attribute with an index of 400 would be four times as important as the average for the set.) Examples of these charts appear in Online Bonus Chapter 1, available at www.koganpage.com/AI-Marketing.

What is a designed experiment?

The term **designed experiment** covers a broad range of approaches. However, all experimental designs for trade-off studies meet one goal: estimating the values of many items cleanly and clearly. Two of the methods, discrete choice and conjoint analysis, also use these designs so that relatively few carefully selected situations or comparisons can estimate what will happen in dozens to thousands of situations.

That is, if we use an experimental design and show just a few **stimulus items** (products, marketplaces or comparisons) then we can estimate accurately what would happen in **hundreds**, or even **thousands**, of different situations.

Conjoint, Discrete Choice and Other Trade-Offs

With conjoint analysis and discrete choice, we also get a clear reading of how strong each item is in influencing some overall measure, such as a choice, or (in some cases) interest in a choice. (This latter measure can be useful in some instances, as we will discuss.)

That may sound abstract, so let's go to a specific example. Suppose you want to measure relative preferences for cars that vary in horsepower, mileage and time to get from zero to 60 miles per hour (roughly 96 kilometres per hour). This example will use a rating scale, in spite of its known difficulties, to make the explanation as simple as possible. (Using a rating scale, it is still possible to get relative preferences based on the fact that we are comparing each person's ratings to her/his other ratings.) Figure 3.7 shows one wrong way and the right way to get at the relative influence on overall ratings of different levels of horsepower, mileage and time from zero to 60.

We would have no idea what is influencing overall ratings using the bad set-up – everything improves in the same way from car 1 to car 3: horsepower gets better, mileage gets better and time from zero to 60 miles per hour gets better. We will get a clear picture from the many variations, where all three factors vary differently.

Figure 3.7 A small and wrong way to measure and a larger correct way

Small and wrong:
How likely would you be to buy each car?

	HP	MPG	Seconds 0 to 60	Rate this car
Car 1	120	30	9	
Car 2	180	40	8	
Car 3	240	50	7	

Larger and correct:
How likely would you be to buy each car?

	HP	MPG	Seconds 0 to 60	Rate this car
Car 1	180	30	9	
Car 2	120	40	9	
Car 3	240	50	9	
Car 4	240	30	8	
Car 5	180	40	8	
Car 6	120	50	8	
Car 7	120	30	7	
Car 8	240	40	7	
Car 9	180	50	7	

Artificial Intelligence Marketing and Predicting Consumer Choice

Figure 3.8 Elements of a designed experiment

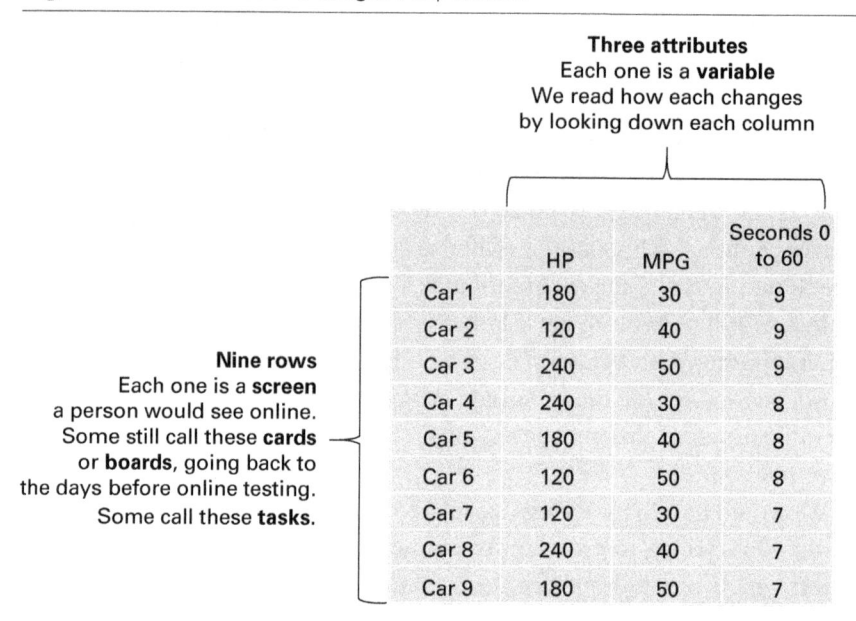

Three attributes
Each one is a **variable**
We read how each changes
by looking down each column

	HP	MPG	Seconds 0 to 60
Car 1	180	30	9
Car 2	120	40	9
Car 3	240	50	9
Car 4	240	30	8
Car 5	180	40	8
Car 6	120	50	8
Car 7	120	30	7
Car 8	240	40	7
Car 9	180	50	7

Nine rows
Each one is a **screen** a person would see online. Some still call these **cards** or **boards**, going back to the days before online testing. Some call these **tasks**.

In the second set-up, with nine different cars, all the features vary in different ways from one car to the next. This in fact is a designed experiment. In Figure 3.8 we review how this works, where the various cars appear in the form of a table. Each car is a row in the table, and each attribute is a column.

Following the usual convention, each column is a **variable**. That is, the attributes get varied from one car to the next. Each row would be shown on a separate screen in a typical online interview.

Looking down the three columns in Figure 3.8 we can determine how variations in each feature or attribute relate to variations in each of the other attributes. We use standard correlations to measure these relationships. As a reminder, correlations measure how well the two variables fall

Figure 3.9 Showing that there are no correlations among attributes

Correlations	HP	MPG	0 to 60
HP		0	0
MPG	0		0
0 to 60	0	0	

NOTE Cells are darkened because a variable cannot have a correlation with itself into a straight line. We showed this in Chapter 2, where variables were plotted versus each other.

In our example, all correlations are zero. That is, there is no relationship in the way the features vary from one car to the next. Recall that the features are **variables**. Figure 3.9 shows the table of correlations. (Some blanks – the black boxes – appear in the table because variables cannot have correlations with themselves.)

This characteristic of designs is key because we do not want the measurement of one variable to get mixed or **confounded** with the measurement of another. When the attributes have no correlation with one another, this is called an **orthogonal** design.

Making it formal

The full name for this type of design is a **fractional factorial orthogonal design**. This is a mouthful and sounds highly impressive. Many years ago, we ran across a person who charged his clients extra for a 'certified' version of one of these. However, at the time, these designs all came from a catalogue that was labelled 'orthogonal designs'. This name simply means that this design uses a fraction of all possible combinations and that the factors are varied so that they have no correlations. Designs later became more varied (and flexible), as we will discuss soon.

Another complication

One other important rule also holds for this type of experimental design: every pair of **attribute levels** will appear at least once. This is not every three-way set, four-way set (or more, with bigger designs). In our example, for instance, a quick review shows:

- 120 HP appears with 30, 40 and 50 MPG each at least once;
- the same holds for 150 HP and 180 HP – each appears with each MPG at least once;
- also, 120 HP appears at least once with 7, 8 or 9 seconds to 60;
- and the same holds for 150 HP and 180 HP versus each time to 60 – and so on.

Getting everything right takes a lot of work. At one time, this kept a lot of graduate students fully occupied as they worked towards their degrees. These designs went into catalogues, which had to be searched for best design for the task at hand. (We will get to how you decide on a design shortly.) Fortunately, any relatively new computer can easily crank out these designs, making custom ones to fit new situations.

The great measurement power of experiments

Two examples will show why we bother with experiments. For instance, suppose you had a product with six attributes, each having three levels, and one attribute with six levels. This would mean that you could have: 3 x 3 x 3 x 3 x 3 x 3 x 6 or some **4,374 possible variations** on this product.

Using an experimental design, we can accurately estimate the value of all 4,374 possible variations using only 18 product descriptions.

Next, suppose you have a product with 18 two-level attributes (these could be 'feature is there' versus 'feature is absent' or 'colour is red' versus 'colour is blue', for instance). This would give you 2^{18} (2 to the 18th power) or **262,144** combinations. You can measure all these possible combinations using only 20 carefully selected product descriptions.

Even more combinations can be tested and compared in real time using a **market simulator program**. These run under Microsoft Excel (or more rarely, PowerPoint or in Adobe Acrobat PDF format) and feature easy-to-use controls. (Your computer also needs to have Flash Player installed for the PowerPoint and PDF versions to work.) We discuss simulators in Chapters 4 and 5.

> **Designed experiments** allow you to measure the effects of varying many attributes accurately and cleanly. Used with discrete choice modelling and conjoint, they also allow you to accurately forecast responses to dozens or even thousands of alternative product/service configurations by showing just a small scientifically selected subset. Designed experiments have tremendous power. For instance, with 18 two-level attributes, you can determine the worth of 262,144 possible combinations using only 20 experimentally designed product configurations.

What you measure and the size of experiments

The more attributes and variations of attributes (or levels) that you need to measure, the larger your experiment needs to become. That is, as you vary more attributes and levels, you will need to show people more screens or pages with varying products. But how many?

This is a rough rule of thumb – the exact formula is a little more complicated. As we did in Figure 3.8, below we express this both as rows in a design or as screens that you need to show with different products:

- two-level attribute: one row in a design or screen shown;
- three-level attribute: two rows or screens shown;
- four-level attribute: three rows or screens shown;
- five-level attribute: four rows or screens shown;
- six-level attribute: five rows or screens shown.

And then we need to consider a bit more. We need two more rows or screens:

- One for measuring the **error** in the model. This allows us to know how well we are measuring – basically how consistent each person was in answering. Otherwise, when we run the model, this will be reported as 100 per cent regardless of how well people did when answering.
- One for a very useful term called the **constant**. This has mathematical meaning, but we can use it to measure the value of the brand or the choice outside the attributes being tested.

One last wrinkle

You must count the number of variations or levels in each attribute and check the design against these. The design must be at least as big as the product or the two attributes with the most levels. In our example, three three-level attributes would suggest that we need 3 x 2 or six screens, plus our two extra for measuring error and the constant, or eight. However, we must have at least 3 x 3 (the product of the two attributes with the most levels) or nine screens.

Getting more from experiments: HB to the rescue

It is a sad but definite fact that people tire quickly of evaluating alternative products or marketplaces. Depending on the audience, this could start as soon as six or eight being shown. (When study participants are very involved with the product or service, and have good ability to concentrate, they can complete up to 21 or so before they get too tired. Engineers and farmers have done very well with evaluating a great many alternatives.)

When experiments got too large, measuring many attributes and levels, one strategy was to split up the design, giving a fraction to each person, and then adding more people to compensate. For instance, a client goes nearly crazy and wants this:

- six four-level attributes;
- six three-level attributes;
- twelve two-level attributes.

We would need 48 screens to measure this. This of course is far too many to show in its entirety to one person without some illegal stimulative substances. The old solution was to show each person a fraction of these, for instance 12 of the 48 required, and then multiply the number of study participants to make up for it. Showing one-quarter of all the screens to each, we would multiply study participant by four.

That is, each person counted as one-fourth of a total experiment or **replication**. To get to the right number of experiments to analyse, we just increased the count of people. In Chapter 4 we talk about how many people you need to measure.

With choice models, adding more people like this worked! But it made for much bigger and costlier studies. Splitting up designs for traditional full-profile conjoint was highly messy and likely to explode. Clearly, as demand increased for more complex and realistic representations of products and services, we needed something better.

Enter HB analysis

Hierarchical Bayesian (HB) analysis was developed in the 1990s to address the above problem. It is a machine learning method that stretches how much we can measure in trade-off studies, relying upon immense numbers of calculations and some fairly mind-boggling concepts. Fortunately, it has been proven under fire – for over 25 years.

With HB, we can measure up to four times as many attributes in choice models/conjoint as we could before this method was developed. We could, for instance, reasonably split a 48-screen task into 12-task sets, show each person one 12-task set and not increase the sample. (Please note that some authorities say you should not try for more than a twofold increase or threefold increase in what you measure before you compensate by increasing the number of people you interview.)

As a big bonus, we also could get data for individuals from discrete choice models (and MaxDiff studies). That was never possible before HB. All answers could be only for groups. Those were the bad old days.

But what is HB analysis?

Briefly, **HB analysis** fills in data that is scant or missing for a respondent by repeatedly **borrowing** estimates from other respondents. That is, it keeps sampling other respondents and storing values from those who have the missing information, then running calculations. It usually does this 20,000 or more times for each attribute level for each respondent, keeping a running average of its estimates.

It may or may not compare the respondent to the sample it is drawing and make adjustments based on their similarities. Estimates will settle down to steady values (or **converge**) if you have set up the problem correctly. If you have not, then maybe they will not – and you need to root out problems. A solution that does not converge usually means errors in set-up, data collection or coding of values.

This method gives your PC (or Mac) more of a workout than almost anything else you might ask it to do. Unlike nearly any other task we throw at a computer, these analyses will leave you waiting. It could take many minutes for a complicated discrete choice modelling run to finish, even hours.

HB analysis: it works and it's not magic

Hierarchical Bayesian (HB) analysis is a machine learning method that allows us to generate far more information from a designed experiment than formerly was possible. This allows us to measure more attributes and attribute levels than used to be possible for a specific number of marketplaces (or products) shown in a study. Some experts say this is about twice as much, but about 25 years' experience shows that we can safely measure three to four times as many as used to be possible.

In the bad old days, if we needed to run an experiment requiring us to show 48 screens of marketplaces in total, we would have needed to boost our sample by three times if we showed each person 16 of these. With HB, we get almost exactly the same result with no increase in sample. And we get data for each individual.

This sounds like sorcery, but it works, relying on the power of the computer doing many millions of calculations to reach an answer.

Amazingly, all this borrowing of information works – and we get highly accurate estimates. It seems almost supernatural and even somewhat suspect, but with HB analysis we encounter one situation where we can get much more thanks to the great power of modern computers.

We could argue about counting this as artificial intelligence, but you will note that we have called it a **machine learning method**. That is, the computer stores calculations and incorporates them into later ones, thus learning from what it has done. We will get into what makes analyses **Bayesian** in more detail in later chapters. For now, this has to do with the way that later estimates incorporate and modify earlier ones.

A brief talk about origins

The origins and evolution of discrete choice modelling

Work on discrete choice modelling started in the 1960s. Daniel McFadden eventually won a Nobel Prize in economics for this work. (This appears to be the only method we discuss anywhere in this book that has this distinction.)

The first widely cited application of discrete choice modelling, published around 1980, answered this question: How we can predict choices when the alternatives do not have any attributes in common? This was in transportation, where the choices were taking a train, bus or car to work. The authors aimed to determine the factors that would incline people more towards choosing each type of transportation.

The three choices have no common attributes except time door-to-door. For instance, you do not care about the cost of parking downtown if you take the train to work, or the fare on a train if you are taking a bus – and so on.

Analysing choices without common attributes posed many thorny problems, involving difficulties that can scarcely be imagined until you see the proofs involved. Fortunately for all of us, the method is on a solid footing. And the study worked!

And indeed, this method has a remarkably strong track record as well as excellent theoretical underpinnings. It remains the most realistic and most predictive method for determining the specific attributes and variations in attributes that influence consumer decisions – and how much influence those attributes have.

Conjoint analysis from start to its many varieties

Conjoint analysis was developed in the 1970s by market researchers, largely due to frustration with the poor predictive ability of scaled importance ratings. As we mentioned, these ratings do not work well as predictors of behaviour in nearly all instances. They are generally unreliable, in that their connection to what people will actually choose is tenuous at best.

One possible exception, just to remain fair, would occur if you have a lot of historical sales data, a lot of historical ratings data, a product or service category that is not changing, and consumers who are not changing. As you might guess – this is not too likely.

Conjoint proved it was better than scaled ratings in real-world applications, even in its earliest incarnations. It was rapidly and widely adopted. Early conjoint (before about 1970) looked a little like magic squares – people put numbers in boxes ranking pairs of attribute levels as in the sample in Figure 3.10.

The guest imaginary study participant in Figure 3.10 best likes the car with the most horsepower and best mileage (MPG), shown by the number 1 in that box. Next, she sticks with the highest mileage car but with the next most horsepower (150). In her third choice, though, she does not opt for the lowest horsepower car with the best mileage, rather taking the highest horsepower car with the next best mileage. The rest of the squares are given values down to the obvious worst choice, with the lowest horsepower and worst mileage.

Our presumably patient participant would then need to do another grid like this for horsepower versus time 0 to 60, then another for MPG versus time 0 to 60, etc. Not only is an exercise like this tedious with four or more attributes, the approach remains distant from what people do when selecting a product or service. And so improvement of this method continued.

Figure 3.10 Our guest fictional study participant ranks cars on two features

		Horsepower		
		120	150	180
MPG	30	9	8	7
	40	6	3	4
	50	5	2	1

NOTE '1' is the best and '9' is the worst

The big development: full-profile conjoint analysis

This form of conjoint arrived in the mid-1970s. It shows a series of whole products or services and asks the study participant to evaluate each in turn. Because it shows full descriptions of a product, it has the name **full profile**. Respondents typically rate these product profiles, or (very rarely now) sort and rank them.

This was immediately hailed as a great advance and gained widespread adoption. It often worked well, particularly with widely known brands that were similar to each other. But it also broke down mysteriously in other situations – and as these were understood better, the use of discrete choice modelling rose.

Also, with standard analytical tools, the ability of conjoint analysis to measure was quite limited. Most studies stuck to six or seven attributes at most, with just a few variations of each.

As mentioned above, HB analysis broke the barriers on how many attributes and levels might be tested. Before this method was developed fully (around 1990), a number of alternative forms of conjoint analysis attempted to deal with these limitations.

Perhaps best known among these was a software product called **Adaptive Conjoint Analysis (ACA)**. This took each person down a slightly different route based on what they said about what they found acceptable before seeing any product profiles. This method received some strong criticism, with some justified complaints about the assumptions behind it.

That is, concerns were voiced about the lack of realism involved in pulling attributes out of a product and asking for which levels were acceptable, without seeing how they fit with the other features of the product. For instance, you might say off the top of your head that you would never buy a condominium with a balcony (perhaps for fear of being mistakenly serenaded at midnight by some wandering Romeo). However, if you found a condo that was perfect in all other regards, you might then decide that you could put this fear aside and buy it after all.

So there were credible objections about both calculations and the realism of the task. In spite of these, this product enjoyed considerable popularity until discrete choice modelling supplanted conjoint as the strongest method for determining a product's optimal features and prices.

Another method that attempted to deal with limitations of traditional conjoint is called **partial profile conjoint**. The idea here was to simplify what study participants saw and evaluated, by showing just a few features of the product or service in question. This also suffered from an obvious problem in its lack of realism. We do not evaluate actual product or service choices with some of them hidden from view, making the assumption that what we cannot see is acceptable.

The start of trade-offs: Q-Sort and Thurstone's Case 5

Thurstone's work on these methods was done before any of the other methods were even considered, all the way back in the 1920s. He developed the analyses needed to turn rankings of different items into **ratio-level** scaled data. As already mentioned, because this was still early days, he got to call his scaling procedure 'The Law of Comparative Judgements'. Nothing, no matter how clever, gets to become a law any more.

The procedure for solving this problem is called **Case 5**. (Originally the '5' was written as a Roman numeral, or 'V'.) We will not be discussing the other four cases, but these are discussed in an imposing paper by Thurstone.

We use Case 5 analysis following guided sorting. It works only at the group level because you need to find how many times each item ranks better than each other. This produces a so-called **win-loss matrix**, in which the item with the better ranking 'wins'. An example of a win-loss matrix is shown in Figure 3.11.

Thurstone's work underpins much of the later work done in analysing how people trade off features. His method still remains highly useful for determining the relative importances of long lists of attributes or messages.

Figure 3.11 A win-loss matrix

	A	B	C	D	E	F	G
A		69	75	65	79	78	72
B	60		69	59	71	73	68
C	53	60		55	74	67	60
D	63	69	74		83	74	71
E	49	58	54	46		58	52
F	51	56	61	55	71		60
G	57	60	69	58	77	68	

NOTE Part of a 'win-loss' matrix: for instance, A wins against B 60 times and B wins against A 69 times.

Maximum difference scaling (MaxDiff)

Maximum difference scaling (MaxDiff) is both the name of a piece of software that follows an analytical routine and an established statistical procedure that is different. The software appeared around 2000, but other similar methods existed for many years before then. MaxDiff software does this:

- It starts with a list of items.
- It generates a special experimental design.
- This design makes sure that items are compared with each other in a balanced way.
- It merges data gathered from study participants and the design, and prepares a file that can be analysed by special HB software.
- The HB software then generates data on the importances of the items for each person.

Otherwise, comparisons of items several at a time could be analysed just as we analyse rankings with Case 5, at the group level. The software implementation of MaxDiff is a direct outgrowth of Thurstone's method.

Applications in brief

We will have much more to say about these methods in Chapters 4, 5 and 6, and in Bonus online Chapter 1. However, a brief review of their best applications might be useful as a way to conclude our introduction to them.

Both **conjoint** and **discrete choice** have enjoyed long histories as methods for creating the best possible new products and services. **MaxDiff** and **Q-Sort/Case 5** have worked well for many years in prioritizing specific claims, messages or product features. Given below are a few more specifics.

Discrete choice modelling

This method does best at determining the **marketplace effects** that will follow if products or services in a competitive environment get reconfigured, introduced or dropped. **Discrete choice modelling** excels in realism, both in the way it represents the choice in the marketplace and in the way it asks people to make choices just as they would in an actual purchase decision.

This also is the best method to determine what could happen following changes where there are several products or services of the same brand. These effects include the egregiously named **cannibalization**, which refers to the way that changes in one product might take (or 'eat') some of the sales from another product offered by the same brand. It can also reveal so-called **product line synergies**, in which the presence of two or more products leads to greater sales than you would expect from each product separately.

Conjoint analysis

Conjoint analysis, in its traditional full-profile format, considers **one product at a time**. Therefore, it makes sense to consider conjoint when there is no true competitive context for your product. Sometimes products do not get evaluated alongside competitors – for instance, direct-mail insurance offerings. (People indeed do not keep folders filled with old offers to compare.)

Alternatively, if you have some really special offer on your website, people may act on it without doing any further comparisons. Conjoint does well at creating the best alternative to display for this application.

Conjoint analysis also can work highly effectively in optimizing any type of message, determining the best combination of elements to include. If you have, for instance, a message where you want to test seven elements (such as headline, headline placement, contents of text, graphics and so on) and each can vary in three ways, that would make for **2,187 possible ways** of varying the message. Conjoint analysis can determine the worth of all of these by testing **only 18** experimentally designed variations. We show an example of this in Chapter 5.

Consider conjoint as well when your product will get chosen only infrequently. Since discrete choice modelling uses choices, it might not pick up what is driving decisions if the brand you are interested in rarely gets chosen.

You also could consider narrowing the scope of competition to get a better answer, if your brand is rarely chosen from a wide field. For instance, suppose you are doing a study for everyone's breakfast favourite, SoggyOs. A brand such as this could have a 0.5 per cent share of the entire breakfast-food market and still make a lot of money. Looking at this broader market, you probably could not determine with any accuracy which changes might most increase sales – any effect would be vanishingly small in the context of all other possible product choices.

You could instead look only at those specific brands that are your close competitors, that is, other fine shredded cellulose-enriched food-like substances. In that arena, you might have a 10 per cent or 20 per cent share, and so be able to get a more accurate reading of how much changes will affect your sales.

MaxDiff and Q-Sort/Case 5

These methods provide clear readings of the relative importances of individual features, messages or claims. They do not provide any reading of how varying features will affect acceptance of a whole product or service. They, in fact, do not work well with levels or variations of features.

You cannot use either of them to configure an entire product or service. Rather, you can weigh elements that you might include in, for instance, a special-features add-on package (as for a car), or assess the importance of broader claims you might make about a product or service.

You will get ratio-level information from either of these methods. That is, after the analysis, you can for instance say that, 'Message N was twice as important as message R'. This, and the clear differentiation of items into most and least important, provide strong advantages over the use of scaled ratings.

MaxDiff is good for evaluating about 8–35 items in a list. Q-Sort can determine relative importances for many more items – up to 100 have been reported in the literature. However, MaxDiff has the advantage of providing importances for every person. Q-Sort provides answers only for a group of people.

Every time you want to analyse another group within your sample with Q-Sort, you must run another analysis. With MaxDiff, to analyse a new group, you merely need to average the individual data that you already have for the people in that group.

Summary of key points

The **experimental** or **trade-off methods** were developed to deal with a salient problem with scaled importance ratings, that is, the unfortunate fact that these ratings are highly unreliable in predicting behaviour. When you ask people to rate directly what they find important (in a survey), they tend to identify nearly everything as critical. Reliance on direct importance ratings has led many an unsuspecting organization down a wrong path, wasting time and resources.

The great advantage of all the trade-off methods is that they force people to prioritize, just as in real life. They cannot say that everything is important.

The more complex methods, **conjoint analysis** and **discrete choice modelling**, forecast marketplace responses to product or services (or communications or web pages) when features and/or prices are varied. There is some confusion about the differences between these two methods, and some treat the term conjoint analysis as a broader heading that includes discrete choice. However, because these two approaches developed in different disciplines and work in somewhat different ways, we will be treating them separately.

Discrete choice modelling was developed by econometricians to address the question of how we can predict choices when the alternatives do not have features or **attributes** in common. The theoretical and mathematical work going into this method is truly impressive. This appears to be the only approach we discuss throughout this book that was awarded a Nobel Prize.

In a discrete choice study, people are shown products in a **marketplace** or **market scenario**, where the main competitive offerings are described alongside each other. In a typical web survey, one hypothetical marketplace is shown on one computer screen, and people are asked which product they would choose if all were configured as shown. Then they are shown another screen in which the features of the products have been varied and are asked to make another choice. It is also possible to include 'none of these' as a choice – greatly increasing realism – since people almost always can opt out if all alternatives are truly unacceptable. People might make a choice like this in the region of 6–20 times.

Conjoint was developed by market researchers and originally focused on single products. In its traditional form, it shows a **whole product** described as a series of features or attributes, and asks for a rating – hence the name **full-profile conjoint**. While conjoint analysis does ask people to weigh features in the context of all other features, it typically asks for a rating. This is less closely tied to what people do in the real world than the choices made in a discrete choice modelling study.

Both conjoint analysis and discrete choice modelling can lead to powerful **market simulator programs**, which show in real time how marketplace responses vary as features and/or prices of products, services or messages are changed. The typical **market simulator** runs under Microsoft Excel and has easy-to use controls.

Maximum difference scaling (**MaxDiff**) and **Q-Sort/Case 5** are the simplest of this group of methods. They give us clearly differentiated importances for a list of items, such as claims about a product, or features that do not make up an entire product or service. They cannot measure the relative worths of different variations or **levels** of features. They can, however, provide a clear reading of the relative importances of features, and at the ratio level. That is, we can say, for instance, 'feature N is twice as important as feature R'. We cannot do this with scaled importance ratings.

MaxDiff can provide importances for every person, while Q-Sort does so only for groups of people. However, Q-Sort can get a fix on the importances of many more items than MaxDiff, with up to 100 reported in the literature for Q-Sort as compared to about 35 for MaxDiff.

Designed experiments

The term **designed experiment** covers a broad range of approaches. However, all experimental designs for trade-off studies meet one goal: estimating the values of many items cleanly and clearly. Two of the methods, discrete choice and conjoint analysis, also use these designs so that relatively few carefully selected situations or comparisons can estimate what will happen in dozens to thousands of situations.

These designs have great measurement power. For instance, if you have a product with 18 features that each vary in two ways, this gives rise to 2^{18} (2 to the 18th power) or 262,144 combinations. Using a designed experiment, you can determine the value of all of these with 20 carefully selected product configurations. A market simulator program would allow you to determine the values of all these combinations (assuming you had the time and patience) in real time.

Traditionally, all experimental designs used in conjoint analysis and discrete choice modelling were the **orthogonal, fractional factorial** type. This is a mouthful but it simply means that a fraction of all possible combinations is carefully selected and that there are no correlations in the ways that the attributes vary from one product or marketplace to the next.

Basic rules for designed experiments

The more attributes and variations of attributes (or levels) that you need to measure, the larger your experiment needs to become. That is, as you vary more attributes and levels, you will need to show people more screens or pages with varying products. In this chapter we gave some rules about how much you need to measure (that is how many screens you need to show with different products or marketplaces) for different numbers of attributes and levels.

HB analysis gets more from experiments

It is a sad but definite fact that people tire quickly of evaluating alternative products or marketplaces. Depending on the audience, this could start as soon as six or eight have been shown. (As mentionned earlier, when study participants are very involved with the product or service, and have good ability to concentrate, they can complete up to 21 or so before they get exhausted.)

We get much more than we used to from experimental methods by using a machine learning approach, **Hierarchical Bayesian (HB)** analysis. Most experts agree we can measure twice as much as was traditionally possible, with no accompanying increase in the number of study participants.

In the old days, if you constructed a very large experiment, you simply split it among people taking the study. Each person might do one-third of an entire experiment requiring (for instance) 36 marketplaces or products. Then you multiplied the number of people in the study by three to make up for this. It worked – but led to considerable increases in time and expenses in doing the study.

HB has been pushed to get three to four times as much information without increasing the number of people in the study. It has still returned excellent results.

HB analysis sounds almost magical, and relies on some fairly mind-bending concepts, but it has definitely proven itself under fire for over 25 years. It might not quite count as artificial intelligence, but it definitely can be considered machine learning, as the computer makes many thousands of repeated estimates and uses the earlier ones to inform the final result.

Best applications

Discrete choice modelling remains the best method for predicting the effects of changing products in a competitive marketplace. It also is the only method that can truly address what happens when there is more than one product from a given brand in the set of competitive entries. That is, it can determine when there are so-called product line **synergies** (effects from two or more products together that are greater than we would expect from either product alone). It also can diagnose the awful-named product line **cannibalization,** where one product cuts into (or 'eats') the sales of another product from the same brand.

Conjoint analysis, developing as it did with a focus on a single product, remains useful where a product does not have true competitors. For instance, this might happen with a direct-mail offering for an insurance product. (People of course do not keep portfolios of these, waiting for the best one to happen into their lives.) Also, conjoint can be useful in creating the best product where the product has a very small share of the entire market. Since discrete choice modelling is based on choices, if a product gets chosen infrequently, you may not get enough data to determine which variations in its features are driving levels of marketplace acceptance.

MaxDiff and Q-Sort do not evaluate entire products or services, but rather are useful for evaluating the relative importances of a series of claims, message or features. You might use either method, for instance, to find the most important items to include in a special features package for a car, or the best absolutely free gift that a person gets for signing on with their friendly telecommunications provider. MaxDiff can provide importances for every person if analysed using HB analysis, while Q-Sort provides information only for groups of people. Q-Sort can prioritize many more items than MaxDiff, though – up to 100 as compared to up to 35.

Take extra care with projections

As a reminder from Chapter 2, conjoint analysis and discrete choice modelling can get you to **share of acceptance**. This differs from market share in that you must factor in how aware people are of the product and how widely distributed it is (at a minimum) to get to actual marketplace levels. If you hope to make **projections**, you must also know the size of the entire market (generally not easy to determine), and account for any problems in areas such as communications, how the product or service is displayed, how salespeople treat it, and so on. You must be extremely well prepared to make a good projection.

Creating the best, newest thing

04

Discrete choice modelling

In this chapter we discuss arguably the most powerful of all methods for determining the best mix of prices and features to include in a product or service. **Discrete choice modelling** centres on determining exactly what people will choose. We review the basics, and then tremendously effective outputs, ie market simulations and market simulators. We show how they solve problems that are otherwise impossible to address.

Key features

Let's start with what may seem an extreme statement – and then explain the reasons for making it. **Discrete choice modelling** arguably is the most powerful of all methods for determining the best mix of products and features to include in a new product or service in a competitive market.

This method centres on determining how changes in the features of products or services influence choices. If it is set up and analysed well, it has tremendous power to predict how new or modified products or services will fare in the actual marketplace.

Before we start, it is worth a mention that we will be metaphorically treading on the edges of some deep theoretical and mathematical waters. We will be manoeuvring around much that is abstruse, instead focusing on explaining clearly what you need in order to make effective use of these remarkable methods. We hope that those with more academic experience do not find any of their favourite theories slighted.

Why we do this: payoff in market simulations

The greatest power of this method resides in its ability to simulate what will happen in a changing marketplace over the near term. Later in this chapter, you will encounter an example where the outcome of a competitive response showed so much potential risk that the sponsoring organization decided to lock up the reports. They actually feared that a leak could undermine their market position.

Figure 4.1 shows some aspects of a Microsoft-Excel-based market simulator program. Not all simulators have these features – some are important and yet sometimes omitted, as we will discuss.

You see a portion of the simulator in this figure. The controls that adjust the products' features and prices appear only in part. The rest would be reached by scrolling down in the workbook.

This program opens like any Excel workbook. The example shown in Figure 4.1 is from an actual study done among doctors, determining what they would prescribe if a new drug had certain features and prices. It has been disguised by modifying names and some numbers. The circled letters in the figure are not part of the simulator itself, but rather appear to help identify different features.

Near letter **A** you see a graphical display of the outcome of the simulation. These are the **shares of preference** expected after the controls for the simulator have been changed to reflect a specific combination of pricing and features. This information appears in table form near letter **C**.

Two adjustments for external market conditions appear near letter **B**. As we mentioned in Chapter 2, without adjustments like these, you cannot expect the **share of preference** found by the calculations behind the simulator to approach **actual market share**. This is because all those who responded to the study were made 100 per cent aware of the products – and that needs to be adjusted down to reflect marketplace conditions. In this specific simulation, the percentage of patients who are newly diagnosed will affect product choices, so another control was included to adjust for that.

Letters **D** and **F** are respectively controls for configuring the state of the marketplace that you want to estimate, along with a **reference** or **base marketplace** to which you will compare. This reference case is included so that you can get an accurate fix of how much the changes you are trying will affect marketplace acceptance of your new product or service.

This is an important feature because of the way that utility – the abstract quantity this method assumes is traded off – gets translated into marketplace behaviour. We will be talking about the way utility works in more

Figure 4.1 A portion of a market simulator

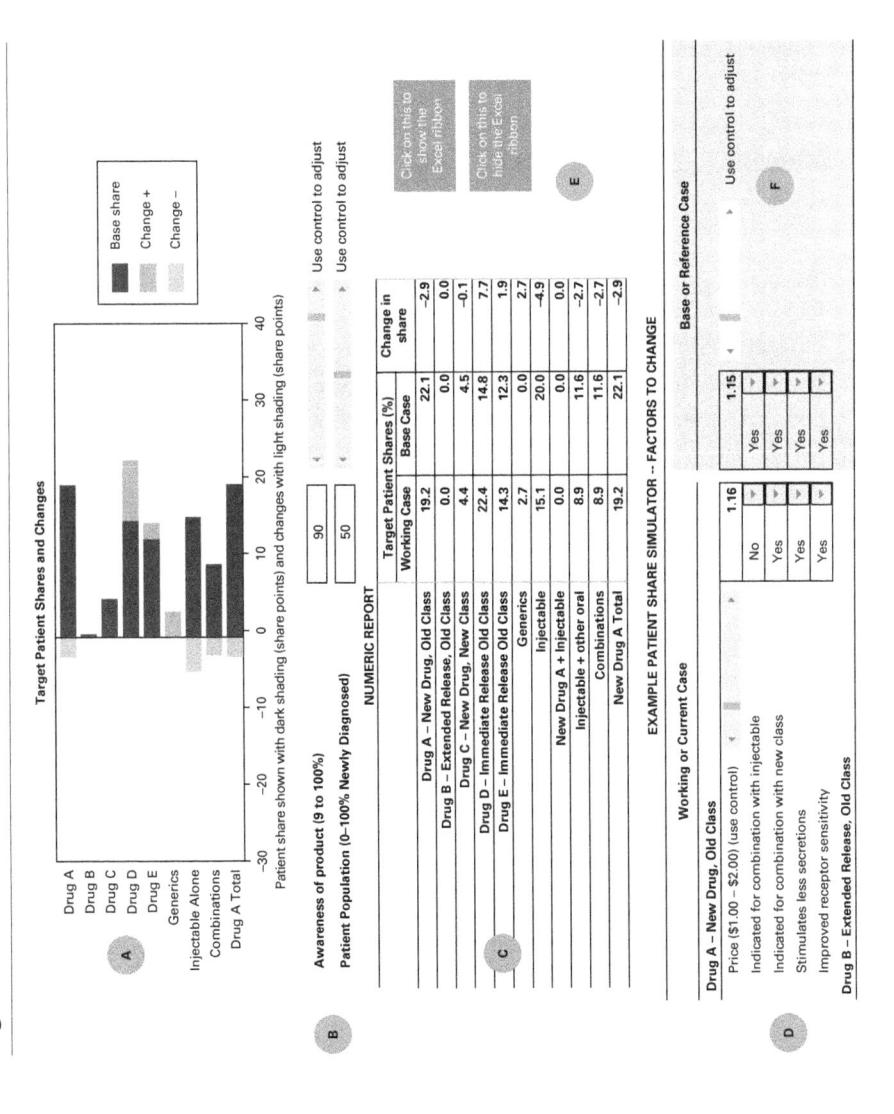

detail. For now, though, we just need to understand that this is key for seeing the strengths of effects from changing features and prices.

Finally, near letter E, we have some controls that allow you to modify the basic Excel display. The program opens with the Excel ribbon – the control panel across the top of the screen – hidden from view so that you can see more of the simulator. Clicking the upper button restores the Excel ribbon to view, and clicking the lower button hides it again.

These are the basic ingredients that make a simulator a formidable forecasting tool. Now that we have seen this incredibly powerful form of output, let's go through some of the basics and steps that you need to get there.

As real as it gets

Discrete choice modelling is based on a survey that exposes products to study participants in the context of realistic marketplace situations. The products that people evaluate can have their own features and their own prices. This realism – and the fact that we are observing choices – provides a very strong analytical advantage. Consumers evaluate alternative products while considering competitive offerings, just as they would in the marketplace.

Study participants get a set of **tasks** or **scenarios** or **market scenarios**, each one describing a set of realistic branded service/product alternatives. They then simply say which product in each market scenario – if any – they would choose. They do not need to rate alternatives, or rank items they would never select. They simply need to pick whatever they would choose. They also can have the option of saying that none of the alternatives would appeal to them.

Alternative products from one brand can appear competing against each other. **Market scenarios** can be set up precisely reflecting the important alternatives likely to appear in the actual marketplace. Therefore, you can determine consumer responses in the specific competitive situations that you would need to test.

No need for unrealistic introspection

Discrete choice modelling has another advantage over ratings-based methods in that it does not force buyers to dissect and to explain their reasoning in making decisions. Extensive research has shown that most consumers do not give accurate descriptions of what goes into their decisions.

As we discussed in Chapter 3, most buyers will **rate** all or nearly all proposed features as 'highly important' or 'critical' when asked to answer direct importance-rating types of questions. They will faithfully do this whether they truly need those features or not.

Similarly, most people say little about why they did not choose a product beyond observing that they 'don't like it', 'it wasn't for me', or 'it wasn't right'. Asking directly about what falls short in a product can prove to be a frustrating task.

Approaches to understanding what consumers will choose need to go beyond these usually inaccurate ratings patterns to discern what influences buyers' behaviour – starting with essential feature-related, provider-related and pricing-related needs.

Although discrete choice modelling market scenarios present more information than many other research study methods, people generally have little trouble completing the task – even when evaluating 10–15 marketplaces. (They may grumble after seeing six or so, but typically keep working with good levels of consistency.)

After all, in each market scenario shown, people need only do something that they do all the time – look at alternatives and make a choice. Study participants typically report that the task engages their attention, and that it sometimes even is **fun**. That is a rare word in connection with most research studies. The generally high rates of study completion with this method support this description.

An experimentally designed approach

Discrete choice modelling studies are constructed according to strict experimental designs, as we described in Chapter 3. The exact number of marketplaces or scenarios required in a study will depend upon the precise number of **attributes** and **attribute levels** (or variations) to be tested. As the numbers of attributes and attribute levels to be varied increase, so do the number of scenarios required by the design.

Accurate analysis of findings from discrete choice modelling requires experimental designs that are **orthogonal** or very nearly orthogonal (that is, in which there is **zero correlation** or nearly zero correlation in how attributes vary from one marketplace to the next). Zero correlation means that the way one feature varies, going from one marketplace to another, has no relationship to the way that any other feature varies.

Large experimental designs are difficult to construct properly, and in those cases we need the computer's help to generate them. Larger designs are typically very nearly **orthogonal** (usually the specific type called **D-optimal designs**). These designs work just as well as standard orthogonal ones, but cannot be found in catalogues in most cases. They require computer time to develop.

Keeping the experiment a reasonable size is important. One key part of any discrete choice modelling study, then, would be a thorough discussion of the number of attributes and attribute levels to be varied – and of the implications that these variations will have on the final study design. Measuring just what is needed – and no more – is a critical consideration.

Worth saying again: the payoff in market simulations

The real power of this method is its ability to simulate what will happen in a changing marketplace over the near term. If you can manage to think ahead to what competitors most likely will do, then you can cover not only what would happen if you change your own fine product or service, but also what would happen when competitors respond.

Later in this chapter, you will encounter an example where the outcome was so revealing – and showed so much potential vulnerability – that the sponsoring organization decided to lock up the reports. They actually feared that a leak could undermine their market position.

Thinking through and setting up the problem

Thinking in terms of choices

Discrete choice modelling, like all **trade-off study** methods, envisions products or services as a set of distinct features. In discrete choice modelling, these definite features have distinct variations that are assumed to be measurable and comparable. This means that the value of each can be traded versus other features.

This is about as far into the psychology of decision making as these methods go. Discrete choice modelling can be seen as aiming to forecast the outcomes of decisions, rather than as trying to follow the inner workings of the human mind. This method is very much about **what** needs to happen with features and prices to attain greater acceptance of a product or service, rather than digging into **why** people behave as they do.

Each choice in a discrete choice modelling study can have its own features and prices. Comparing choices that do not share attributes is one key problem that this method was developed to solve. Some of the earliest widely cited applications for this method involved transportation, where (for instance) the choices were car, bus or train. These clearly do not share common attributes except for time door-to-door. For instance, the cost of parking downtown does not apply to the train or the bus, the distance between bus stops does not apply to car or train, and how often the trains run does not apply to car or bus.

These early studies worked – forecasts were borne out in the real world. A large body of important work in this subject is still related to transportation. (You can learn much more about this method in some excellent courses from the MIT school of Civil and Environmental Engineering.)

The first step is a large one

You must first consider how your fine product or service can vary, and then how competitors might vary either at the same time or in response. This first step can prove to be surprisingly difficult and often takes as much time as everything else done in the process.

For instance, working with the marketing team at a major US insurer, it quickly emerged that they had no idea about the details of their competitors' products. Worse, what they had imagined was available among their products was not all what they could offer. After a few weeks of digging, one of their team announced that the whole project was 'giving us a headache'. Fortunately, all involved took the appropriate analgesics, survived this phase and went on to do a successful update on their offerings.

Setting up a study: an example

Let's go back a number of years to when debit cards were still not ubiquitous. The client, here called Quiet Financial Services (QFS), was an extremely wealthy company that only recently had abandoned the practice of solely serving those who had been recommended by other clients. (Their motto could have been, 'If you have an in, we might be inclined to offer you financial services'.) They wanted to develop a high-limit debit card for the right kind of people. Their two key competitors in this market were Citibank and American Express (Amex).

They did not want to offer all the same features in the key areas of interest rate, credit limit and annual fee as the other two companies. They set out to test credit limits of $20,000 and $80,000, while Amex offered $50,000 or $120,000 and Citibank a whopping $90,000 or $120,000. They also wanted to test three different interest rates from those their competitors were offering, and to anticipate what might happen if their competitors changed their interest rates in response.

In addition, they had absolutely no intention of offering this card with no fee. This was Citibank's key incentive for their customers to accrue a crushing debt. QFS lastly decided to test Amex dropping their relatively lofty $50 fee in response to QFS coming in with a lower one. Figure 4.2 shows each competitor and the features to be tested. The features appear in the boxes over the grey horizontal bars.

In total, we have QFS with two 3-level attributes and one 2-level attribute, Amex with two 2-level attributes and one 3-level, and Citibank with one 3-level attribute and one 2-level. The constant (Citibank offering no fee) does not count as an attribute because it does not change.

> **No change means no measurement**
>
> You cannot measure the impact of any feature that does not change. This is considered a fixed part of the product. You must vary a feature in some way to measure its effect on choices.

Figure 4.2 Discrete choice treats brand as like a container for features

	QFS	Amex	citibank
Interest	QFS Interest 10%, 11%, 13%	Amex Interest 12%, 14%	Citibank Interest 8%, 11%, 12%
Fee	QFS Fee $50, $80	Amex Fee $90, $150	Constant
Limit	QFS Limit $20,000, $80,000	Amex Limit $50,000, $100,000	Citibank Limit $90,000, $120,000

Something may have seemed strange to those of you familiar with traditional conjoint analysis: we **did not** count the brand as an attribute. As we will discuss in Chapter 5, in conjoint analysis (and its conjoint-like descendant, **CBC**) **brand** typically gets included as an attribute that gets varied along with other attributes.

With discrete choice modelling, however, **brand works like a container** that holds the attributes. If we include a term in our model called the **constant** (as discussed in Chapter 3), that can be thought of as the residual value of the brand after we account for all the specific attributes that we are measuring.

The idea that **attributes can be specific to each choice** is a critical concept that makes discrete choice modelling different from, and superior to, traditional conjoint analysis. We will talk more about this difference in Chapter 5.

> **Consider brand as a container for features**
>
> With discrete choice modelling, each choice (or brand) can have its own features, varying in ways specific to that brand. Brand does not need to be counted as a product attribute. Rather, we can think of **brand as being like a container** that holds the attributes.

Limits on how much you can measure

The QFS study we have been discussing would require a total of 12 marketplace scenarios. As a reminder, as you measure more attributes and more attribute levels, you need more marketplace scenarios to measure. Here is how many marketplace scenarios, or computer screens, you need to measure for different numbers of attribute levels:

- two-level attribute: one marketplace scenario or screen shown;
- three-level attribute: two marketplace scenarios or screens shown;
- four-level attribute: three marketplace scenarios or screens shown;
- five-level attribute: four marketplace scenarios or screens shown;
- six-level attribute: five marketplace scenarios or screens shown.

And then we need to consider a bit more. We need two more marketplace scenarios or screens:

- One for measuring the **error** in the model. This allows us to know how well we are measuring – basically, how consistent each person was in answering. Otherwise, when we run the model, this will be reported as 100 per cent regardless of how well people did when answering.
- One for a very useful term called the **constant**. This has mathematical meaning, but we can use it to measure the value of the brand or the choice outside the attributes being tested.

You also must count the number of variations or levels in each attribute and check the design against these. The design must be at least as big as the product or the two attributes with the most levels. So if you have, for instance, a six-level attribute and a three-level attribute, you need at least 6 x 3 or 18 marketplaces. This underlines the importance of going for the simplest model that measures everything you need. Going for the simplest working model covering everything is an extremely well-established practice in the sciences. It is sometimes called **Ockham's razor**.

Ockham was William of Ockham, who lived around 1300, so this idea has a great deal of history. The razor, going along with the idea that you should trim away everything extraneous, apparently came into this around 1840. It is not clear whether William actually even saw a razor.

Even with the near-magic of HB analysis, which we review below, economy in design remains an important principle. You need to know what to measure and how to measure. Understanding the marketplace and your buyers before you start the study is critical.

Reviewing some best practices

These are important to any study, and while some may seem apparent, we have encountered more than a few instances where one or more was not followed. These merit a special call-out.

A few important guidelines

- **Understand your market.** You need to know your market before doing a discrete choice modelling study. For instance, if you were embarking on a study of industrial macerators, would you know how many sparging paddles to include in your test? Nearly 99.99 per cent of us would be completely lost on this question without doing some advanced work on the exciting macerator market. Never plunge forward without getting some preliminary insights – from secondary sources and/or qualitative research.

- **Know how users and prospects talk about the product or service.** Those who work with a product all day tend to believe that all users have their level of interest and knowledge. Particularly in medical, financial and technical fields, users can show an unsettling level of unfamiliarity with terminology and jargon. For instance, doctors who are not specialists or researchers may have little idea of what the client is saying about their fine medical product. Again, qualitative research can delineate how actual users of a product or service talk about it – and what they understand.

- **Focus on benefits to the user, rather than how the product is made.** Engineering types, in particular, can get enmeshed in the intricacies of how the product is made. For instance, a food manufacturer wanted to test written descriptions of how many **foot-pounds of torque** were required to open jars of their Ambrosian substance. They were quite proud of reducing the effort required to open a jar in highly specific terms, and thought everyone else would be also.

- **Keep the attribute levels in order.** It seems this should be obvious, but there have been a few studies where this was not done. So if you are, for instance, measuring prices, make the lowest price the first level and then increase steadily to the highest price. It is not hard to untangle the results if you fail to do this, but not keeping everything in order introduces another chance for confusion and error. Just a few minutes at the beginning of the project can obviate problems later.

- **Again, measure just what you need to measure and no more.** This is worth another mention because you are constructing an experiment, and its size depends on the number of attributes and levels that you include. More attributes and levels means needing to show more marketplace scenarios, and there is a definite limit to how many of these any person can respond to without illegal stimulants. Keeping things under control and focusing on key features is critical. Also, while you should include the **key competitors** in your marketplaces, you do not need to include every small product or service.

- **Measure as much variation for each attribute that you think may reasonably happen.** You can estimate what will happen between continuous attribute levels that you measure at discrete points. For instance, if you measure prices of $2.50 and $4.00, you can estimate what will happen at any price in between. This is called **interpolation**. However, you cannot estimate accurately anything **outside** the range that you tested. If the highest price you tested was $5.00, for instance, you cannot accurately guess what might happen at a price of $7.00. This is called **extrapolation**. It is highly risky because you do not know where responses may shift strongly without testing. Better to go a little outside the expected range than to fall short later and not be able to simulate a new situation.

- **Consider narrowing the field of comparisons if you have too many choices.** You may need to focus in on more direct competitors than the broader marketplace. For instance, a major maker of printers several years ago wanted to 'rationalize' their inkjet printer offerings – that is, offer fewer products that competed closely with each other. However, looking at their own sprawling product line and competitors' offerings, they came up with 57 products that a hapless buyer might choose.

  They did some preliminary investigations with buyers, and after some discussion separated the choices into price ranges. It turned out that someone who wanted to spend about $100 on a printer would not even look at one costing $800, but might consider something for $250 if they found it absolutely wonderful. The sponsoring company constructed five price ranges, with some overlap at ends of each range, bringing the total number of choices that any given person would see down to about 12. This was a lot, but more manageable for all involved. And as a result, they were able to determine which closely competing products they could safely eliminate.

- **Still, make the marketplaces represent the main competitors realistically.** The marketplaces provide the **reference point** for decisions that people will make. (We will get to reference points later in this chapter.) Making this reference realistic helps make decisions in the study more closely reflect the decisions people make in the actual marketplace.

- **If you expect products to move into or out of the marketplace, make sure that they do so in some of the marketplaces you show.** There are well-tested ways to do this. This level of realism is the best for determining exactly what will happen in different situations. Some newer research on how people make decisions (which we will discuss soon) strongly supports the idea that anything you simulate should include only the alternative product sets that people actually saw in the study. Some software allows you to do otherwise, but this is not a sound idea.

- **Tell people to imagine they really need to buy/get one of the choices if any is at all acceptable.** Research shows that this actually helps people to answer more accurately.
- **Include a 'none of these' option.** In the real world, people can defer nearly any decision. Paired with the recommendation directly above, this leads to more realistic responses, with people choosing 'none' only in the rare instance when an experimental design generates a marketplace scenario containing all bad choices.

What happens if these guidelines do not get followed?

Occasionally an organization will launch into one of these studies without doing their homework, or without thinking about the rules. This can result in confusion, delay and ample quantities of blame. The case study below shows what happened in one such instance.

CASE STUDY One that did not start well

A company that made wine wanted to do a pricing study. They selected nine prices per bottle for use in the study, specified in this order: $9.59, $8.39, $11.99, $10.59, $8.99, $12.49, $9.99, $12.00 and $11.00. They also tested three sizes for their beverage, 750 millilitres, 1 litre, and 850 millilitres. They created 12 screens, each of which showed one price and size combination. (They did not show competitors but said that prices could vary from $8 to $14 for a comparable comestible.) Then they collected their data, but could not make any sense of what they got back when they tried to analyse it.

What went wrong?

There are two principal problems here, the first of which has two parts. To start, they tested too many prices. If you know the most and the least you anticipate charging, you need to test no more than four prices to capture the most complex patterns of price versus expected share – although you might possibly go to five (if really not sure, six). You would do this to attempt capturing some price at which responses change drastically. As a reminder, shares almost always go down with sufficient increases in price. There may be some price at which this decline becomes much steeper.

The other part of this first problem was that the prices were not in order from low to high. This is one of the pitfalls pointed out above, and indeed this company did not know exactly how to deal with the data got from doing this. They needed to be shown how to reorder the results just to determine whether they looked sensible.

The second issue was that they did not have enough data to analyse correctly with just 12 products shown (these could not accurately be called **marketplace scenarios**, with just one product). First counting the attribute levels, we find that measurement would require showing eight marketplaces to measure the first attribute and two for the second. That is less than the 12 they had, but they forgot one other rule. The actual minimum would be 9 x 3, or 27, due to the need to cover as many marketplaces as the numbers of attribute levels multiplied by each other.

This last problem proved to be insoluble without more work. The best that could be done was to go back and interview more people with the remaining price/size combinations. We then relied on our faithful HB analysis to help put together the results from the two groups interviewed. This meant delays and extra costs (and considerable grumbling), but going back for more responses did ultimately save the project.

The price is right: price versus change in share

We mentioned above that four different prices would be enough to capture even the most complicated pattern of price versus share. But what are some of the patterns that you might encounter? A **self-effects curve**, as illustrated in Figure 4.3, shows one way a product's share could change as its price,

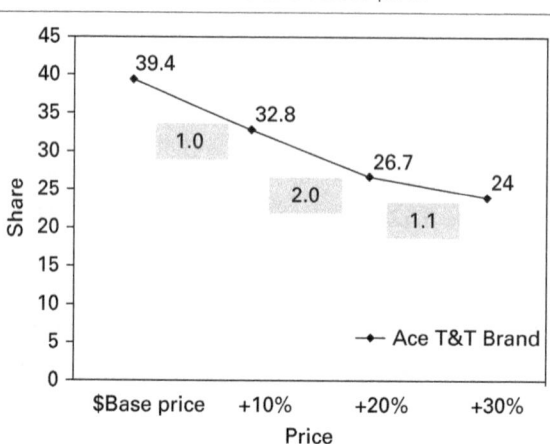

Figure 4.3 A self-effects curve for share versus price

and only its price, changes. We find this by running several simulations and seeing how share shifts.

The numbers in the boxes near the share values represent **price elasticity measurements**. An elasticity measurement is the ratio of the percentage change in the product's share divided by the percentage change in price.

A product's response is considered **elastic** if the value is greater than 1.0, meaning a 1 per cent change in price causes more than a 1 per cent change in sales. An elasticity value of approximately 1.0 means that the changes are sometimes called **revenue neutral** – that is, gross revenues remain approximately the same with increases or decreases in price. Finally, if the value is less than 1.0, the response is considered **inelastic**.

Anything related to **elasticity** seems perpetually confusing. It may be easier to recall that elasticity values higher than 1.0 correspond to a **loss in gross revenues** based on increasing price, and those below 1.0 correspond to **gains in gross revenues** with increases in price.

By the way, for all the discussion of price elasticity, you likely will avoid confusion if you leave it out of **your** discussion. For instance, many years ago, we brought a study to a junior client in which the displays showed how many share points they would lose for a dollar increase in price. This young person got incensed, demanding to see the elasticities. The modified presentation then went to the Really Big Boss upstairs. He listened for a while, then burst out, 'I don't care about these [expletive] elasticities! Show me how [many] sales we lose if we raise the price a dollar!'

Figure 4.4 shows several price versus share curves that you will commonly encounter. If we know where responses are likely to change, four price points will cover all these contingencies. The figure to the left shows an essentially straight-line response to raising prices for TinyCo, and a curved (convex) response for Ace T&T. The Ace T&T curve shows increasing rates of share loss as prices rise.

Figure 4.4 shows two response curves where there is a **point of inflection**, or **elbow**, as prices increase. That is, after a certain price is reached, shares drop off much more sharply. You want to set the prices tested so that any such change is captured. The existence of **inflection points** like these underlines the riskiness of trying to extrapolate beyond the prices you actually test. If you do not test an adequately wide range, an inflection may lie just outside your highest or lowest price.

Gargantuan brand's response curve shows a clear **reservation price**, a point beyond which sales drop rapidly to nearly zero. In some categories there are clear reservation prices. For instance, a number of years ago, almost no bottled juice in the US sold at over $5.00 a container. Those days are no longer with us, but the principle remains.

Figure 4.4 Different responses of share to price changes

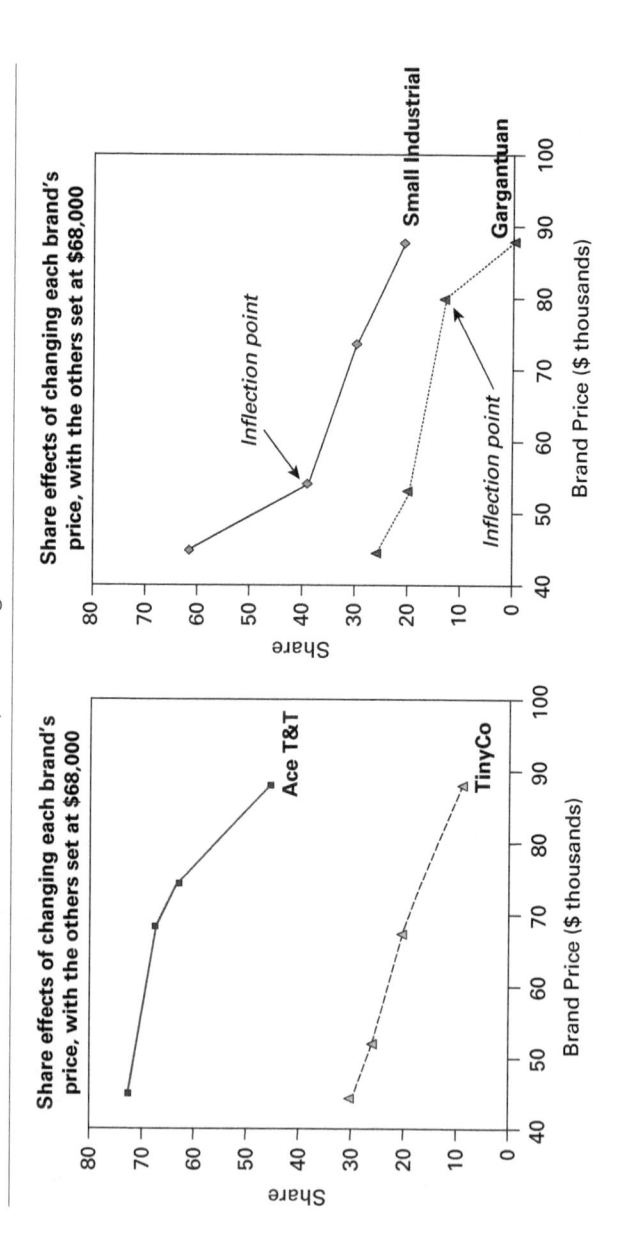

Welcome back to the world of HB analysis

Our cautions about keeping studies compact now have as much to do with not wearing out the people answering as any limits on the size of an analysis. This is thanks to the world of HB analysis, which we will revisit and discuss in slightly more detail.

Briefly, this method of analysis fills in data that is scant or missing for a respondent by repeatedly borrowing estimates from other respondents. That is, it keeps sampling other respondents and storing values from those who have the needed information.

It usually runs 20,000 or more times for **each attribute level** for **each respondent,** keeping a running average of its estimates. It may or may not compare the respondent to the sample it is drawing and make adjustments based on their similarities. Whether these comparisons get done or not, the estimates seem to come out the same in all practical terms.

Estimates will settle down to steady values (or **converge**) if you have set up the problem correctly. If you have not, then maybe this will not happen. A solution that does not converge usually means errors in set-up, data collection or coding of values.

HB gives your PC (or Mac) more of a workout than almost anything else. You will wait for a complicated analysis to run to finish, maybe for hours. Amazingly, all this borrowing works – and we get very accurate estimates.

Figure 4.5 shows the progress of an analysis graphically. Each wavy line represents the history of the average utility estimates for one level of one attribute. At first, these estimates are unstable, but by number 30,000, they are oscillating around a steady estimate – or they have **converged** around a final value.

Before HB analysis, if we wanted to measure more than could be handled by setting up about 15 marketplace scenarios, we had to increase the sample and give each person a fraction of the whole set of marketplaces we needed to get the measurements we wanted. For instance, if we needed 28 marketplace scenarios, we could have given each person half of those, and doubled the sample.

Now we can squeeze much more out of a study without needing to compensate by increasing samples. You can get three or four times more information reliably (although some experts are more conservative and say twice as much and no more). Even doubling the amount of useful information we can get from one person is amazing.

Figure 4.5 How values change as HB analysis runs

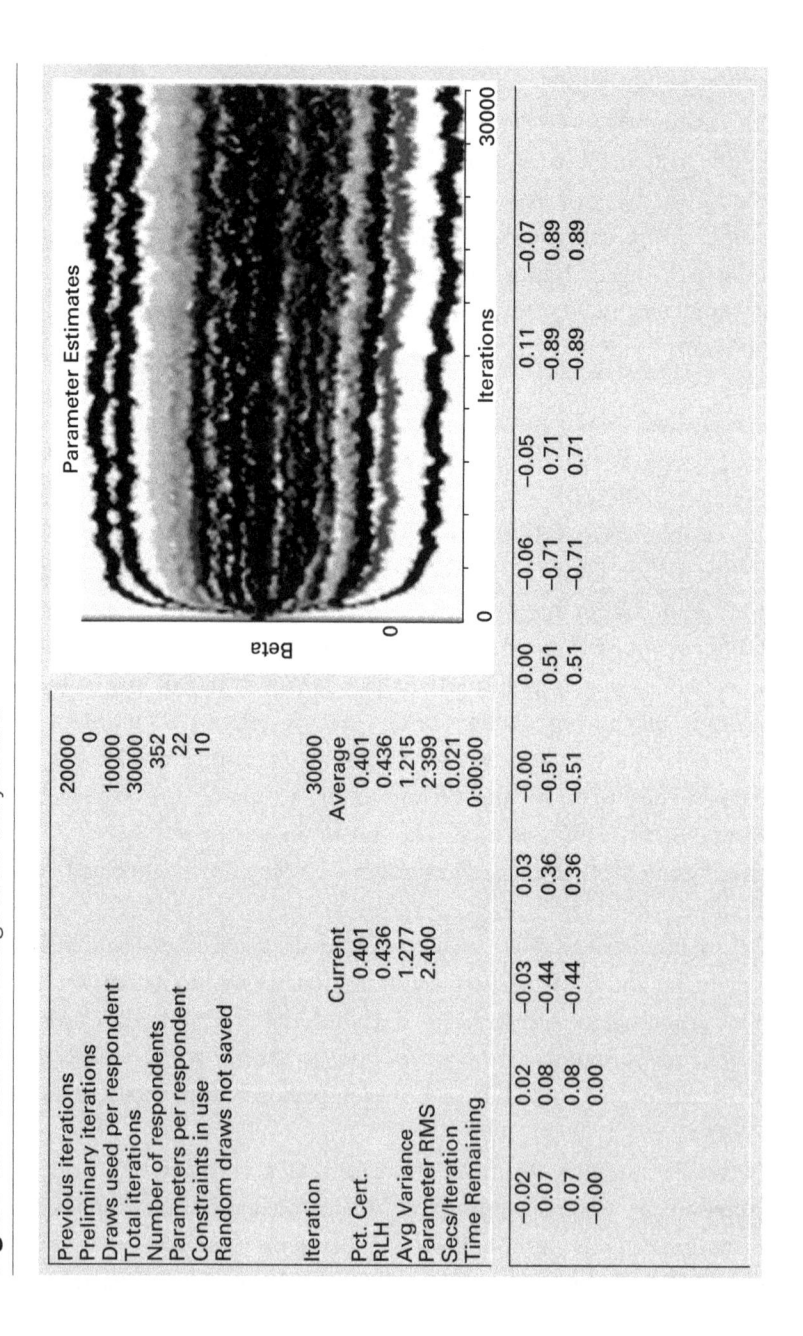

Previous iterations	20000						
Preliminary iterations	0						
Draws used per respondent	10000						
Total iterations	30000						
Number of respondents	352						
Parameters per respondent	22						
Constraints in use	10						
Random draws not saved							

Iteration	Current		Average	30000			
Pct. Cert.	0.401		0.401				
RLH	0.436		0.436				
Avg Variance	1.277		1.215				
Parameter RMS	2.400		2.399				
Secs/Iteration			0.021				
Time Remaining			0:00:00				

-0.02	0.02	-0.03	0.03	-0.00	-0.06	-0.05	0.11	-0.07
0.07	0.08	-0.44	0.36	-0.51	-0.71	0.71	-0.89	0.89
0.07	0.08	-0.44	0.36	-0.51	-0.71	0.71	-0.89	0.89
-0.00	0.00							

Parameter Estimates

Beta

0

Iterations 0   30000

How many people you need

First, no hard and fast rules exist. Discrete choice is based on approaches in the logistic regression family of methods. Some experts say you need 10 people per item you measure. For most related methods, five is often said to be sufficient. Experience shows that, for a reasonably sized experiment, **125 per group** you want to measure separately is safe and reliable. Some are more cautious and say **200 per group**.

As a reminder, all samples have error. Discrete choice modelling may be helped somewhat because the errors in this form of analysis have a tighter distribution than with most procedures. This is called a Gumbel distribution. We can see this in Figure 4.6. Smaller errors mean that samples in discrete choice modelling studies may act like bigger samples with standard measurements.

About those curves

Some of you may look at the normal curve and say something like, 'Oh, yes, that.' Others might have a vague, if not terror-filled, recollection of something you probably should not have dozed through in Statistics 101. So that everyone is up to speed, the **normal distribution** appears many times when we measure physical phenomena (hence its name, normal).

Figure 4.6   Errors in discrete choice versus many other methods

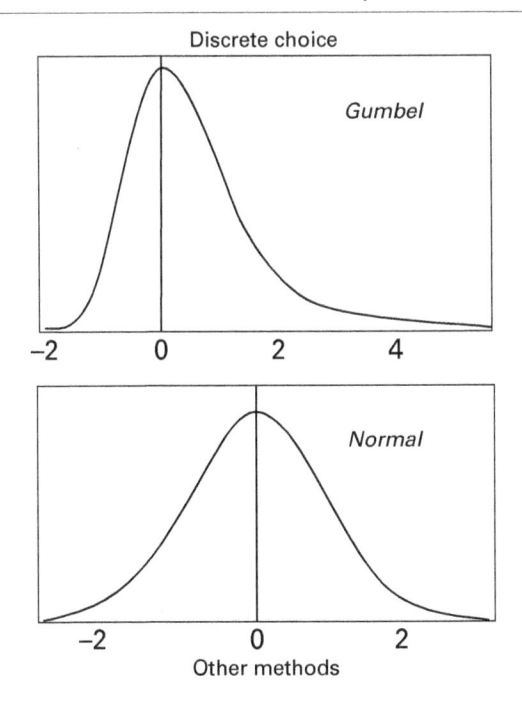

For instance, the belt sizes of men's pants in the army follow a normal distribution. The height of the curve represents how many items or observations fall at that point. We can see that the most fall right at the average. In Figure 4.6, the average is set to zero, and differences from the average are either positive or negative. As we get further from the average, there are fewer observations or items. This curve is symmetrical, with as many below by a certain margin as above by the same margin.

Errors in measurement in mathematical models also often fall into the same kind of normal curve. Not so the Gumbel distribution. By comparison, it is taller and pinched in towards the middle, with relatively more small errors. It also is not symmetrical. It skews out further on the positive side.

That pinching around the average is the important part. Smaller errors mean that measurement is somewhat more accurate for a given sample size than with many methods we typically use.

Back to our topic

Recall that with HB analysis you can create a large experiment, varying many attributes and attribute levels, and not need to make a compensating increase in sample. This helps keep the size and cost of studies involving discrete choice modelling in line. With exceptionally large experiments, you still may need to increase the sample to get enough for making good measurements.

This definitely happens when you need more than 48 marketplace scenarios, equalling 48 screens that you would need to show. Even dividing this by three, this would result in 16 screens per person participating in the study – a hefty burden on the poor study participant.

Some experts would say that dividing the design by three and not increasing the sample is stretching too much. Staying more conservative, any experimental design requiring over 36 market scenarios must have an increased sample. With 36 scenarios, that would involve dividing the total design into two parts, showing each person 18.

Studies can grow unexpectedly. Not long ago, one became monstrous, with 77 candy choices appearing on a simulated shelf. This many is not recommended. The story is tangled, featuring a client that somehow got out of control, and an inexperienced and highly confused person getting into the middle of the planning process. This study set out to measure the effects of certain candies being removed from the market. Some products were considered essential, items that never would be out of stock and so should have been always present. However, 55 candy choices could be there or not. This required 60 marketplace scenarios. Since the average candy buyer was not expected to remain patient with repeatedly seeing simulated store shelves, each person made choices in 10 out of the 60 marketplaces. The study used a sample of 1,000, and then allowed no more than two-way divisions of the total into subsamples; 500 was the minimum group size analysed.

All involved held their collective breaths, due to the difficulties in attempting to measure so much in one study. Fortunately, share predictions proved to be accurate, even for candies with shares that were a fraction of a percentage point. We could make comparisons because the sponsoring company had extensive sales data. When simulations were set to current market conditions, results fitted the marketplace.

Utility and share

Going back to earlier chapters, you may recall that discrete choice modelling uses **utility** as a way of keeping score. This allows various features and prices to be valued on a common footing. However, this method does not assume that utility has a straight-line relationship with more share. Rather, discrete choice modelling uses an **S-shaped relationship** or **response curve**.

This matches how people respond perceptually to their environment. For instance, suppose a light source is slowly increased in brightness from zero. When the light is sufficiently dim, small increases in brightness hardly register as differences. Then when the perceptual threshold is reached, increases in intensity register more strongly. This is the mid-portion of the S-curve. Finally, continuing to dial up the illumination, another threshold is reached where the light becomes too bright. Then further increases cannot be perceived.

This curve also matches marketplace behaviour. Utility must pass a certain threshold to get a noticeable response – that is, smaller products tend to get lost in the shuffle. When a product becomes sufficiently salient, small increments in utility boost responses strongly. Finally, saturation is reached. At that point, big changes in utility are needed to move those strongly committed to other choices. It is hard to move people with entrenched preferences and so approach a nearly unanimous response level.

Recent research into decision making, in particular **prospect theory** (for which Daniel Kahneman won a Nobel Prize) is largely consistent with this view of utility. Prospect theory also uses an S-curve, but one that is less

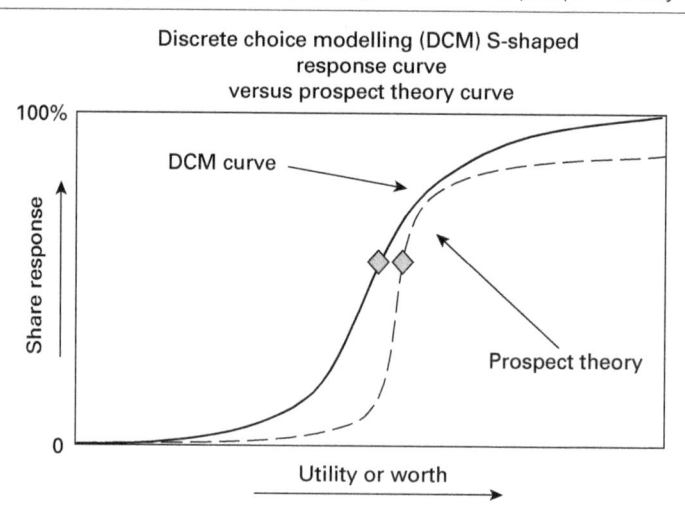

Figure 4.7 Comparing the S-shaped response curve to prospect theory

Discrete choice modelling (DCM) S-shaped response curve versus prospect theory curve

symmetrical. Figure 4.7 shows how the prospect theory S-curve compares with the one hypothesized by discrete choice modelling.

The prospect theory curve reflects the finding that people focus more strongly on losses than on gains. The diamond on the curve represents a 'reference value' – a point above which people see a gain and below which they see a loss.

The various choices in each discrete choice modelling marketplace set a reference point for comparisons – which ones are better and which worse. This underlines the importance of **keeping marketplaces realistic**. The context that the whole marketplace provides is a key factor in the choice a person finally makes.

Mathematically, the symmetrical S-curve is a reasonable approximation for the curve in prospect theory. We could argue about whether it is good enough. Perhaps venturing onto another region of metaphorically thin ice, we can surmise that functionally these models are adequately close. The fact that discrete choice modelling forecasts have held up so well, in instances where they could be checked, argues that this method can capture what people choose. That is of course dependent on the project being set up and analysed with care.

Estimates involve calculations

The realism of the S-shaped response model makes for extra work in calculations. That is, while the analysis leads first to utilities, you cannot know the value of an alternative just by summing its utilities. There is an intermediary step (technically **exponentiation,** which may be familiar to some as the **exp** function in Excel). This gets you from utility to that S-shaped curve.

This curve looks nearly like a straight line over its middle range. Outside that range, shares have a less clear relationship to utility. A product with a share over (about) 60 per cent and under (about) 10 per cent can respond to changes in utility in unintuitive ways.

You need a **market simulator program** to see how shares change as features and prices change. After discussing one last consideration, we will show some examples of simulations in action.

The last wrinkle with HB analysis

Using HB analysis, the utilities produced for each person are scaled differently from those for other people – that is, larger or smaller than for others. This happens for some technical reasons, which we will spare you. The practical upshot of this is that reporting utility values after using HB analysis makes only limited sense.

How we get away from this problem is by solving for 'share' one person at a time and averaging these values into an overall share. Precisely how this happens is just a bit technical, but let's say it and go forward. That is, this gets done (for each person) by first exponentiating the total utility of each choice, then dividing that by the exponentiated sum of all the choices' utilities. We then average all these calculated results.

In any event, remain cautious if you see a report of utilities. Instead, you should be using a **market simulator** and observing the **effects** on share of changing features and prices. And this brings us directly to the topic of **market simulations.**

Market simulations

In a **market simulation program** – perhaps the best thing since sliced bread – all the hard work finally pays dividends. It provides a powerful culmination to everything done in selecting attributes and levels, in getting a good experimental design, in making the marketplaces, in doing the analysis, in giving your poor computer its workout for the month, and in tweaking Excel until it does what you need.

Our first simulator

The first such program we discuss is a relatively simple one, from a study that has been disguised slightly for use here. It involved commercial purchasers of printers. The basic situation was this: if customers committed to buying a certain number of printers, they could get a cash and/or non-cash incentive. The main question addressed was which of these it would be best to offer. Another factor measured was the price of the printer model that might be used in connection with this bulk purchase.

That is, the client wanted to measure how share would be affected by different prices and different incentives. They also wanted to know what would happen if competitors responded by offering their own incentives at various price points.

Figure 4.8 The current case side of the simulator

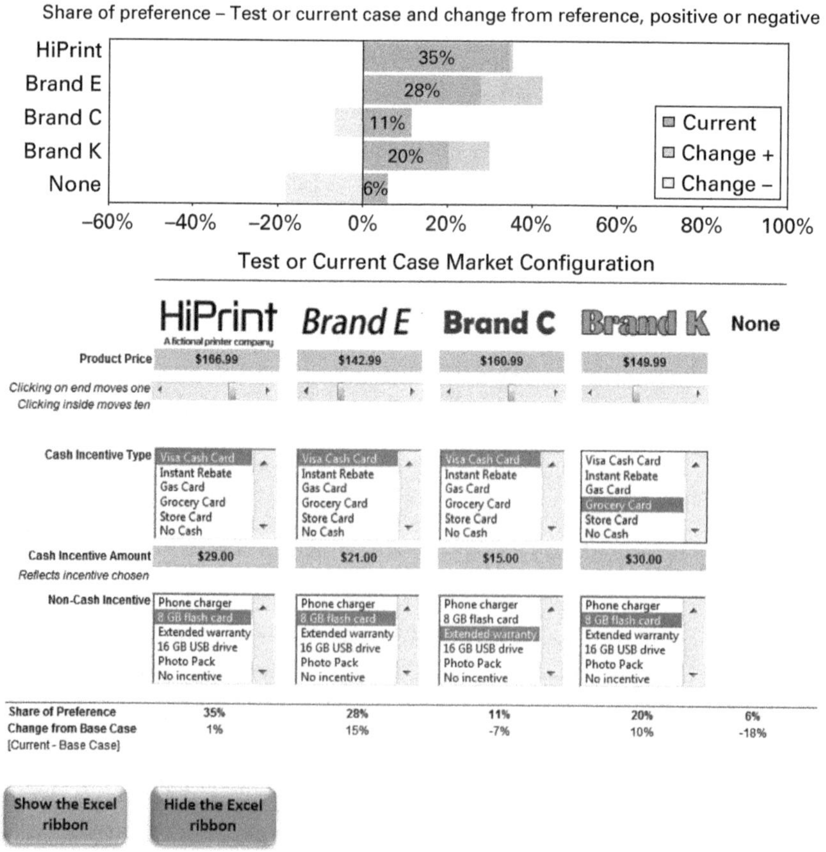

Creating the Best, Newest Thing: Discrete Choice Modelling

Study participants chose among these offerings and could also choose 'none of these' if all the competing offers did not meet their needs. They were told to imagine that they really needed to make such a purchase, but that they could opt out if all the choices were unacceptable. They saw real brand names, which we have altered in this example.

Figure 4.8 shows a part of this simulator. In this the user could set the **current case**. This would be the configuration that they wanted to test in a given simulation. The other part of the simulator, in which the user would set the **reference case**, appears in Figure 4.9. Together both sections are too large to read comfortably in print. (Excel, where this simulator was constructed, allows users to scroll around the screen to see different parts of a given display.)

The changes in the simulator show differences between the **current case** and the **base** or **reference case**. You need to have this comparison if you want to understand the sizes of share changes when features and/or prices change. Again, this is so because utility does not have a straight-line relationship with share. The size of the share effect from changing a feature will depend in part on the share at which you start.

This may seem like a mind-bending concept – but it reflects the realities of the marketplace, and so is important to recall. Where you start in the marketplace can influence how strongly the marketplace responds to whatever you are changing. Starting from a sufficiently low share can cause the share effects of making changes to your product or service **strongly non-linear**. Adding a given amount of utility may produce little effect, then adding the same amount may increase share much more, for instance.

You can see this phenomenon reflected in Figure 4.7. Depending on where you start on that S-curve, effects in share arising from adding a given amount of utility can vary widely. This definitely merits being called out.

Figure 4.9 shows the **reference** or **base case** portion of the simulator. This section can be reconfigured – that is, the features and prices can be changed – so that you can still understand the share effects of any change that you make, should the current or reference situation change.

> Because utility and share do not have a straight-line relationship, it is important to have a **reference** or **base case for comparison** so that you understand the share effects of changing features and/or prices. Depending on where your product starts on the S-shaped curve reflecting the relationship of utility and share, a given change in features or prices can have different share effects.

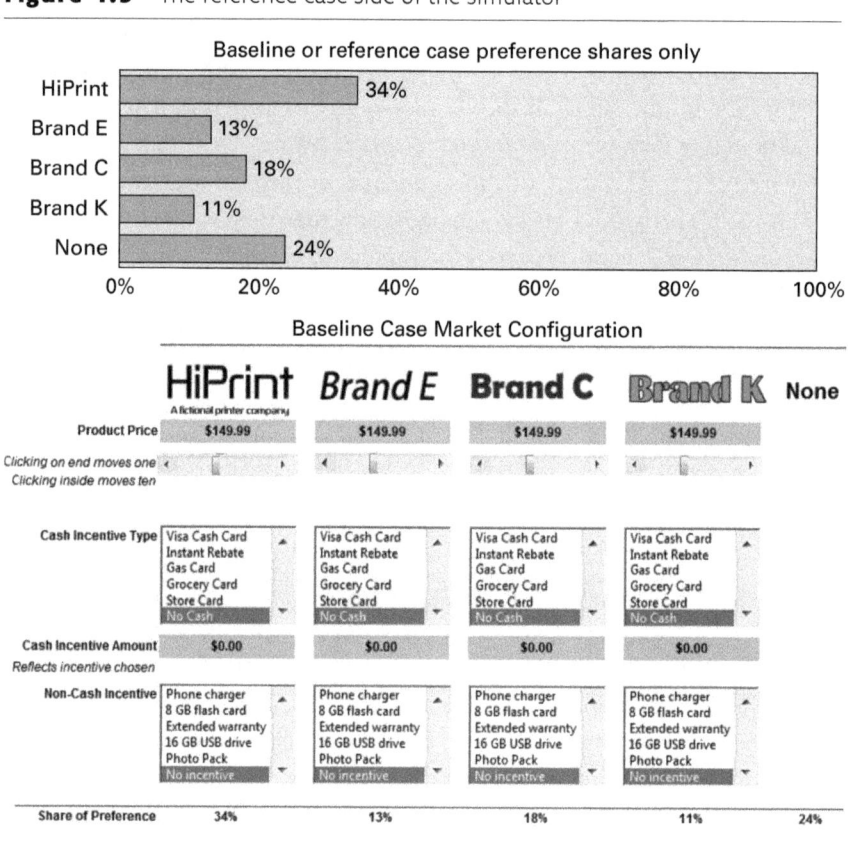

Figure 4.9 The reference case side of the simulator

Baseline or reference case preference shares only

HiPrint	34%
Brand E	13%
Brand C	18%
Brand K	11%
None	24%

Baseline Case Market Configuration

	HiPrint (A fictional printer company)	Brand E	Brand C	Brand K	None
Product Price	$149.99	$149.99	$149.99	$149.99	
Clicking on end moves one / Clicking inside moves ten					
Cash Incentive Type	Visa Cash Card / Instant Rebate / Gas Card / Grocery Card / Store Card / No Cash	Visa Cash Card / Instant Rebate / Gas Card / Grocery Card / Store Card / No Cash	Visa Cash Card / Instant Rebate / Gas Card / Grocery Card / Store Card / No Cash	Visa Cash Card / Instant Rebate / Gas Card / Grocery Card / Store Card / No Cash	
Cash Incentive Amount (Reflects incentive chosen)	$0.00	$0.00	$0.00	$0.00	
Non-Cash Incentive	Phone charger / 8 GB flash card / Extended warranty / 16 GB USB drive / Photo Pack / No incentive	Phone charger / 8 GB flash card / Extended warranty / 16 GB USB drive / Photo Pack / No incentive	Phone charger / 8 GB flash card / Extended warranty / 16 GB USB drive / Photo Pack / No incentive	Phone charger / 8 GB flash card / Extended warranty / 16 GB USB drive / Photo Pack / No incentive	
Share of Preference	34%	13%	18%	11%	24%

CASE STUDY The power of simulations – mobile phone towers

This study concerned the exciting world of mobile phone towers, in particular, the electronic innards that make them work. The sponsoring company, who we will call Ace T&T, had little idea of what their true competitive situation was. Their main source of information was anecdotal reports from the sales force, peppered with some gossip they picked up at various conferences and conventions.

They were fairly sure that they were the leading provider, but had no idea what their lesser-known competitors, who we will call Minor Players, Insignificant Co, and Tiny Industries, were doing with pricing.

Ace wanted to know if they could sell more of these units if they dropped their prices. Also, they wanted to know what would happen if their competitors followed suit. An experiment was set up and interviews were conducted. In the survey, buyers of mobile phone towers saw a series of marketplace scenarios. In each of these, the four brands offered towers at different prices between $48,000 and $88,000.

The client chose four evenly spaced prices for each brand. There also were two non-price features that could vary in a couple of ways, but these proved not to be important to the study, so we will omit them here.

This led to a total of 24 marketplace scenarios. Each study participant evaluated 12 of them and, thanks to HB analysis, this was sufficient.

Lock up those reports!

The simulator was made so that it showed both share and gross revenues per 100 sales. This was critical information, as Ace found out in the first simulations it tried. They set the reference point to the average current price revealed in the research: $68,000.

Note that 'none of these' was a study option but was not reported. This did not exceed 1 per cent until all prices were over $82,000. These were boom times, if not the golden age, for mobile phone towers.

In any event, in simulations, Ace first set all brands' prices to that $68,000 average. They then dropped their price to $52,000. This initially seemed good for them, as their estimated share went from 38 per cent to 46 per cent. This meant a share increase equal to 46/38 or 121 per cent.

However, if the other brands somehow stumbled onto what Ace was doing and matched their price decrease, Ace would end up nearly where they started, at a 39 per cent share. We can see this in Figure 4.10, where the results of these two simulations appear in chart format.

Figure 4.10 Base case and two simulations showing the danger of a price war

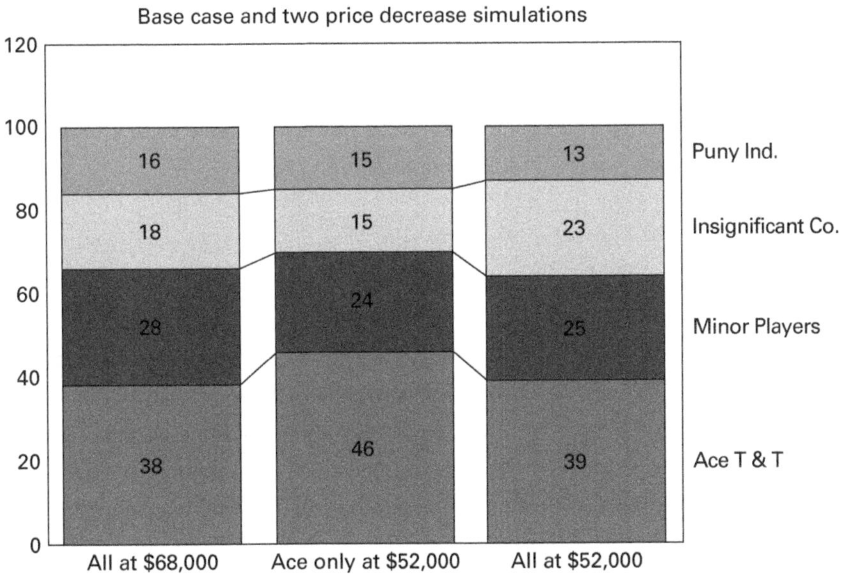

Base case and two price decrease simulations

	All at $68,000	Ace only at $52,000	All at $52,000
Puny Ind.	16	15	13
Insignificant Co.	18	15	23
Minor Players	28	24	25
Ace T & T	38	46	39

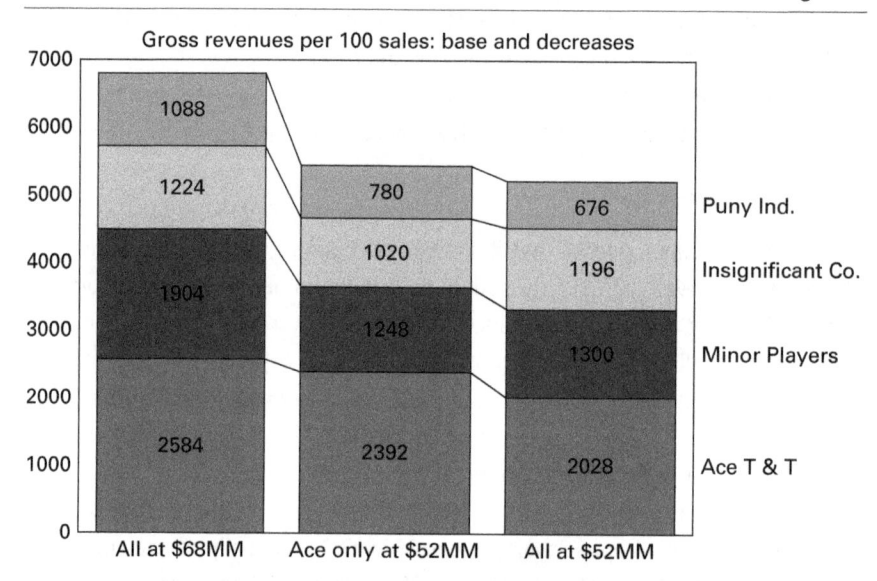

Figure 4.11 Changes in revenues from the simulations underline the dangers

Gross revenues per 100 sales: base and decreases

Bar segment	All at $68MM	Ace only at $52MM	All at $52MM	Category
Puny Ind.	1088	780	676	Puny Ind.
Insignificant Co.	1224	1020	1196	Insignificant Co.
Minor Players	1904	1248	1300	Minor Players
Ace T & T	2584	2392	2028	Ace T & T

This was bad enough, but looking at gross revenues, the picture turned dire. Although Ace's share increased if Ace alone dropped price, their gross revenues actually declined slightly in spite of larger share. If the others followed suit in dropping prices, Ace would end up selling nearly the same amount of units, but gross revenues would go down by about 22 per cent. We can see this in Figure 4.11.

Seeing these simulations, Ace issued the call to lock up the reports. They realized that they would lose terribly if they started a price war – or indeed if anyone else did. Only Insignificant Co. would emerge nearly unscathed if everyone dropped prices. They might find the drop in revenue acceptable for their increased presence in the market. Their share would rise by over 27 per cent, increasing by five points over their initial 18 per cent.

On the upside

Sobered but made more curious by these simulations, Ace T&T tried a few more. Three of these are summarized in the chart in Figure 4.12. The first, under '**A**', shows what happens if they alone raised their price to $74,000. They manage to eke out a small gain in gross revenues, even if selling fewer units.

Then they tested what would happen if they and their competitors all raised prices. This appears under '**B**'. As is the case with other **inelastic** goods and services, if prices were to go up, all competitors win – and consumers lose. This is one reason collusion is illegal.

Figure 4.12 Results from three more simulations

Base case and price increase simulations

	Base	A	B	C
Ace T & T	16	17	16	17
Minor Players	18	19	17	20
Insignificant Co	28	29	26	31
Puny Industries	38	35	40	32

All at $68MM — Ace only $74 — All $74MM — Ace $72MM, all other $64MM

Gross revenues per 100 sales: base and increase

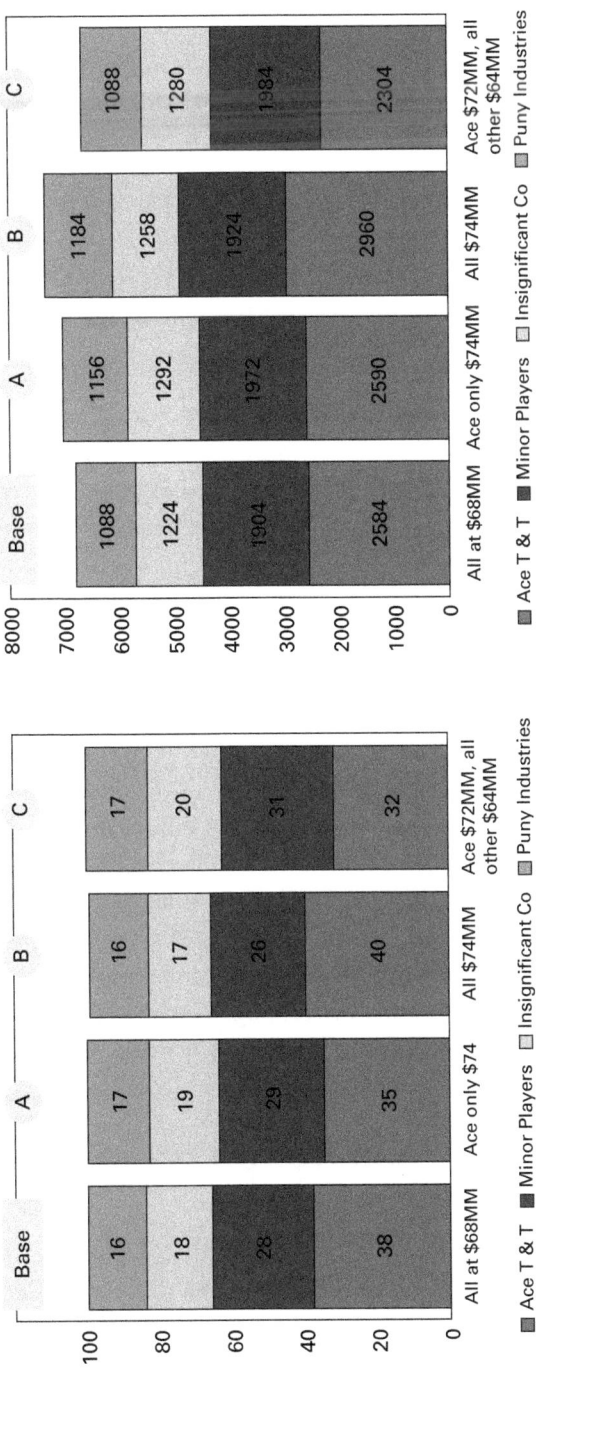

	Base	A	B	C
Ace T & T	1088	1156	1184	1088
Minor Players	1224	1292	1258	1280
Insignificant Co	1904	1972	1924	1984
Puny Industries	2584	2590	2960	2304

All at $68MM — Ace only $74MM — All $74MM — Ace $72MM, all other $64MM

The last simulation, under '**C**', shows what would happen if they raised their price and all others took a modest decrease at the same time. In this instance, they lose, but so does everyone else.

This example underlines the importance of **not focusing solely on share** as the criterion for your success. It also shows how simulations can model both actions and counter-actions, helping to set a more effective strategy.

Making more than one choice: allocating purchases

Discrete choice modelling can forecast what will happen in situations where people might choose more than one item. With everyday consumer products, this might happen in such situations as buying beverages or some food items. Allowing people to choose more than one item is called **allocating purchases**.

Allocation often makes sense with business-to-business purchase decisions. As an example, many studies among doctors ask what they would prescribe for 10 or 20 typical patients and/or patients of specific types. This makes sense because doctors often prescribe several different drugs for the same condition, depending on such factors as other drugs the patients are taking, diseases and disorders that they have, the patient's age and so on.

The simulator we showed at the beginning of this chapter is based on doctors allocating 20 patients to the different therapies available. They did two allocations in each marketplace that they evaluated, one for all patients and one for newly diagnosed patients.

While it is possible to allow people to choose as many items as they like, this can get messy to analyse. Asking people to allocate across a set number of purchases, such as the next 10, always works well.

Using the simulator program in the online resources

Download the program (available at www.koganpage.com/AI-Marketing) and open it with Microsoft Excel. If Excel is feeling reasonably well, the program will open and the Excel ribbon (the bar across the top with menus and commands) will temporarily vanish. Two buttons on each page of the

Creating the Best, Newest Thing: Discrete Choice Modelling   115

Figure 4.13   Page display controls in the downloadable simulator

| Click to hide the Excel ribbon | Click to show the Excel ribbon |

simulator allow you to control whether the Excel ribbon appears or not. These buttons are shown in Figure 4.13. If you cannot see them, and need to use them, please scroll down until they are visible.

If you want to continue working in Excel after using the simulator, **restore** the ribbon to view, and then close the file using the menu. If the simulator is the only file open, using the small 'X' that appears in the uppermost right corner of the screen will make Excel close.

If Excel is baulking at opening the simulator, please reassure it, clicking the option it presents to say it is fine to run macros. If this still does not work,

Figure 4.14   The left side of the downloadable simulator

Current Case				Reference Case			
Brand R				**Brand R**			
Horsepower	◄ ▬ ►	250		Horsepower	◄ ▬ ►	250	
Price	◄ ▬ ►	15099		Price	◄ ▬ ►	13999	
Features		Yes	No	Features		Yes	No
✓ Cruise control with No-Wake Mode		○	●	✓ Cruise control with No-Wake Mode		●	○
✓ Learning Key		○	●	✓ Learning Key		●	○
✓ MPG Mode for saving fuel		○	●	✓ MPG Mode for saving fuel		●	○
✓ Adjustable handlebar with Electric		○	●	✓ Adjustable handlebar with Electric		●	○
✓ Off-throttle steering control		○	●	✓ Off-throttle steering control		●	○
Brand G				**Brand G**			
Horsepower	◄ ▬ ►	270		Horsepower	◄ ▬ ►	278	
Price	◄ ▬ ►	13499		Price	◄ ▬ ►	13999	
Features		Yes	No	Features		Yes	No
✓ Cruise control with No-Wake Mode		●	○	✓ Cruise control with No-Wake Mode		●	○
✓ Remote control Learning Key		●	○	✓ Remote control Learning Key		●	○
✓ MPG Mode for saving fuel		●	○	✓ MPG Mode for saving fuel		●	○
✓ Adjustable handlebar with Manual		●	○	✓ Adjustable handlebar with Manual		●	○
✓ Dual brake system		●	○	✓ Dual brake system		●	○
Brand N				**Brand N**			
Horsepower	◄ ▬ ►	260		Horsepower	◄ ▬ ►	260	
Price	◄ ▬ ►	12899		Price	◄ ▬ ►	13999	
Features		Yes	No	Features		Yes	No
✓ Cruise control with No-Wake Mode		●	○	✓ Cruise control with No-Wake Mode		●	○
✓ Learning Key		●	○	✓ Learning Key		●	○
✓ Fly-by-wire throttle		●	○	✓ Fly-by-wire throttle		●	○
✓ Adjustable handlebar with Electric		●	○	✓ Adjustable handlebar with Electric		●	○
✓ Dual brake system		●	○	✓ Dual brake system		●	○

| Click to hide the Excel ribbon | Click to show the Excel ribbon |

go to the third tab in the simulator, 'Security in Excel 2007 and beyond'. Follow the instructions there and Excel should at last cooperate.

The first page of the simulator has some general instructions. These are important to include with any simulator that will find its way around an organization, or in case someone opens it after a few months have passed.

The next sheet is the actual simulator. Figure 4.14 shows the left side of the screen that you will find on this sheet. Here you have all the controls for setting the **current case** and for establishing a **reference** or **base case**.

Prices and amounts of horsepower run using sliding controls. You either can pull these to the desired values or click on the ends or inside the control. Clicking on an end (arrow) of the horsepower control changes it by one unit; clicking inside it changes it by 10 units. Clicking on an end of the price control changes it by 10 units, while clicking inside changes it by 100 units.

Figure 4.15 The right side of the downloadable simulator

Shares

	Brand R	Brand G	Brand N
Current	22.4%	44.0%	33.7%
Reference	30.4%	39.1%	30.5%
Difference	−8.0%	4.8%	3.2%

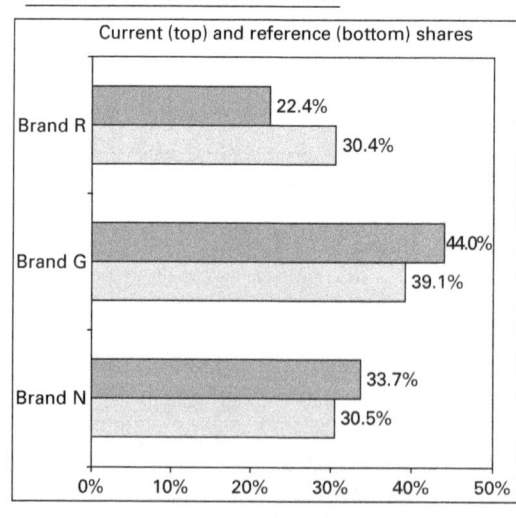

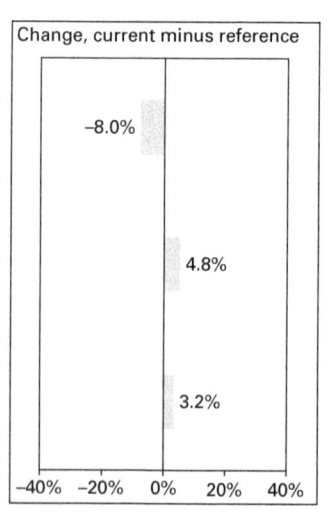

Gross Revenue per 100 prospects

	Brand R	Brand G	Brand N
Current	$ 315,406	$ 615,308	$ 471,423
Reference	$ 425,723	$ 547,730	$ 426,447
Difference	$ (110,317)	$ 67,578	$ 44,976
% change	−25.9%	12.3%	10.5%

All the other features are either present or absent. You choose whether each is a part of the feature package by clicking either on 'Yes' or 'No'.

At the bottom of this side of the page you will find a set of control buttons that allow you to control whether the Excel ribbon is visible or not. A last set of identical controls also appears at the bottom right of the page about security in Excel.

Figure 4.15 shows the various displays in the simulator that result from the chosen values of the current and reference cases. The top section has numerical information.

Next to this chart you will find two additional control buttons. One returns the current case to preset values built into the simulator. The other returns the reference case to a set of preset values. Controls of this type can be useful after a few simulations have been run and you would like to get a fresh start.

The middle section of this page shows the information in the number chart in a graphical format. Seeing the differences in changes can help make their sizes more easily understandable.

At the bottom, you will find calculations for gross revenues per 100 sales. These are gross revenues because no costs (such as distribution, advertising or other kinds of overhead) are offset against them.

Again, in many cases, going for the largest share may not be the best policy for getting the most revenue. This chart allows you to keep track of both share and gross sales.

Using Excel to optimize

A powerful **optimizer** is built into Excel itself. This allows you to find the simulator settings that lead to the best possible outcome in specific situations. It is called the 'solver'. It is not part of the simulator itself, but runs in conjunction with the simulator's controls.

You need to load the solver before you use it. The instructions from Microsoft for loading and running this add-on are clear and easy to follow. You could use the optimizer to answer questions such as, 'What is the mix of price and features that will optimize my revenues if competitors stay as they are now?' You could then answer another question, such as, 'What will optimize revenues if my competitors then drop their prices by 10 per cent?'

Addressing questions like these can add a new dimension to predicting changes in share and revenue. Depending on the objectives of the project, **optimization** can provide valuable strategic insights.

Rounding out the picture

This chapter has become the longest and most complex in this book. First, congratulations for persevering. We have actually omitted much, in particular vast swaths of a more technical nature. Still, we have just a few last topics to consider.

Compensatory versus non-compensatory: what is this all about?

Some criticisms of discrete choice modelling have arisen based on theories that people do not weigh attributes and sum utilities to make decisions. These so-called **non-compensatory** theories seem perfectly non-objectionable, as we indeed have no clear idea of how decisions get weighed. However, and let us speak plainly here, the argument that this somehow invalidates choice modelling is nonsense.

Some of these criticisms say that people pick certain features first, eliminate choices based on those, and then narrow down in some way. To these critics, this throws into question what people do in choice models.

We understand what these critics are saying and can sympathize with it, but they are wrong. Just because choice modelling presents a product as a set of attributes, this does not force people to weigh and balance everything they are seeing. People indeed can look at the marketplaces presented to them and use any decision strategy that they would use in the actual marketplace.

We can see by watching how people decide that they have different strategies. One part of many studies is sitting with a few people before the formal interviews start and going through the marketplaces. During this phase, you ask people to talk about what they are doing, ask questions and do a great deal of observation. Some people do indeed focus in on a single attribute, such as price or brand, some balance two or three of them, and some make an earnest effort to balance multiple factors.

Discrete choice modelling can accommodate and reflect any of these strategies. The problem with arguments about 'non-compensatory' decision making seems to lie in confusing a capability of discrete choice modelling with a requirement of discrete choice modelling. That is, it can model people making complicated decisions where they try to trade all attributes. But that does not mean that anyone **has to** do that. People can make decisions according to simpler rules and the method will still work accurately.

Some less fortuitous applications

We have already spoken about the dangers of poorly defined projects, unclear terminology and unrealistic representations of the marketplace. Earlier we reviewed the pitfalls of talking to (or about) the wrong people, and of putting so many restrictions on selecting people for a survey that you lose track of who they represent. But what if you get all the basics right? When could discrete choice modelling not work well?

We have seen problems with certain types of products or services. First, let's consider products as ranging along a continuum, from more cognitive (or having more to think about) to more affective or sensory (or more feeling-based). Trade-off methods work best where products have more cognitive elements.

Sometimes it is very difficult to get people to trade affective or sensory elements. For instance, in a trade-off exercise, people do not accurately trade off 'tastes good' against other product attributes. We know that in real life, people will consume some fairly awful items in the interest of saving money. For instance, certain store brands of non-fat cream cheese are indistinguishable from window caulking except that they do not hold up as well as the caulk to the elements. Yet these remain on sale.

However, you will almost never encounter a person who will admit in a survey to eating something that tastes worse than the container it comes in, just to save a few pennies. Such a purely sensory trade-off is a rare instance where the in-market experience does not translate well into the setting of an interview. In any event, never try to trade off worse taste, aroma or feel versus other features in a discrete choice model.

However, people can show that they respond differently to various brands. For instance, Sony once commanded a higher price than other brands for the same set of features. Therefore, features once were worth more with the Sony name. This shows that a rather amorphous quantity such as 'brand identity' can in fact be measured in a choice study – by the hard-edged metric of what people choose.

Variants of choice modelling

A number of variants of discrete choice modelling have been proposed. Some of the better-known ones come from one company, Sawtooth Software. These include menu-based choice based modelling, which aims to address the specific problem of modelling choices from companies that offer a menu of choices, such as phone companies on their websites. You can set up a standard discrete choice modelling study to get close to this, but not exactly what you would see on such a website. Another offering is adaptive choice-based modelling, which seemingly chases the chimera of non-compensatory decision making.

These are interesting ideas, but so far have been supported only by papers published on the company website, or in some cases by papers from loosely vetted industry conferences. This does not mean that there is anything wrong with the work involved, just that these have not yet been held up to rigorous academic standards.

As mentioned in Chapter 1, every method we discuss in detail has to pass in both the sphere of peer-reviewed papers and in the test of practical application. So far, then, these variants have intriguing ideas, but no more.

Perhaps the best-known alternative, a software product called **Choice-Based-Conjoint**, or **CBC**, has gained many followers. To some, this (wrongly) is seen as the same as synonymous with discrete choice modelling. Actually, though, the name of this product is honest. It is partly conjoint analysis and partly discrete choice modelling.

Because of this hybrid nature, CBC will appear in Chapter 5, where we explain conjoint analysis. There, you will be able to see what CBC takes from this approach and what it takes from discrete choice modelling.

Summary of key points

Discrete choice modelling is arguably the most powerful and sophisticated method for determining the exact mix of features and prices to include in a product or service. It focuses on what people will choose. It provides some of the most powerful outputs of any analytical method, in particular interactive market simulator programs. These show you precisely what will happen to share of preference when products' features and/or prices are changed.

If you can manage to think ahead to what competitors most likely will do, then you can cover not only what would happen if you change your own fine product or service, but also what will happen when competitors respond.

The method uses a survey that shows people realistic representations of the choices they have to make. Each person will see a series of these **marketplace scenarios**, and in each they simply say what they would choose, just as they do in real life. The problem can also be set up so that they can say they would choose 'none of them' in each marketplace. This greatly increases the

Creating the Best, Newest Thing: Discrete Choice Modelling

realism of the exercise. There are very few situations indeed where people cannot sit out making a purchase, even when the need is strong.

Discrete choice modelling considers products or services as collections of **attributes**. In the study these attributes are varied in specific ways. For continuous attributes, such as car horsepower, only certain specific values are tested. The different values that are tested are called **levels**. For instance, if the engine could have anywhere from 150 to 240 horsepower, we might test 150, 180, 210 and 240 as the levels. To determine the values in between we would **interpolate**.

Discrete choice modelling is based on strict experimental designs that govern which level of each attribute appears in a given marketplace scenario. As you measure more attributes and levels, the experiment must grow larger to measure them.

It is important to measure exactly what you need – and no more. People doing a discrete choice study typically start to tire after evaluating 6–12 marketplaces. Most people will stick with it for a few more, but about 21 is the limit even for highly analytical study participants.

Therefore, careful discussion of precisely what goes into a discrete choice modelling study is critical. So is a good understanding of the marketplace itself before you start the study. You truly need to zero in on what matters.

Recall that you need to have one marketplace scenario to measure a two-level attribute, for instance, and three to measure a four-level attribute. This underlines the need for economy.

Utilities and choices

Discrete choice modelling uses abstract quantities called **utilities** as a kind of bookkeeping. These units allow us to compare the effects of different attributes and prices. This use of utilities does not mean that the method assumes people will look at and weigh all the attributes that they see. People can focus on a single attribute, such as price, they can look at a few of them, or they can make careful, exacting decisions. Whatever their strategy, this method will accommodate it.

The aim of this method is to model what people will choose. It does not delve deeply into psychology or hidden motivations. Its focus is always on the value of features and how changes affect that value.

Features are specific to the choices

Each choice can have its own features and prices in discrete choice modelling. The brand or choice acts as a kind of container for those features. We can get an idea of the residual value of the brand, aside from the attributes that are varied, by looking at a term in the model called the constant. We get this as part of the model, if we set it up properly. We therefore do not need to specify brand as an attribute.

This is an important consideration, and one that may be puzzling to people used to the thinking behind conjoint analysis. In the basic form of that type of analysis, brand is an attribute rather than a place where other attributes live.

Best practices

Here is a basic outline. Please refer back to this chapter for more about each:

- **Understand your market.** Too many of these studies fail before they start because of inadequate preparation. Measuring the wrong attributes or focusing on inessential concerns inevitably leads to poor results.
- **Know how users and prospects talk about the product or service.** Makers of technical, medical and professional products are particularly prone to believing that all users of their products really understand them and know all the corporate lingo. It is better to assume that users know no such thing. It is best to find out how users talk about the product or service and use precisely that language.
- **Focus on benefits to the user, rather than how the product is made.** Again, makers of a product may believe the technical details are fascinating, and providers of a service often think that everyone is engrossed by the organizational processes that underlie their work. Users care about what a product does for them, not how it is put together. Focus on the functional benefits, not the technical specifications.
- **Measure as much variation for each attribute that you think may reasonably happen.** That is, you want to measure as much change in each attribute as you expect to see. Suppose you want to measure responses to price and your highest price is $5.00. Yet at $5.01, people start considering the price too expensive and sales fall off drastically. You will have no way to know. You need to measure up to the point where you think no sudden changes in response are likely.
- **Consider narrowing the field of comparisons if you have too many choices.** If you are studying SoggyOs breakfast substance, for instance, you likely would not include all things a person could have for breakfast as a competitive set. Indeed, any specific cereal-like substance would

likely have a minuscule share of the total market. Measuring what drives changes is difficult for items that rarely get chosen. Instead, you should compare to the close competitors. In the case of SoggyOs this might be other fine cellulose-enhanced, overly sweetened breakfast-like treats.

- **Still, make the marketplaces represent the main competitors realistically.** We know from recent research on decision making that the context for decisions is very important in determining what people will choose. The marketplace scenarios provide that context. Make sure it allows people to choose much as they would in the real world.
- **Tell people to imagine they really need to buy/get one of the choices if any is at all acceptable.** Research and experience shows that this leads people to make better and more consistent decisions.
- **Include a 'none of these' option.** Together with the instruction directly above, this makes the exercise realistic. People will think as if they are in a frame of mind conducive to buying, but they also will know that they can sit out the decision if the experimental design generates a marketplace where all choices are not acceptable.

The price is right

Discrete choice modelling is the method par excellence for testing responses to changes in price. This comes from the realism of showing products side by side in a marketplace, from asking people to choose, and from each choice having its own pricing variable. This means that the prices can be fit exactly to each choice.

If you have a good sense of pricing in the marketplace, four prices should be all you ever need. As we showed in several charts, four points will capture the most complex price versus share relationships you will encounter. If you are not certain, you might go to five prices or even six, but we have never seen a need for more.

The Bayesian advantage

Hierarchical Bayesian (HB) analysis has opened up the world of discrete choice modelling. It is an incredibly complex method of calculations, and it will give your computer its workout for the week – or year. We have seen massive problems take hours to run on the largest and speediest computers. It seems almost magical in how it works – and yet it does work. It has been validated time and again over the last 20 years.

It allows you to double or triple the amount of information you can get from a given study participant. Suppose you have a study that requires 24 marketplaces based on the experiment you have set up. You can show each person half of those and get a nearly perfect reading on all the attributes. In the old days, before HB analysis, you would have to double your sample to compensate for splitting the task in half.

Also, you get data for every person. Before this form of analysis, you could only get data for a group of people. Data for each individual is a remarkable advance.

Utility and share

Utility is an abstract quantity and it must get translated into share in some way. Discrete choice modelling uses a sophisticated model that is in line with how we respond perceptually to the environment. This model also is at least a reasonable approximation for the biases in decision making that recent research has revealed.

This response model is an S-shaped curve. This is realistic but it also makes translating utility into share difficult. The relationship is not a straight line. This makes sense looking at a marketplace, though. If you brand has a low share, you have to do more to stand out from the noise. If your brand is reasonably visible, people will respond more readily to changes. Then if you have a really large share, it becomes increasingly difficult to convert those who are intensely loyal to other brands. That is the top of the S-curve, where you can really pour on extra value and still see only small shifts in the marketplace.

You cannot just look and guess

You must run a simulator program to see how share changes when a product or service changes. Looking at utilities and guessing is inaccurate. Utilities are doubly inaccurate if you use HB analysis, as each person's utility values will be larger or smaller than each other person's. You need to get all the utilities on the same footing by first solving for 'share' within each person and then averaging.

Allocating choices

Discrete choice modelling allows you to model people making more than one choice at a time. For instance, we can ask doctors to allocate different drugs to 10 or 20 typical patients. We also do such things as asking ordinary consumers to choose their next 10 or 12 soft drink purchases.

Table 4.1 Setting up contingent pricing

	Very low	Low	Medium	High
750ml or 850ml	$8.39	$9.59	$10.59	$11.99
One litre	$8.99	$9.99	$11.00	$12.49

Contingent attributes

We also can make the values of one attribute contingent on another. For instance, suppose we have two size classes of wine bottle, and three prices that we conceptualize as low, medium and high. Each size can have its own set of low, medium and high prices (Table 4.1).

We also can make one attribute (or more) disappear entirely based on the value of another attribute. The way to do this was first proposed over 20 years ago. Blanking out attributes in an experimental design does not introduce correlations or hurt the statistical performance of the design.

Cautions and where this may not work

It is worth saying again that discrete choice modelling, for all its incredible power, produces **share of preference**, not market share. To get to market share, you must adjust for marketplace factors such as comprehension and awareness of the product and how widely the product is distributed. To go to projections, you must know the size of the entire market, which is often difficult to determine.

Lastly, you must know what part of the total market your particular sample of study participants represent. This makes drawing projections extremely difficult. We often include extra controls in the simulator that the sponsoring company can manipulate, seeing what projected sales would be under a wide range of different assumptions.

We also need to recall that forecasts are necessarily short term. Once market conditions change, they lose much of their precision and power. With sufficient change, they can become highly inaccurate.

These methods seem to break down most severely with purely sensory attributes. People do not seem able to trade a product 'tasting worse', 'smelling worse' or 'feeling worse' for other attributes in a discrete choice study. This is so even though they obviously do so routinely in real life.

Overall

Market simulations (and market simulator programs) may indeed be that elusive best thing since sliced bread. When discrete choice modelling studies are done with care and understanding, these models can have incredible predictive power in the short term. This need for care, for advance thinking, and for measured consideration of the results may work against truly widespread adoption. Those seeking a quick fix, or those who hope a machine will solve the problem for them, will quickly look elsewhere.

A sample simulator is included in the online resources for this chapter, available at **www.koganpage.com/AI-Marketing** – it should give you an idea of the tremendous power that discrete choice modelling can have. We encourage you to follow the instructions, use it and see how it works.

Conjoint analysis and its uses

05

This chapter addresses the other main method for getting to the optimal product, service or message. Conjoint analysis has been described as outmoded by some, but in the right applications it remains a powerful method. In particular, it can work remarkably well in optimizing communications, such as advertisements and web pages. It totally outdistances the traditional A/B testing used with web pages. It also can precisely optimize delivery of complex services. We will compare and contrast conjoint with discrete choice modelling, showing where this method has unique applications.

Thinking in conjoint versus thinking in choices

Conjoint analysis developed largely in the market research community. As you may recall from Chapter 3, its earliest incarnations looked something like magic squares, where levels of two features were crossed versus each other and the resulting combinations were ranked. You will find this back in Figure 3.10, which shows how this looks.

Conjoint became a widely used and useful tool with the development of traditional **full-profile conjoint** in the mid-1970s. This shows a series of whole products or services – hence the name **full profile**. Study participants typically rate these product profiles.

Before online interviewing became so prevalent, people could also sort and rank the profiles, which appeared on cards. You will still encounter the term **conjoint cards**, meaning the product profiles, as a remnant of this now rare practice.

Conjoint was quickly hailed as a great advance over traditional rating scales, and gained widespread adoption. It overcame many of the problems with ratings, such the tendency of people to rate everything highly important if given the chance, and the tendency to give socially acceptable answers in ratings. (We discussed these concerns in greater detail in Chapter 2.)

Conjoint often worked well with widely known brands that were largely similar to each other. But it also broke down mysteriously in other situations. There also was a logical disconnect in using it with multiple products. That is, it presented products one at a time, but then attempted to simulate how they behaved side by side in a marketplace. The task posed in the interview was clearly less like the real world than the one in discrete choice modelling.

And indeed, the underlying conjoint analysis model as a whole was less realistic than the model used in discrete choice. As a reminder, with discrete choice, each choice can have its own features. With conjoint analysis, features were considered as applying across all the choices, and compromises often had to be made.

Figure 5.1 goes back to our earlier example in Chapter 4 with Quiet Financial Services (QFS); it shows the framework for discrete choice modelling, and how it contrasts with the one for conjoint analysis.

With discrete choice modelling, the brand (or the choice) is a container and attributes are specific to each choice. With conjoint analysis, brand is an attribute that can combine freely with the others. Note that with conjoint, some attribute levels that were specific to each brand had to be eliminated so that the experimental design would remain a reasonable size. If we were to have two five-level attributes, for instance, that would require 5 x 5 or 25 product profiles. That would be too many to show using the traditional conjoint analysis methods.

Another salient problem is that attribute levels that do not belong with each brand would need to appear with that brand. For instance, 'no fee' would have to appear with QFS, which has no intention of offering 'no fee'.

That problem was addressed imperfectly by using 'prohibitions'. Basically, this meant swapping in another attribute level for the one specified by the experimental design, whenever two attribute levels could not appear together. This could damage the design and make the attributes correlated.

If you were lucky, the correlations would still be low, and the design would not be weakened too much. But with the wrong swap or too many swaps, the experiment would fall apart, undermined by strong correlations among the attributes. (If this seems confusing, please go back and look at the section in Chapter 3 on designs and why they need zero or near-zero correlations.)

Figure 5.1 Attributes in discrete choice versus attributes in conjoint

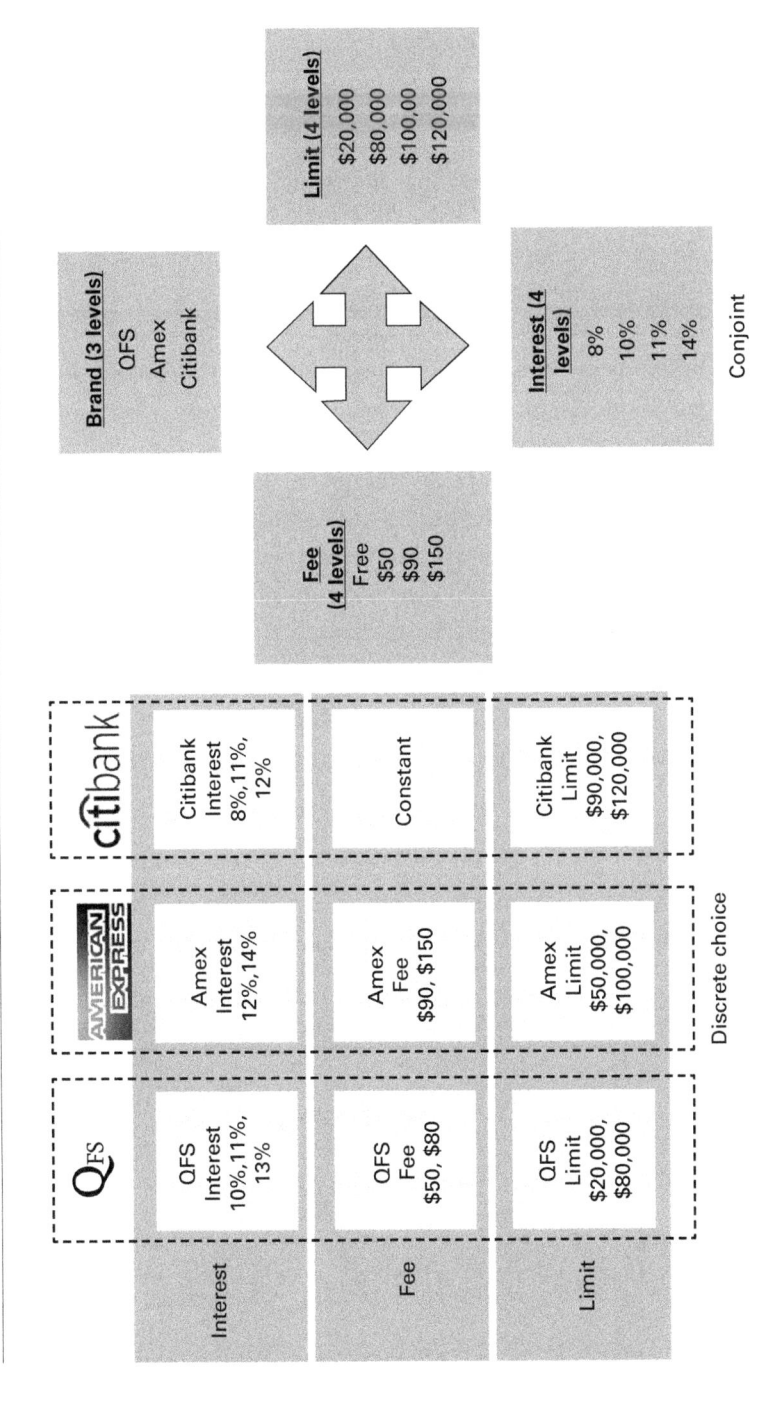

Lack of realism in how conjoint treats utilities

Conjoint analysis started with an overly simple view of how utility becomes share in the marketplace. More utility equals more preference, in a straight-line relationship. More formally, the relationship is seen as linear and additive. As we discussed in Chapter 4, the S-shaped relationship postulated in discrete choice modelling closely fits what we know about decision making and how products fare in the marketplace. Figure 5.2 shows how the traditional treatment of utility by conjoint compares with relationship captured by discrete choice modelling.

We use the word 'traditional' because conjoint can be retooled to perform better in this area. With a few tweaks, we can solve a conjoint problem just as we would an **allocation problem** in discrete choice modelling. Then we have at least overcome one salient issue.

All of the remaining problems, though, make conjoint less than ideal for estimating how products will behave in a competitive environment when they are varied. The problem of attributes not being specific to the choices also makes measuring responses to changes in the attributes less accurate. It is no wonder conjoint analysis has been eclipsed by discrete choice as the leading method for predicting acceptance of products in a competitive marketplace.

Then how (and why) do we use conjoint analysis?

Conjoint analysis can provide valuable insights in situations where the product would have a minuscule share, and so get completely swamped by

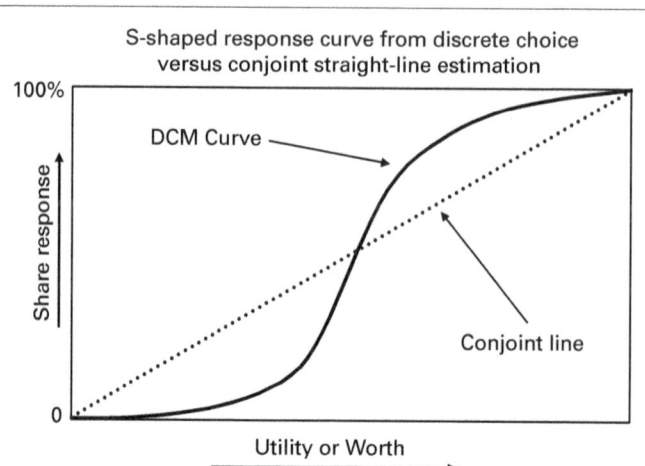

Figure 5.2 Differences in how discrete choice and conjoint treat utility

> Traditional conjoint analysis shows one product at a time and asks for a rating of that product. In conjoint analysis, if you include brand, it becomes an **attribute** rather than a **container for attributes** (which is the case with discrete choice modelling). Since brand is an attribute, each brand must appear with each level of each other attribute. This can lead to impossible combinations. Even if it does not, the conjoint approach is less realistic and less precise than one used by discrete choice modelling. Discrete choice modelling is now strongly preferred for predicting acceptance of products in a competitive marketplace.

other choices when people are asked to choose. That is, if a product is rarely chosen, there would not be enough information from the few times it did get selected to determine what was driving that choice. Conjoint analysis allows you effectively to put that infrequently chosen product 'under a microscope' and determine its best possible configuration.

Conjoint also can do remarkably well in optimizing communications, in particular print advertising and websites. You can test the equivalent of thousands of alternative configurations in one study. It completely overwhelms the more usual A/B testing done with websites – as we will see.

In addition, conjoint analysis can do remarkably well in determining the specific levels of service that need to be offered in complex customer relationships, such as those between a utility and its commercial customers, or a pharmaceutical company and the doctors and clinics it serves. We will see all three of these applications.

> While conjoint analysis is not the best choice for determining how products will behave in a competitive marketplace, it still has some important uses. These are three principal applications:
>
> - **Where competitive context would be overwhelming**: this would be the case when you wanted to make the best product and the product had a very low share. Because the product would get chosen only rarely, patterns of choices would not accurately reveal which changes worked best. Conjoint analysis, with its single-product focus, can put that product 'under a microscope' and show how to select the best variations of its features.

- **For optimizing communications**, such as print advertisements and websites. You can get the relative appeal of thousands of alternative configurations, completely surpassing such current methods as A/B testing.
- **For determining the exact levels of service in complex customer relationships**, such as between utilities and their commercial customers. The many elements in customer interactions can be carefully tailored, leading to the best mix.

Conjoint analysis for single-product optimization

An example from a good number of years ago involves a maker of disposable pens. These are the inexpensive pens that eventually run out of ink and are discarded, or mysteriously disappear forever and are not worth retrieving, as when you lend them to a friend.

There are dozens of alternative brands and models to choose from, so a new pen entering this crowded field would garner at best a very small share. This would have posed a problem in testing reactions to the new pen if it had been tested alongside competitors. It might been chosen rarely – or never. Zeroing in on the product itself with conjoint analysis therefore made sense.

This approach also worked because of the way that consumers make purchases. The manufacturer noticed that buyers would purchase more pens if they had a positive experience writing with a certain pen. The company had identified a number of factors that could make the pen better to use, including the barrel width, roller-ball composition, viscosity of the ink, drying time of the ink and so on.

They decided to test five features that could each vary three ways and one that could vary six ways. This would be 3 x 3 x 3 x 3 x 3 x 6 or **1,458** possible configurations.

An experimental design led to 18 different prototype pens. The makers produced a batch of these to be used in testing. People were invited to interviewing facilities, where they found the pens and plenty of paper. They tried the 18 pens, then put them in order from favourite to worst. These rankings can be used in conjoint analysis just as numerical ratings can.

The main output of this study was a simulator accurately showing the relative appeal of all 1,458 possible pens. In fact, many more configurations were possible, because the simulator allowed **interpolation** between the values tested for continuous variables, such as drying time of the ink. After carefully considering the results, the company was able to make a new pen that people liked using and that succeeded in the market.

Using the single product simulator in the online resources

Our next example concerns a new type of dietary fibre that came in the form of a large tablet. There are many products that contain dietary fibre, so the sponsoring company was concerned that their new invention might get lost in the mix if it were tested in marketplace scenarios alongside the more established brands.

The study therefore used full-profile conjoint analysis, showing this new product alone. Study participants evaluated a series of 16 hypothetical new products. Each product they saw differed in level of dietary fibre, formulation, flavour, numbers of days of supply and price.

Price was shown both as price per tablet and price per package. Price per tablet was **contingent** on the formulation, with four different prices, depending on how the product was made. Total price was contingent on both the price per tablet and days of supply.

The main results of the study can be seen in the simulator (available at www.koganpage.com/AI-Marketing). There are three versions, one that runs under Excel, one that runs under PowerPoint, and one that runs in the Adobe Acrobat PDF format. All versions are fully interactive.

PowerPoint version

Download the file and open PowerPoint. The program works in presentation mode. To get to presentation mode on a PC, press the F5 function key at the top of the keyboard. On a Mac, you need to press Option-Return. (You need to have Flash Player on your computer for the PowerPoint and PDF versions to run.)

Figure 5.3 shows what you will see when you open this simulator. We have added letters that do not appear. These will aid in quick location of the features being discussed.

The controls for the simulator appear under 'A'. These are all select-one type controls, with the darker shading appearing over the level selected. The total appeal of the product, and how that compares to the best possible product, falls under 'B'. More detail related to this chart follows under 'C',

Figure 5.3 Sample basic-one product conjoint simulator

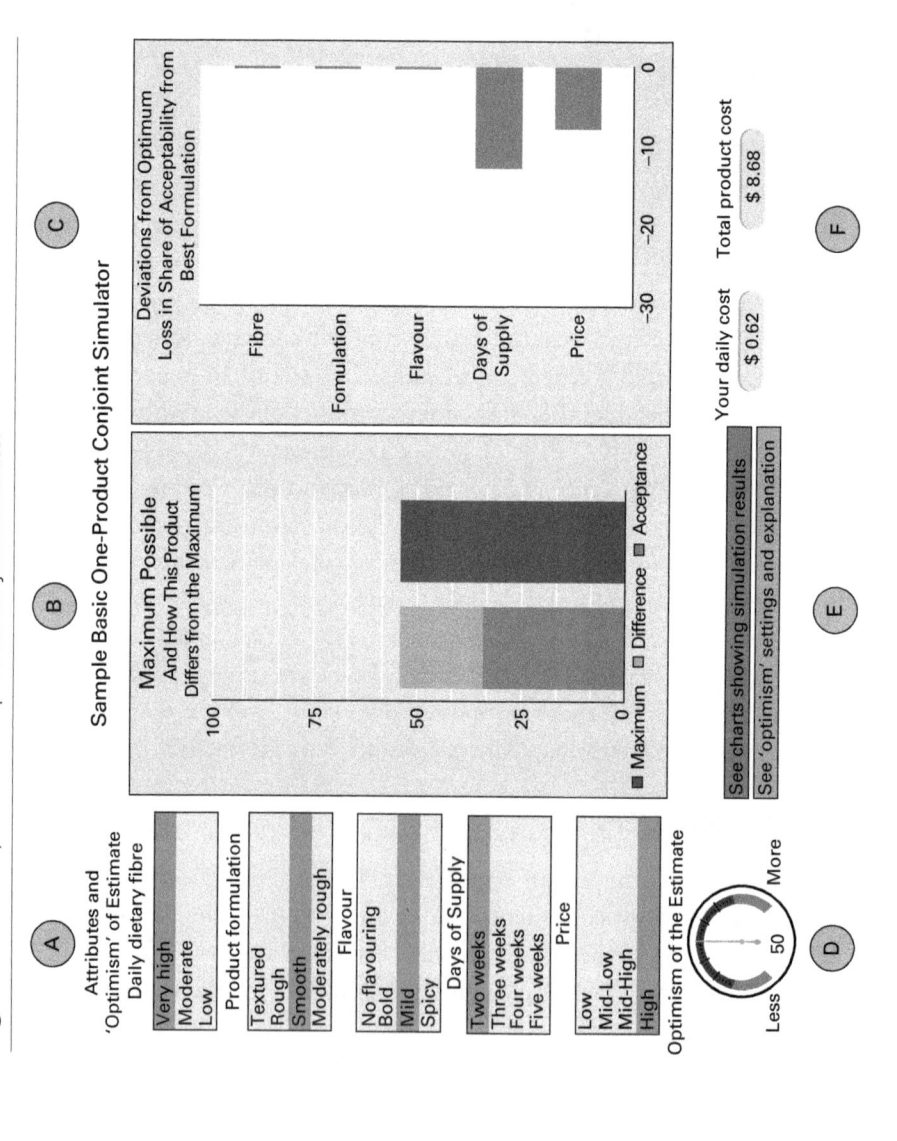

where a chart displays differences between the attribute levels chosen and the best possible level.

This simulator has a special control that the sponsoring company requested. You see this near 'D'. This deflates the so-called 'optimism' of the estimate. That is, study participants estimated their likelihood of buying the various products they saw on a 0–100 scale. Because they rated the product in isolation, there was some concern that this rating was inflated. Therefore a control was added to deflate this estimate if needed.

Near 'E', there is a two-item selector, a kind of mini-menu. Clicking on the bottom bar switches to another page that shows how estimated share of preference changes as the so-called optimism changes. The least optimistic curve aims to look like the bottom part of the curve in prospect theory (which we discussed in Chapter 4), which was postulated to be a bottom limit for how quickly share versus utility could decline.

Figure 5.4 shows how the relationship between utility and share can be changed by the dial-shaped control (this control appears on both pages of the simulator). Moving the control counter-clockwise with the pointer will move the line down to the least optimistic relationship.

Similarly, dialling the control clockwise makes the estimate more optimistic, until it finally reaches the straight-line approximation traditionally

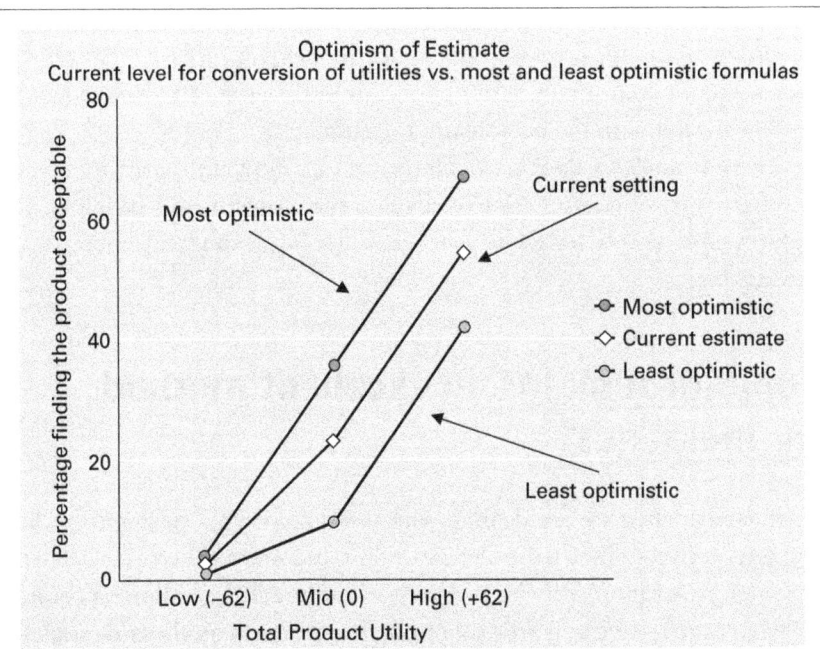

Figure 5.4 Details of how utility becomes share of preference

used in conjoint analysis. That is as optimistic about share effects as you can become.

In Figure 5.3, pressing on the top bar of the two-item menu (above letter **E**) brings you back to the simulator itself. We have one more feature to describe. Prices, both per tablet and in total, appear above letter **F** in Figure 5.3. These reflect the actual prices that people participating in the study saw. The controls under letter **A** reflect the way that prices were set up so that the correct price could appear with each formulation. (As a reminder, Table 4.1 on page 125 shows how contingent pricing can be done.)

Excel version

This works very much like the PowerPoint version, but due to differences in how graphics are handled in each program, has a slightly different look and feel. Again, you need to download the file and open it with Excel. If Excel asks whether you really want to run the content, answer in the affirmative. Should Excel still refuse to function fully, please refer to the instructions on the third sheet, 'Security in Excel 2007 and on'.

Problems with estimating actual effects in the marketplace

This simulator underlines the problems inherent in moving from ratings to market share. We do not know which model will forecast changes most accurately. We must make assumptions, or at the least test various assumptions as we did with the demonstration simulator.

Conjoint analysis does particularly well at showing the relative values of different features, and relative changes that come from varying in those features. But again, it is not the best choice for showing effects in the marketplace.

Conjoint remains an excellent method for messages

Fortunately, when we are dealing with messages, we are trying to pick the best alternative – so the issue of how utilities become marketplace behaviour becomes irrelevant. And with websites, even though we still use a conjoint-style approach, we can go directly to behaviour, such as clicks or stickiness

Conjoint Analysis and its Uses

(how long a person stays on the page or site). Using conjoint, we get the equivalent of testing hundreds or even thousands of alternative message configurations, all in one test.

Our first example: an unwanted message

This is a direct mail piece, one of those insurance offers we all look forward so much to receiving. This happened many years ago, and may be one of the first applications of conjoint to developing the best mix of elements in a message.

Because these insurance offers are designed to work with very low level of responses (often under 1 per cent), even a fractional improvement can make a vast difference. If you move from 0.8 per cent to 1.0 per cent response, you have increased your sales by 25 per cent (that is, this is the 0.2 per cent increase divided by the 0.8 per cent base rate).

There are two components to this offering: the envelope and the letter. Figure 5.5 shows a disguised version of the items tested. Six features or **attributes** were varied. Counting the variations or **levels** we get to how many **message profiles** we will need to show.

Specifically, here we have four attributes each with four levels, one attribute with three levels, and one with five levels. Let's go through the formula for how many profiles this will require. First, we take the number of attributes times the number of levels. Specifically, we have (4 x 4) + (1 x 3) + (1 x 5); that comes to 16 + 3 + 5, or 24. Then we subtract out the total count of attributes, which is six. That gives us 18. We need to add back two more so that we can measure error and we can estimate a term called the constant.

We finally used 24 message profiles, and showed each person eight of them. That is, everyone saw just one-third of the total. So, in effect, everyone counted for just one-third of a complete set of responses, or perhaps, one-third of a whole respondent.

Each profile was rated on a 0–100 per cent scale, with the dependent variable being how likely the person felt they would be to read and consider the message. (Recalling that expected purchases hit about 0.8 per cent on a very good day, the sponsoring company did not make 'actually buying' the criterion.)

When we did this many years ago, it required us to triple our sample. As a reminder, now that we have **HB analysis**, we actually can get much more per respondent. We might possibly even get away with no increase in sample.

Back to our main story, Figure 5.6 shows the way the **effects on acceptance levels** looked. This clearly delineates what is most and least attractive to prospective customers.

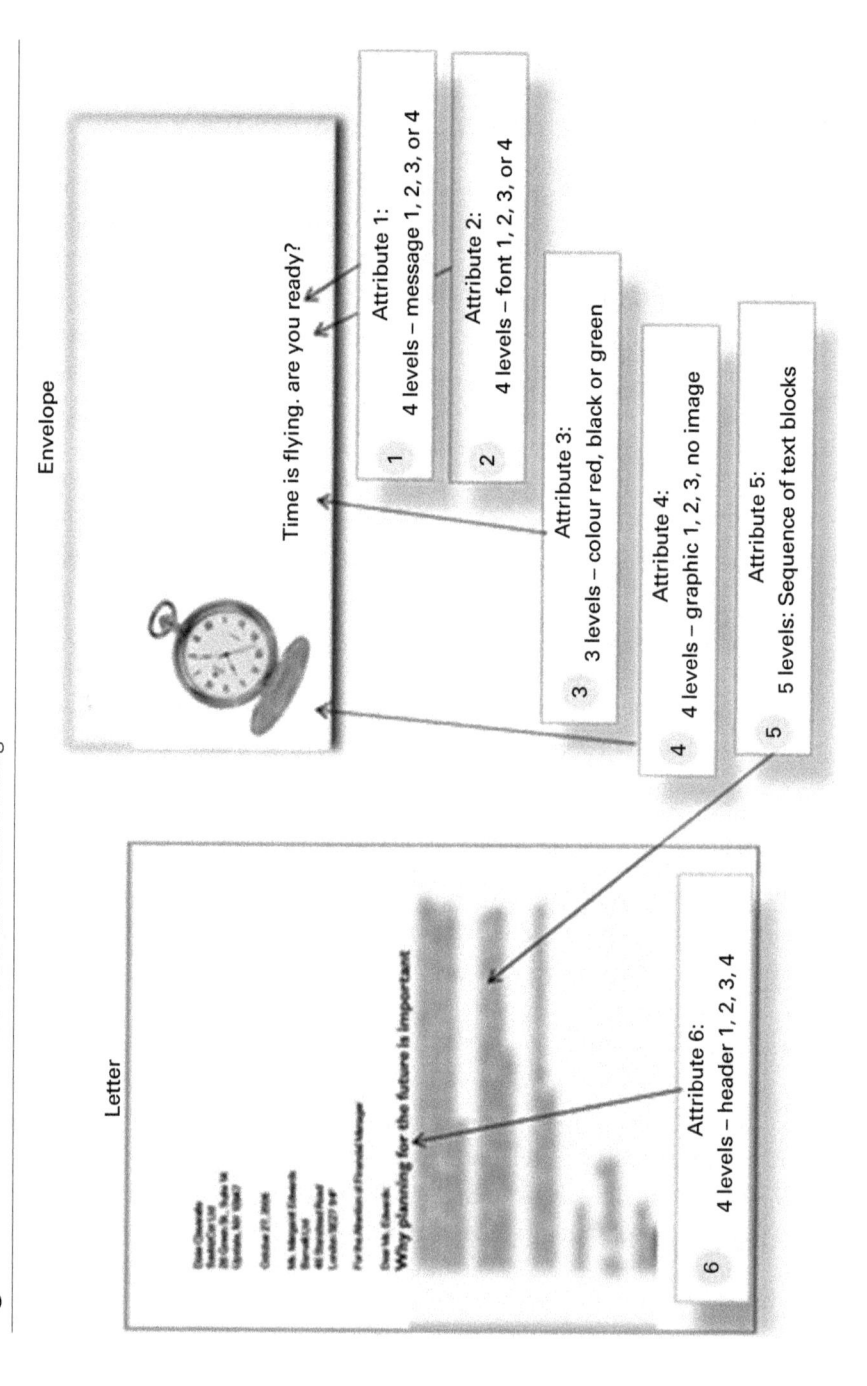

Figure 5.5 Elements varied in the direct mail offering

Figure 5.6 Responses to the elements of the direct mail offer

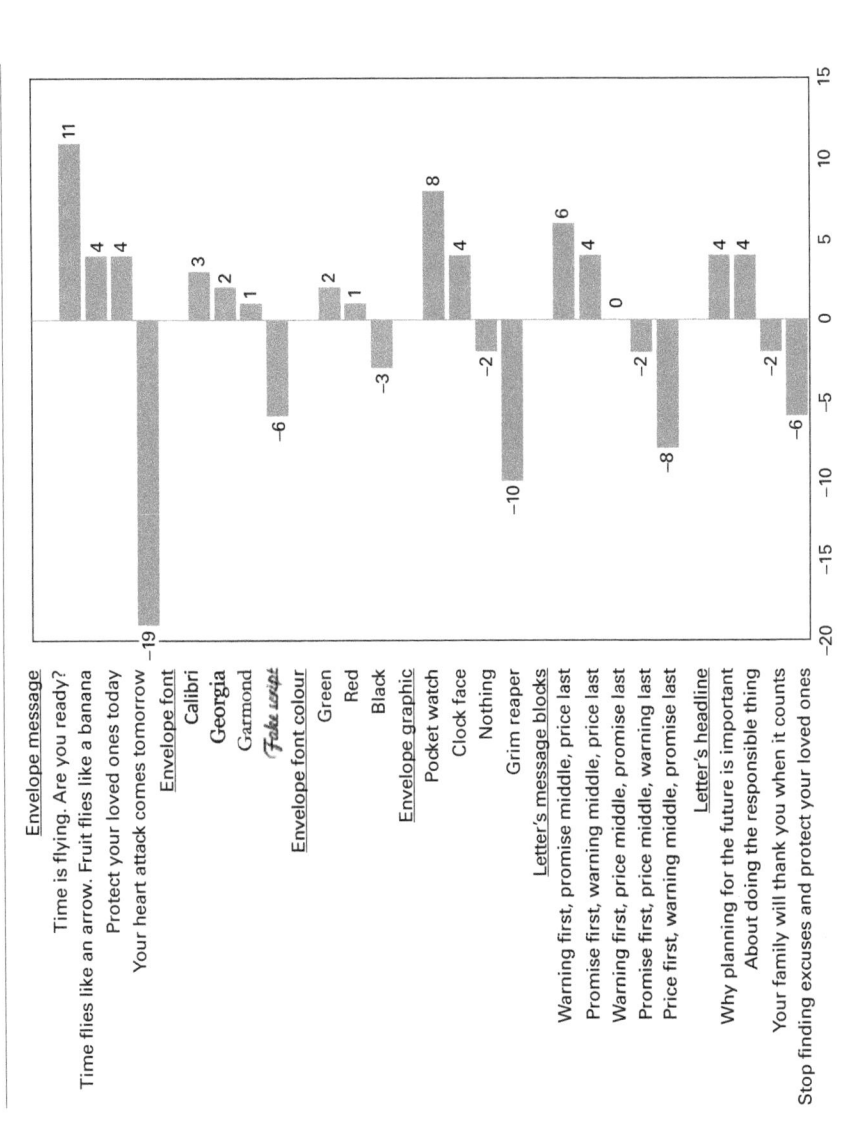

Element	Value
Envelope message	
Time is flying. Are you ready?	11
Time flies like an arrow. Fruit flies like a banana	4
Protect your loved ones today	4
Your heart attack comes tomorrow	−19
Envelope font	
Calibri	3
Georgia	2
Garmond	1
Fake script	−6
Envelope font colour	
Green	2
Red	1
Black	−3
Envelope graphic	
Pocket watch	8
Clock face	4
Nothing	−2
Grim reaper	−10
Letter's message blocks	
Warning first, promise middle, price last	6
Promise first, warning middle, price last	4
Warning first, price middle, promise last	0
Promise first, price middle, warning last	−2
Price first, warning middle, promise last	−8
Letter's headline	
Why planning for the future is important	4
About doing the responsible thing	4
Your family will thank you when it counts	−2
Stop finding excuses and protect your loved ones	−6

Here we have tested the equivalent of 4 x 4 x 3 x 4 x 5 x 4 or some **3,840 alternative combinations** of message elements, and have found the best one:

- Time is flying. Are you ready?
- Calibri font on envelope.
- Green ink on envelope.
- Letter: Warning first, promise next, message last.
- Letter: Why planning for the future is important.

We had a direct way to test whether this combination worked, as the design the client was using already was one of the combinations with lower total utility. By switching they actually improved their response rate by some 25 per cent, just passing the magic 1 per cent acceptance mark. So this was an early success story.

Using this method with a print advertisement

The next example comes from a test of a print advertisement. The same principles hold as in the direct mail test. Figure 5.7 shows our slightly fictionalized ad and the elements varied in it.

There are three alternative photos, and a variety of areas in the headline and text that would be varied. Here we would have an immense number of possible variations. That is, we would have: 3 x 3 x 3 x 3 x 2 x 3 x 3 x 3 or **4,374** possible ways of combining these elements. We can determine the value all of them with **24 experimentally designed combinations**.

How would this look to a study participant? In Figure 5.8, we see how one profile in the test would look, using a combination of elements based on the experimental design. This was an online test, with each person exposed to eight alternative combinations or profiles out of a total of 24 used for the test.

How this worked

Based on this test, the client was able to determine easily which of the over 4,300 possible combinations generated the most interest. This was done with a chart showing the basic effects of changing each measured attribute, just as we did in the last example. This study, however, involved another interesting issue, which we could call the presence of a HIPPO. A HIPPO is simply the Highest Paid Person's Opinion (so, no indeed, we have not gone crazy). The Big Boss really wanted to know how a few of his favourite ideas played out against the best combination.

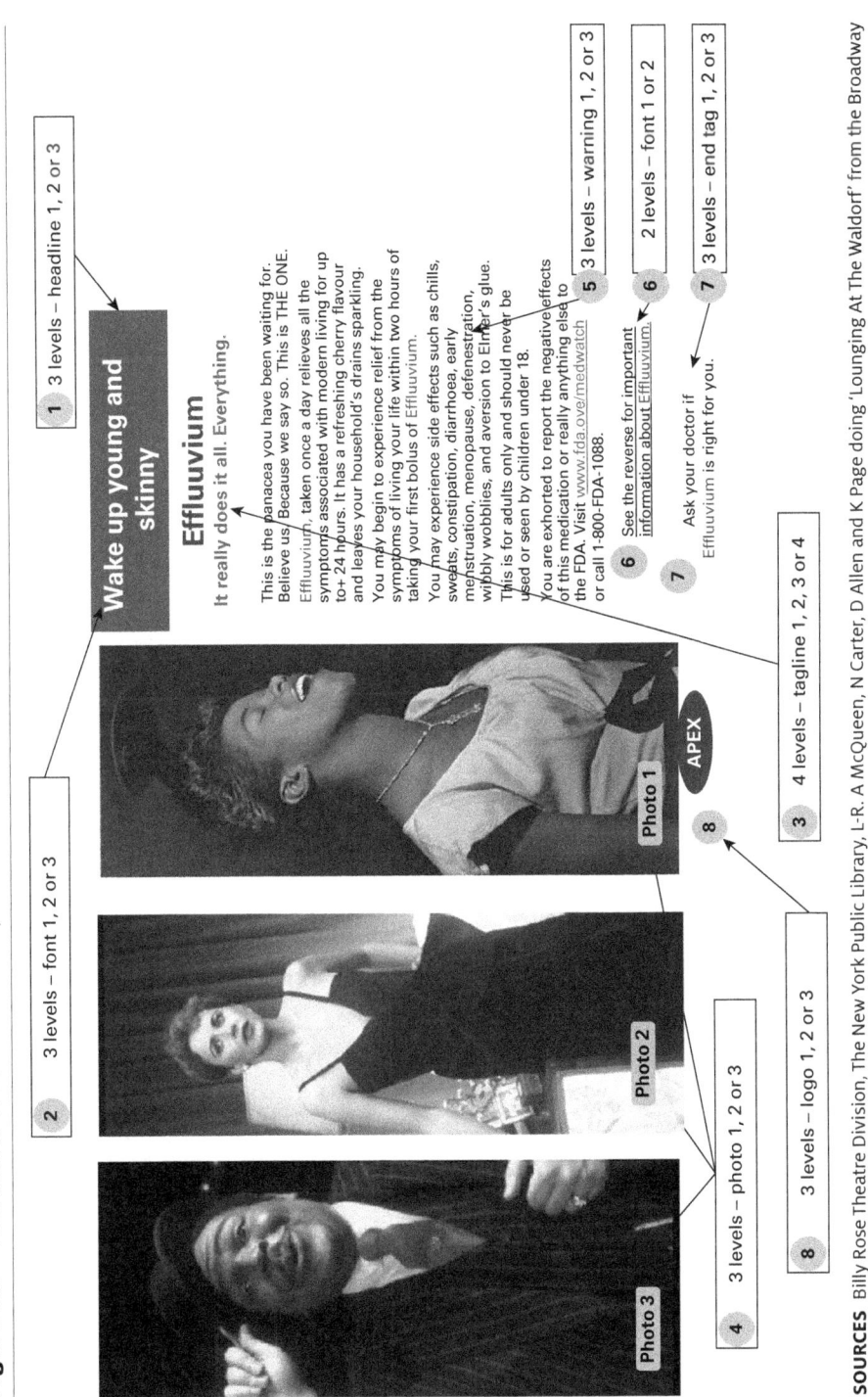

Figure 5.7 Alternatives to be tested in the print advertisement

1 3 levels – headline 1, 2 or 3

2 3 levels – font 1, 2 or 3

3 4 levels – tagline 1, 2, 3 or 4

4 3 levels – photo 1, 2 or 3

5 3 levels – warning 1, 2 or 3

6 2 levels – font 1 or 2

7 3 levels – end tag 1, 2 or 3

8 3 levels – logo 1, 2 or 3

Wake up young and skinny

Effluuvium
It really does it all. Everything.

This is the panacea you have been waiting for. Believe us. Because we say so. This is THE ONE.

Effluuvium, taken once a day relieves all the symptoms associated with modern living for up to+ 24 hours. It has a refreshing cherry flavour and leaves your household's drains sparkling.

You may begin to experience relief from the symptoms of living your life within two hours of taking your first bolus of Effluuvium.

You may experience side effects such as chills, sweats, constipation, diarrhoea, early menstruation, menopause, defenestration, wibbly wobblies, and aversion to Elmer's glue. This is for adults only and should never be used or seen by children under 18.

You are exhorted to report the negative effects of this medication or really anything else to the FDA. Visit www.fda.ove/medwatch or call 1-800-FDA-1088.

6 See the reverse for important information about Effluuvium.

7 Ask your doctor if Effluuvium is right for you.

Photo 1 — APEX

Photo 2

Photo 3

SOURCES Billy Rose Theatre Division, The New York Public Library, L-R: A McQueen, N Carter, D Allen and K Page doing 'Lounging At The Waldorf' from the Broadway production of the musical *Ain't Misbehavin'* (New York). The New York Public Library Digital Collections. http://digitalcollections.nypl.org/items/acfeeb2d-5cbe-4ce7-e040-e00a180644aa, Billy Rose Theatre Division, The New York Public Library, actress Kate Nelligan in a scene from the New York Shakespeare Festival's production of the play *Plenty* (New York), The New York Public Library Digital Collections 1982. http://digitalcollections.nypl.org/items/c3b01b10-dab7-0131-de35-58d385a7b928 Sarah Vaughan, possibly at Cafe Society, NYC, ca August 1946. Photography by William P Gottlieb, from the William P Gottlieb collection at the Library of Congress https://en.wikipedia.org/wiki/Sarah_Vaughan#/media/File:Sarah_Vaughan_-_William_P._Gottlieb_-_No._1.jpg

Figure 5.8 One of the ads tested

Assuming this was the only message about this product, how likely would you be to prescribe the product to a typical patient with atypical depression? Please think of just this message and use the 0 to 100 scale where 0 means 'absolutely unlikely' and 100 means 'absolutely likely'. You can use any number from 0 to 100, but try not to rate any two messages the same, as they are all different.

The cure for the common life

Effluuvium
Beat back all the blahs. Really.

You have to trust us this time. We admit to having told you just a few, tiny whoppers and don't even think about all that press for the last two or three lawsuits. These are trifles compared to the relief you will feel. All at once.

Effluuvium, taken once a day relieves all the symptoms associated with modern living for up to+ 24 hours. It has a refreshing cherry flavour and leaves your household's drains sparkling.

You may begin to experience relief from the symptoms of living your life within two hours of taking your first bolus of **Effluuvium**.

You may experience all sorts of terrible side effects but we are putting those on the other side in even smaller type. You won't be able to read it.

This is for adults only and should never be used or seen by children under 18.

You are exhorted to report the negative effects of this medication or really anything else that could cause trouble to the FDA. **Visit** www.fda.ove/medwatch

See the reverse for important
information about Effluuvium.

Synthandroid, a division of APEX drug

Tell your doctor that
you **need** some **Effluuvium**.

How likely would you be to prescribe based on what you see in this message? Please write in any number from 0 to 100.
0 ← → 100
Absolutely unlikely   Absolutely likely

SOURCE Photo from Billy Rose Theatre Division, The New York Public Library, actress Kate Nelligan in a scene from the New York Shakespeare Festival's production of the play *Plenty* (New York), The New York Public Library Digital Collections 1982. http://digitalcollections.nypl.org/items/c3b01b10-dab7-0131-de35-58d385a7b928

This seemed to call for a simulator, similar to a market simulator, but in this case with the overall rating as the outcome. Figure 5.9 gives an idea of how the simulator looked.

Figure 5.9 The simulator used for optimizing the ad

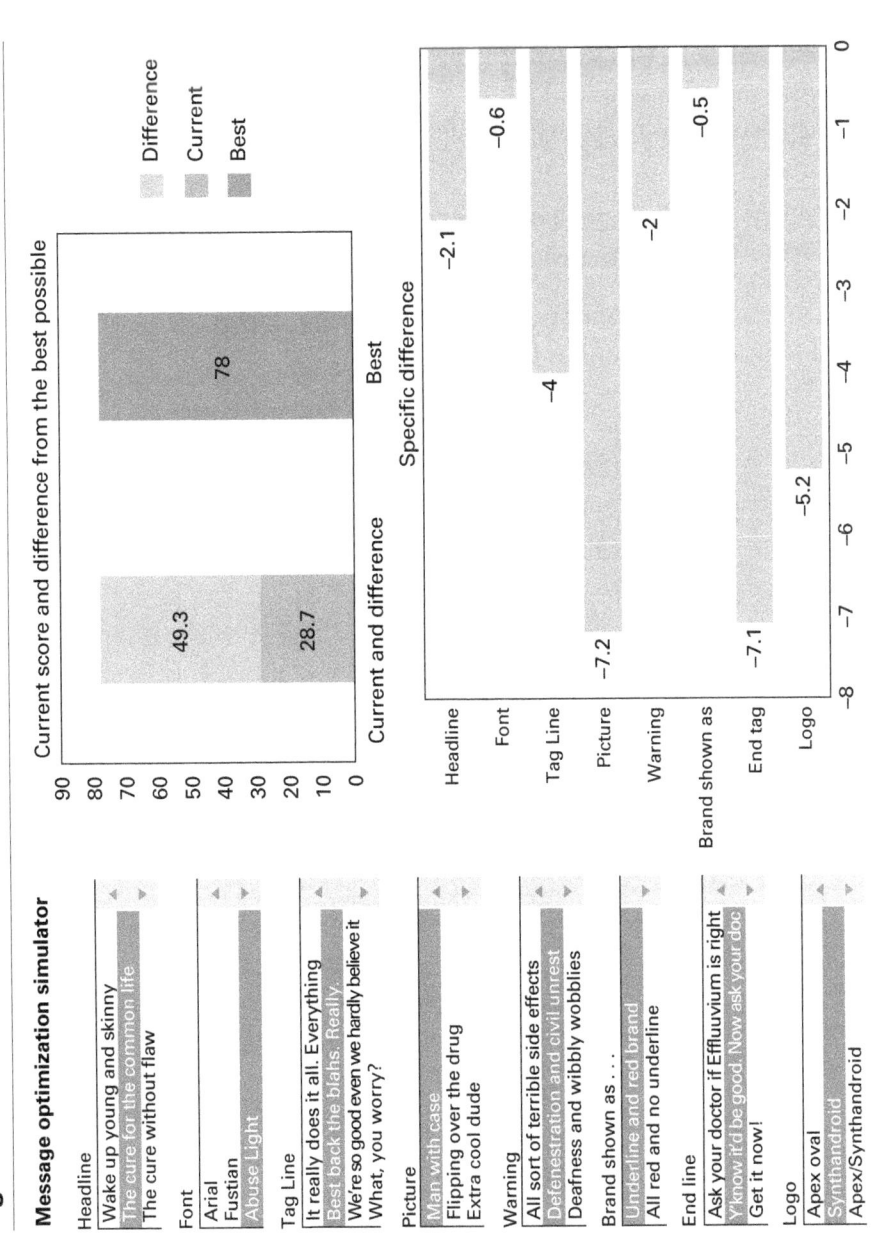

Message optimization simulator

Current score and difference from the best possible

- Difference
- Current
- Best

Current and difference: 49.3 / 28.7
Best: 78

Headline
- Wake up young and skinny
- The cure for the common life
- The cure without flaw

Font
- Arial
- Fustian
- Abuse Light

Tag Line
- It really does it all. Everything
- Best back the blahs. Really.
- We're so good even we hardly believe it
- What, you worry?

Picture
- Man with case
- Flipping over the drug
- Extra cool dude

Warning
- All sort of terrible side effects
- Defenestration and civil unrest
- Deafness and wibbly wobblies

Brand shown as . . .
- Underline and red brand
- All red and no underline

End line
- Ask your doctor if Effluuvium is right
- Y'know it'd be good. Now ask your doc
- Get it now!

Logo
- Apex oval
- Synthandroid
- Apex/Synthandroid

Specific difference

Element	Difference
Headline	−2.1
Font	−0.6
Tag Line	−4
Picture	−7.2
Warning	−2
Brand shown as	−0.5
End tag	−7.1
Logo	−5.2

As we can see in Figure 5.9, the Big Boss's favourite is roughly one-third as well received as the best possible combination (this appears in the comparison of the current share bar to the left and the maximum possible share to the right in the chart labelled 'Current score and difference from the best possible'). This led to the truly difficult part of the study: the researchers in the organization would spend the next several days trying to figure out exactly how to convey this information.

Testing websites: completely outdoing A/B testing

This approach works extremely well with websites, as testing can take place using the actual behaviour of visitors to the site, rather than asking people to provide ratings. This is how it works:

1 Just as for print, the list of features to be varied is created.
2 The variations are put into an experimental design.
3 Alternative configurations are made up.
4 When people visit the site, they are randomly assigned to one of the alternatives.
5 Clicks and/or 'stickiness' (amount of time a person spends on the page) get measured.
6 With extreme values removed or rolled back to more reasonable levels, we solve for the target variable (clicks or stickiness).

Getting rid of extreme values is important – a person may appear to stay on a web page for a long time for many reasons (answering the phone, doing several things at once, putting out a kitchen fire, and so on). Also, vanishingly small times suggest a mistaken click on the site – and so likely are not a reflection of interest levels.

In Figure 5.10, we see how a disguised web page looks with five elements being varied. (The superimposed numbers (1–5) are there just for our reference – they would not appear in the test.)

These five elements each varied in four ways. This comes to some 1,024 alternative combinations of the varied elements (or 4 x 4 x 4 x 4 x 4). To test the value of all possible combinations, we needed to develop and test 20 alternatives in an experimental design to get accurate measurements.

Needing 20 alternatives leads to a caution: you need a fairly well visited website to do behaviour-based testing of this type. If each person sees just **one** of those alternatives, then that person is just 1/20 of a complete set – or that person counts as just 1/20 of a complete respondent.

Figure 5.10 Elements on a web page varied for testing

SOURCE Image on the right: James Tissot, Holyday

146 Artificial Intelligence Marketing and Predicting Consumer Choice

Sticking with a fairly slender requirement of 125 complete respondents, we would need 2,500 visitors to complete one test. So you do need a relatively busy site to do this kind of testing. However, considering that a recently reported A/B test involved over 1 million visitors who were shown either of two alternatives, perhaps this is not asking that much.

Testing by showing an alternative to hundreds of thousands of viewers seems to hearken back to the old days of direct-mail testing, before conjoint analysis-based methods of message optimization were developed. A test then consisted of sending out 700,000 or 1 million pieces and seeing what came back.

There is of course less direct cost and effort involved in passively allowing visitors to see the website in alternative configurations than in developing mailings and sending them. However, there is still considerable waste in showing that many people a message that is less than the best.

Certainly, by using just a few thousand people and being able to determine responses to 1,000 alternative configurations, conjoint message testing has completely surpassed A/B testing.

In Figure 5.11, we have the outcome of the web test, with fictional slogans. (The actual ones really were a little better.) Finding the best alternative from the 1,000 possible configurations has become a simple task.

Figure 5.11 Effects of changing elements of the web page

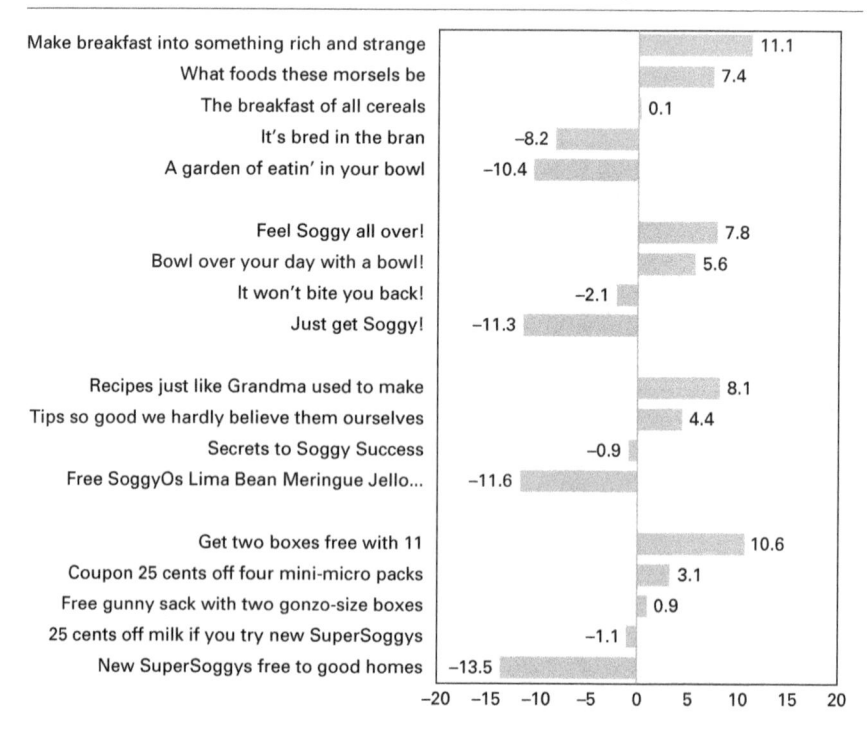

Slogan	Value
Make breakfast into something rich and strange	11.1
What foods these morsels be	7.4
The breakfast of all cereals	0.1
It's bred in the bran	−8.2
A garden of eatin' in your bowl	−10.4
Feel Soggy all over!	7.8
Bowl over your day with a bowl!	5.6
It won't bite you back!	−2.1
Just get Soggy!	−11.3
Recipes just like Grandma used to make	8.1
Tips so good we hardly believe them ourselves	4.4
Secrets to Soggy Success	−0.9
Free SoggyOs Lima Bean Meringue Jello...	−11.6
Get two boxes free with 11	10.6
Coupon 25 cents off four mini-micro packs	3.1
Free gunny sack with two gonzo-size boxes	0.9
25 cents off milk if you try new SuperSoggys	−1.1
New SuperSoggys free to good homes	−13.5

The survey alternative

If waiting for thousands to visit a site still seems like too many, then nothing prevents you from evaluating the elements for a website in the same way as you would test a print advertisement. That is, you would recruit people to a survey, and then show each person a number of alternative site designs.

The live test has the advantage of measuring actual marketplace behaviour, and presumably among people who are interested in the product or service. In the survey's favour, if we questioned people, we would be able to select people of most interest to interview, zeroing in on the responses of important audiences. We also could ask other questions about who the respondents are, their usage of other products, and so on. We would get a more comprehensive picture of who responded.

Conjoint analysis for the best service delivery

Many companies have complex service relationships with their customers. For instance, consider telecommunications and utility companies with their commercial customers, cable companies and insurance companies with their users, and medical device and pharmaceutical companies with doctors and clinics.

All of these companies do more than provide a product or basic service. They may also instal equipment and maintain it, bring samples of supplies, provide ongoing education for professional certification – and have many other interactions. These different areas of interaction are sometimes called **touch points**.

Given the often vanishingly small difference between companies' basic offerings, these other services can loom large in the decision to use one provider, to renew a contract, or simply to continue buying.

A better answer than ratings

We already have discussed at length the pitfalls of asking customers directly what they find important in the services they receive. When asked to provide these ratings, people almost invariably decide it is best to rate nearly everything as highly important.

Conjoint analysis allows to you show an entire service profile, with all the elements in place. You ask study participants to give a rating reflecting how satisfied they would feel if the entire service package could be reliably delivered at that level. Since all the features are evaluated in the context of the whole service experience, this avoids the problem of nonessential features being rated as important. The result is avoiding the dual pitfalls of underdelivering and overdelivering in key areas of customer interactions.

Our example: the pharmaceutical company with nothing special

Pharmaceutical companies often follow a successful competitive product introduction with their own offering that does something similar. This is one reason that we have, for instance, so many drugs that lower cholesterol. Their motivations are understandable, because a so-called blockbuster drug can garner well over $1 billion in sales.

One such company, who we will call NewInnova, had largely used a strategy sometimes labelled 'me too'. Most of their products came about from following a market leader into a new and profitable category. Then one day, they took a long look and realized that they offered nothing distinctive.

Their answer (until such a time as they actually developed something new), would be to focus on their professional relationships with their customers. They had to take careful stock. Many once-favoured interactions (that were in fact bribes) have been outlawed. Still, these companies can do a great deal for their customers.

They can send cheery young representatives to talk with doctors about what they are doing, answer questions about the drugs, and outline new research and developments. This is called detailing. They also can drop off numerous samples of their fine products. This is called sampling. Many companies will produce extensive materials to educate patients and staff members. Some will even send in-person trainers for complex devices and products.

Companies also offer education, including continuing medical education (CME), which in the United States is required in order to retain a medical licence. They offer seminars, conferences and, sometimes, something called medical thought leadership programmes. This last item is new, and seems something like a novel way to offer the now-outlawed bribes. They also send out colourful newsletters, either on glossy paper or on the web. And there are still other ways that they can insinuate themselves into their customers' professional lives.

The key question conjoint service optimization addressed

The sponsoring company, NewInnova, had this question: given that they could perform all these services, how should they offer them? For instance, how much should they sample, and how often should they do detailing? To determine the right balance, they turned to conjoint optimization of their service offerings.

They looked into 11 service areas, of which we show nine in the disguised example below, in Figure 5.12. NewInnova came up with enough variations to require a 42-profile experimental design. Each person saw and evaluated 14 of these. They rated how satisfied they would be on a 0–100 scale, if service could be delivered consistently at the level shown.

This was analysed with HB analysis, using the tweak of conjoint we mentioned earlier, where it is analysed like an allocation exercise in discrete choice modelling. The first output, in Figure 5.13, shows a clear prioritization of the various service areas. The importance of each area is proportional to its effect on overall ratings. Areas with a stronger effect are accorded more importance.

Values have been scaled so that the most important area is set to 100. These values are ratio-level, so that the sampling with an index of 100 would be nearly three times as important as continuing medical education, with an index of 37.

Figure 5.12 A service profile for conjoint-based optimization

Service profile 403

Service area	How delivered
Frequency of detailing	4 weeks
Frequency of sampling	2 weeks
Patient education materials	Fact sheet
Staff education materials	In person and booklet
Continuing medical education	4 online courses offered
Conference	San Jose, 4 days
Adverse effects reporting	Website
Thought leadership programme	Yes
Frequency of news letter	Quarterly

Touch points { ... } Specific Levels

If Company X offered this level of service, how satisfied do you think you would be with your relationship with Company X, all other things being equal? Please write in any number from 0 to 100.

0
Completely
Dissatisfied

100
Completely
Satisfied

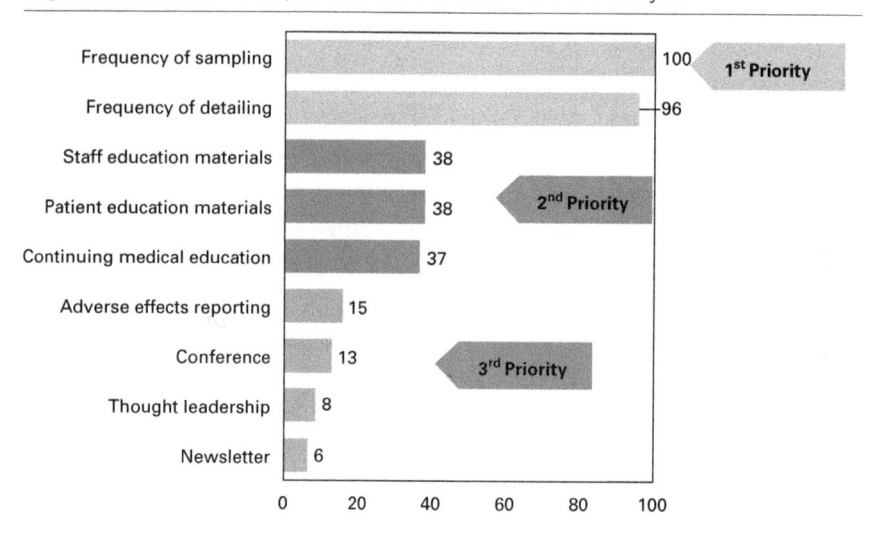

Artificial Intelligence Marketing and Predicting Consumer Choice

Figure 5.13 Priorities' place on service areas from the analysis

Service Area	Value	Priority
Frequency of sampling	100	1st Priority
Frequency of detailing	96	
Staff education materials	38	
Patient education materials	38	2nd Priority
Continuing medical education	37	
Adverse effects reporting	15	
Conference	13	3rd Priority
Thought leadership	8	
Newsletter	6	

There are three clearly defined groups of features. Note also that the least important feature, the newsletter, has an index of only 6. This means that sampling is over 16 times as important as the newsletter in determining levels of satisfaction (100/6 is 16.67).

Speaking of the newsletter, while showing details about how its different levels compared, we saw the senior marketing person's eyes light up for the first time. He was worried that they would have to produce a monthly edition. As you may remember, this was a company that did nothing special – so on a monthly schedule they definitely would not have had enough to say. In Figure 5.14 we can see how the levels of this variable affected satisfaction.

We ran into a more serious concern when analysing the sampling this company did. Part of the survey asked about how often customers now

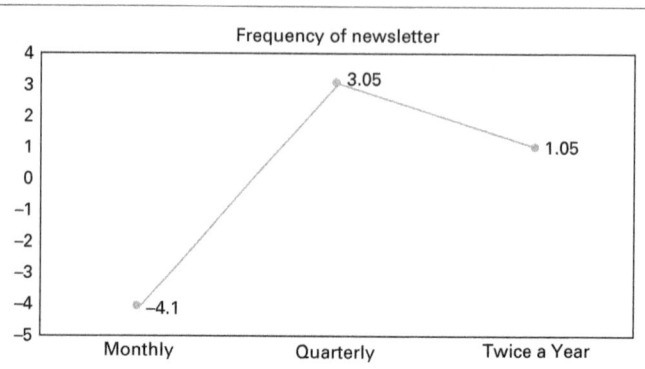

Figure 5.14 Effects from changing the frequency of the newsletter

Frequency of newsletter

Frequency	Value
Monthly	–4.1
Quarterly	3.05
Twice a Year	1.05

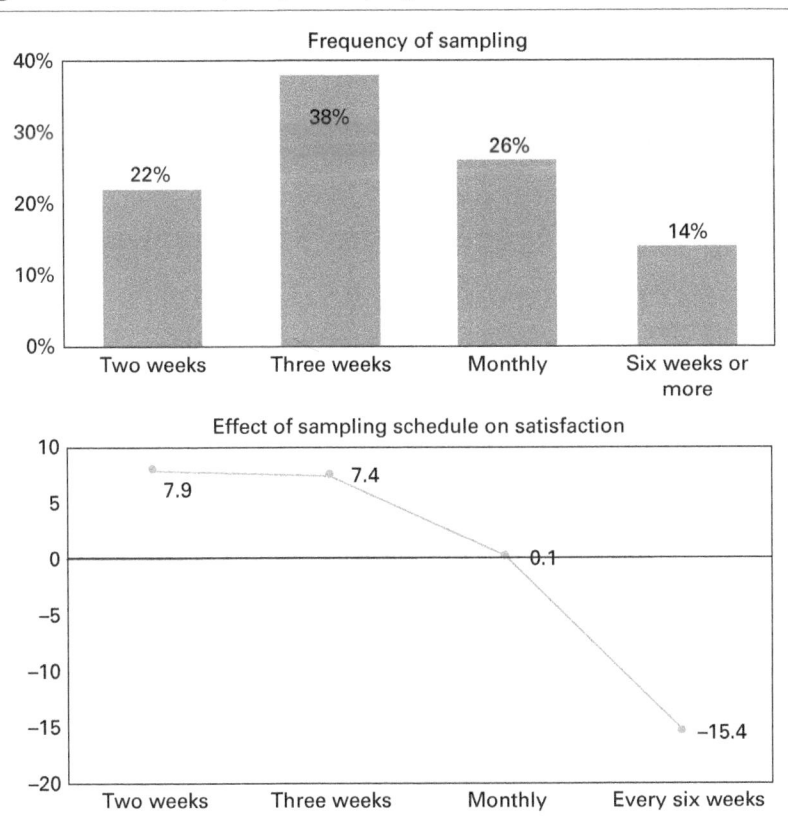

Figure 5.15 How frequency of sampling is overdelivered and underdelivered

Frequency of sampling

- Two weeks: 22%
- Three weeks: 38%
- Monthly: 26%
- Six weeks or more: 14%

Effect of sampling schedule on satisfaction

- Two weeks: 7.9
- Three weeks: 7.4
- Monthly: 0.1
- Every six weeks: −15.4

received each of the services, including getting samples. In the bar chart at the top of Figure 5.15 we can see that 60 per cent received samples every two weeks or three weeks. Some 22 per cent got the samples every two weeks.

However, we see that satisfaction with sampling is nearly identical whether timing is two or three weeks. This means that the client company was **overdelivering** this service to nearly one-quarter of their customers. This is both expensive and wasteful.

On the low side, they were **underdelivering** to some 40 per cent of their customers. Those getting samples every six weeks or less, which emerged as highly dissatisfying, account for a substantial 14 per cent of customers.

Clearly, work needed to be done on how samples were given out. This is a critical area for boosting customer satisfaction, and some customers were getting needless extra sampling, while four out of 10 were getting samples too infrequently.

Because they did this conjoint service optimization, NewInnova could realign sample delivery and so become a more desired provider of all their fabulous 'me too' products. They could similarly refine and revise all their other service offerings, truly meeting customers' service needs. This kind of precise guidance is what makes this method so powerful.

Using the message optimization simulator in the online resources

You can download from the online resources a simple simulator for optimizing messages (available at **www.koganpage.com/AI-Marketing**). Once you have done this, if Excel asks if you really want to run it, say 'yes'. If Excel still does not want to go forward, please refer to the instructions on the third tab, 'Security in Excel 2007 and on'.

This simulator will hide the Excel ribbon (the bar with commands and menus at the top of the screen) when you open it. Two buttons on each page of the simulator control whether the ribbon is visible or not.

You will find these buttons on the bottom of the opening 'Welcome' page and at the right of the simulator page. Make sure you restore the ribbon to view and exit using the 'File' menu if you want to continue working in Excel after closing the simulator.

The story behind the simulator

The sponsor, a magazine we will call *Today's Troubles*, wanted to show how much better a larger ad did in stimulating interest among readers. They also were confident that they were a stronger publication than their similar competitors and very much wanted to show that as well.

They took an ad that they felt was relatively neutral, advertising a vacation. They made 16 prototype ads, varying in size from spot to full page, with different levels of colour, different imagery and different levels of detail in the text. They placed the prototype ads alongside bland 'filler' content if they were not full page. Some ads had an added border and some did not.

Most importantly, some of the ads were identified as being in their fine publication, and some as being in each main competitor's magazine. This gave them a total of six features to be varied and some 864 possible configurations.

Figure 5.16 The downloadable advertising optimization simulator

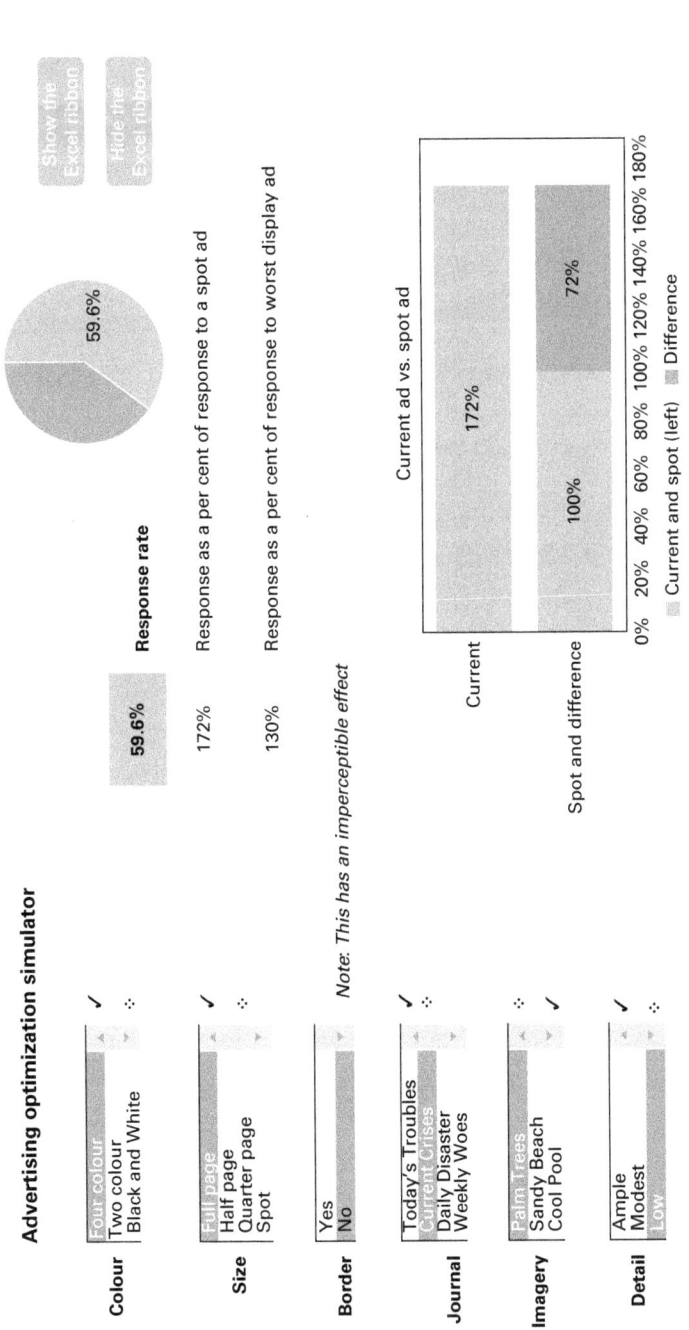

Each person interviewed saw 8 of the 16 prototypes. They reviewed each and said how likely they would be to follow up looking into the vacation listed, using a 0–100 likelihood scale.

The displays in the simulator

The simulator appears in Figure 5.16. As you move the controls on the left, the displays will change in real time. You will see both the estimated response rate and how this compares with the sponsor's least desired choice (the spot ad). This information appears as both a number chart and a bar graph. There also is a numerical comparison to the weakest display ad. This was to provide further impetus to prospective clients to get a better (more expensive) ad. The differences can be quite dramatic. This simulator was judged to have done its job extremely well.

Conjoint analysis and interactions

Now that we have covered several important applications, it is time to circle around to discuss more about the world of variables and how they behave. The subject of **interactions** can become important with conjoint analysis. It certainly is important whenever brand is treated as an attribute and allowed to mix and match freely with other attributes.

An interaction occurs when two or more variables together behave in ways we would not expect from seeing each of them separately. For instance, for men of a certain age and mind-set, **red** and **sports car** interact. That is, a **red** car is nice, and a **sports car** is nice, but put them together into a **red sports car** and you have something truly extraordinary. It is worth far more than you would suspect from the attractiveness of red cars or the attractiveness of sports cars.

Interactions mattered a great deal in the early days of conjoint, because attributes applied evenly to all brands. This was particularly problematic when brands responded differently to changes in price.

An example comes from the golden days of Sony electronics, when this brand could charge more for their products because their name carried a special cachet. As we can see in Figure 5.17, where we plot sales versus price, Sony would always sell more at a given price than all their competitors. Their competitor RCA could sell nearly as much but had to lower prices to attain the same level of sales. Two other brands, the one offered by the store under their own name, and the mysterious Nonameo (the brand

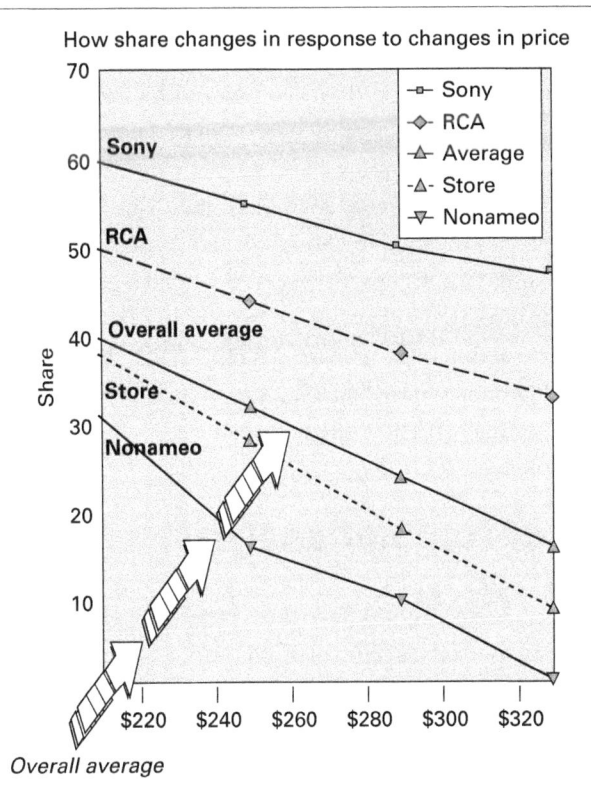

Figure 5.17 Average response to changes in price versus each brand's changes

How share changes in response to changes in price

Overall average

you never heard of) would fare considerably worse. This is what we see in the Figure 5.17 price versus share curves for small televisions offered by these four brands.

If you were to use a single price attribute that applied across all the brands, your estimates would be wrong for all of them. This would be the average line in the middle of Figure 5.17, pointed out by the white arrows.

Errors in estimating price responses probably contributed as much as anything to conjoint falling out of favour. Because conjoint treated brand as an attribute and price as an attribute, you needed to build in special **interaction terms** to get good measurements.

Yet the experimental designs usually used were not large enough to pick up those interactions. For instance, if you had four brands and four prices, the **interaction term** would contain 4 x 4 items or 16 **parameters**. These would be in addition to the four brands and four prices, which together amounted to **eight parameters**.

You could create a larger experiment to make sure that you were measuring this large 16-item **interaction term** accurately, but this kind of planning did not seem to happen much in practice. Missing this interaction could have disastrous results. For instance, if you had followed the average price-response curve and were selling the Nonameo brand, you would probably go out of business. At the very best, you would be sitting on mountains of unsold inventory, as you consistently overestimated how much you could sell.

Interactions usually are not a concern with discrete choice modelling, because each choice can have its own attributes. For instance, if you want to measure responses to changing Sony's pricing, you would have a variable, **Sony price**, specific to the Sony brand. You would get a direct and clean measurement of how share changed by measuring this variable.

However, interactions still matter a great deal with a popular variant of conjoint called choice-based (CBC), and so it is best to remain aware of them. We discuss this further in the next section.

Variants of conjoint analysis

Many modifications of conjoint have been proposed. Two of the best known are the so-called **partial profile** method and a software product called **Adaptive Conjoint Analysis (ACA)**. Partial-profile conjoint was designed to shrink the task that study participants needed to do. The idea was that only a part of the product would be shown and the rest would be 'assumed' to be acceptable. Behind doing this, there were some arguments about the interview otherwise imposing too complex a task. Yet these concerns do not seem well-founded. Research has been published that suggests people can evaluate quite a few complex marketplace scenarios or product profiles. One careful study showed that people were still going strong after 21 market-places. How many you can use in practice depends on how engaged the person is with the category and their native skills in figuring out problems.

Engineers and farmers, for instance, do particularly well evaluating many complex scenarios. (Farmers must be very good at calculating and problem solving to stay in business. They really miss very little. The idea that they are not on top of things is doubly false.) Children and people who rarely read tend to do poorly after just a few scenarios.

ACA had a period of wide adoption. It also was roundly criticized and deserved some of it. It allows people to eliminate some attribute levels before they see them in the context of the whole product. As we have mentioned several times, looking at the entire product often leads people to revise their ideas about what is acceptable. In addition, the maths used to score the items rated unacceptable was subjective and unsubstantiated.

Conjoint Analysis and its Uses

This method also was promoted in part as a means of making the interview less onerous. However, much of the impetus behind it may have been in cutting down the required size of experiments. In the early days of conjoint, measuring only a handful of attributes was possible.

Because we now can use HB analysis, and measure far more attributes than used to be possible, this reduction is no longer needed. Indeed, the popularity of the ACA method appears to be waning, although you will still encounter some individuals who want to use it.

Choice-based conjoint (CBC)

This is a do-it-yourself software approach. It makes the process relatively easy, but simplifies the approach enough to sap some of its power and even to allow misapplications. However, it appears to be quite popular. And indeed, to some, it is seen as synonymous with discrete choice modelling.

However, its name is accurate. It takes something from conjoint and something from discrete choice modelling. (And as you may have guessed from the initials CBC, it comes from the same people who offer us the ACA software product.)

As you can see in Figure 5.18, it shows alternatives and asks for a choice. However, note that brand is missing. It actually is offering a choice between three variants of one product. This is not a realistic representation of what consumers will find in the marketplace.

Not as readily apparent is that all the choices have the same attributes. Having choices share the same attributes is the conjoint part of the CBC approach. If you use this program as it is set up, you will not have any chance to see if an attribute level works better within a specific branded option. You can try to get by this with 'prohibitions', which swap attribute

Figure 5.18 An example of CBC-style conjoint analysis

Features	Which mobile phone plan would you choose?		
Data included	6 GB	4 GB	3 GB
Rollover	Rollover 2 MB unused	No rollover	Rollover all unused up to 10 GB
New phone	Every two years	Every year	Every 18 months
Free calling	Domestic only	Domestic and no roaming in Canada or Mexico	Domestic and no roaming in Mexico
Costs	$100 one line	$140 for two lines	$90 for one line
Which would you choose?	○	○	○

levels. But this can make for design problems. Otherwise, you cannot test any feature unique to a given brand.

For instance, if you want to say your brand is the 'most reliable cellular network' in a standard conjoint model, that claim would have to be tested with all the brands. Yet there can only be one best network, in spite of what some television commercials seem to imply. Attaching this claim to all the choices would lead to some highly unrealistic combinations.

The CBC program does offer an extra-cost 'advanced' option that allows you to get closer to the experimental designs you would use with standard discrete choice modelling. But there is no requirement that you use it. And indeed, we have encountered a good number of studies where none of the people involved had any idea that you could set up attributes as specific to choices.

You may come across studies set up like the one in Figure 5.18. However, we can do better. The lack of realism in having three variants of a product compete against each other, when that would never happen in the actual marketplace, is a serious shortcoming. And the absence of branding is another problem. Everything that we buy anywhere, except certain 'generic' medications, will come with clear brand identifications.

Also, if you include brand as an attribute in this set-up, that then opens up the need to add interaction terms. (You also can avoid this by breaking with the program's default method of setting up problems.) As a reminder, interaction terms are large, having many parameters that need to be estimated. You definitely cannot estimate all possible interaction terms in even a small problem – there are too many items to get an accurate fix on all of them.

Therefore, unless someone is doing considerable extra work with CBC, we should not expect it to provide wholly accurate readings of how products perform in a competitive marketplace. It should give you an excellent reading of the relative appeal of features within a product, just as full-profile conjoint will. However, finding how appealing features are – versus each other – falls far short of estimating share, even share of preference. So use particular care if the CBC approach is being used to estimate marketplace behaviour.

To compare CBC to full-profile conjoint, on the plus side for CBC, it asks for a choice. This is more like what people do every day than the ratings that traditional conjoint requires. On the down side, CBC asks people to process much more information than conjoint does. That is, each screen a person sees with CBC could contain three or four product profiles side by side. Full-profile conjoint shows just one profile.

> Choice-based conjoint (CBC) is a popular software application that many see as synonymous with discrete choice modelling. However, its name is accurate. It has some features of conjoint, and some of discrete choice. It is easy to use, but unfortunately also makes it easy to commit mistakes. It is not the best choice for seeing how products will behave in a competitive marketplace, because of the way it sets up comparisons and its default handling of attributes. It should do an excellent job of determining the relative appeal of attributes – and of the levels of those attributes – just as traditional full-profile conjoint will. But be very cautious if someone has used it and is attempting to forecast share.

Which one is better for a conjoint-like task? There is no clear answer. Some would say that the **choice** involved in CBC makes it more realistic and so superior. Others (your author included) have noticed that most people do not like to read while doing a survey. The fact that full-profile conjoint shows just one product at a time helps study participants. This allows people to see what they need more easily, and so to respond more thoughtfully. Which one to use is an area that those disposed to arguing could argue about all night. But let's not, and let's leave it up to your preference.

Summary of key points

Conjoint analysis is the other method intended to develop the best possible products and services. While discrete choice modelling was developed by economists and econometricians, conjoint analysis developed in the market research community.

The first truly useful, and widely adopted form of conjoint analysis is called **full-profile conjoint**. This shows an entire product represented as a set of specifically described attributes, or a **product profile**. Study participants see a series of these profiles, and in each the levels of the attributes that appear vary. Study participants rate these profiles, or sort and rank them. (The ranking approach is rare now that interviews typically are done online.)

Like discrete choice, conjoint relies on strict experimental designs to make sure that the effects of varying one attribute do not get mixed up with the effects of varying another. Without the designed experiment, attributes can get more or less attractive from one profile to another in highly similar ways. If this happens, we then have no clear way of telling what is driving product preferences.

A simpler model

Conjoint analysis is based on a simpler view of attributes and utility than is discrete choice modelling. In conjoint, brand is an attribute and all other attributes apply equally to all brands. This can lead to unrealistic combinations of attribute levels with a given brand, and so is a salient drawback.

This underlying conjoint model also makes it much more difficult to determine what happens to a specific product when its features change. This becomes particularly problematic with price, as in every category we have ever studied at least one product behaves differently from all others when its price changes.

Assuming all products behave in the same way when their prices change actually makes it nearly certain that all estimates of share changes will be wrong. You can try to avoid this in conjoint analysis by adding a large **interaction term** to the model. For example, with price variable having four levels and a brand attribute having four levels, the interaction term would have 4 x 4 items or 16 **parameters** that need to get estimated. (This is in addition to the eight parameters represented by the four price levels and the four brand levels.)

Estimating all these extra parameters would require making a bigger experiment. The basic design typically used for conjoint analysis would in fact be too small to measure all these extra items accurately.

About utility

Traditionally, conjoint analysis took the very simple view that utility and share have a straight-line relationship. This does not reflect the realities of the marketplace. Fortunately, you now can retool conjoint, solving it like a discrete choice allocation problem. Once you have slightly recast the analysis, then you can handle it like discrete choice by using HB analysis. This gives a more realistic view of how utility becomes preferences.

Not best for estimating effects in competitive marketplaces

The remaining problems, though, make conjoint less than ideal for estimating how products will behave in a competitive environment when they are varied. The problem of attributes not being specific to the choices also makes measuring responses to changes in the attributes less accurate. It is no wonder conjoint analysis has been eclipsed by discrete choice as the leading method for predicting acceptance of products in a competitive marketplace.

Still highly useful in three important applications

Although we do not recommend conjoint as a replacement for discrete choice modelling, it has other highly useful applications. Here are three compelling uses:

- **Where competitive context would be overwhelming**: this would be the case when you wanted to make the best product and the product in question had a very low share. Because the product would get chosen only rarely, patterns of choices would not accurately reveal which changes worked best. Conjoint analysis, with its single-product focus, can put that product 'under a microscope' and show how to select the best variations of its features.

- **For optimizing communications**: such as print advertisements and websites. You can get the relative appeal of thousands of alternative configurations, completely surpassing such current methods as A/B testing.

- **For determining the exact levels of service in complex customer relationships**: such as between utilities and their commercial customers, or telecommunications or insurance companies and their users. The many elements in customer interactions can be carefully tailored, leading to the best mix.

Variants of conjoint analysis

Conjoint has had a number of variants, including most notably choice-based conjoint (CBC). As its name says, it has something from conjoint and something from discrete choice, and yet is neither. This makes it relatively easy to set up a problem involving choice. However, if left in its default settings, it treats the choices as they would be in a traditional conjoint analysis. If brand is included, it is treated as an attribute and allowed to combine freely with all other attributes. (You can buy an extra cost 'advanced' module that allows you to get closer to designs like those used by discrete choice modelling.)

This method also allows you to make highly unrealistic comparisons, such as comparing three unbranded variants of a product versus each other. This is nothing you would ever see in the actual marketplace, and its lack of realism makes any estimates of real-world behaviour suspect.

This method, like traditional full-profile conjoint, should give you an excellent picture of relative preferences among different levels of the various features. However, preference is not choice. We hope you all recall the story about the little girl who loved spinach, but not enough to eat it.

It is an open question whether CBC is better than full-profile conjoint for those questions that conjoint is suited to answer. Some would say that the fact CBC asks for a choice, rather than a rating, makes it superior. Some (your author included) have noticed that nearly all study participants do not like reading while doing a survey. Showing them one product at time, as in full-profile conjoint, encourages more attention and thought to how features are being varied than seeing three or four product variants side by side.

Overall

Although supplanted by discrete choice modelling for forecasting how products will behave in a competitive marketplace, conjoint analysis still has important uses. You can use it to zero in on a low-share product that would hardly ever get chosen in a competitive marketplace. Its ability to put a product 'under a microscope' can be useful in any exercise where you want to optimize the user's experience with that product.

We reviewed a successful example of this, in which study participants evaluated 18 disposable pens configured according to an experimental design. This close attention to one product allowed the manufacturer to create a pen that had the best possible writing characteristics.

Also, conjoint analysis can do remarkably well in finding the best mix of elements to include in a message or on a web page. You can test the equivalent of hundreds or thousands of alternative configurations in one simple test. This method completely surpasses traditional A/B web testing where, at most, two to four alternative pages are tested.

Lastly, conjoint can optimize how services are delivered in complex customer relationships. Where there are many ways that companies interact with their customers, sometimes called customer touch points, conjoint can define the best possible configuration. Companies that have complex service relationships can be found in areas such as telecommunications, utilities, insurance social networking, and the medical and pharmaceutical industries.

Four simulators are available in the online resources for this chapter (available at **www.koganpage.com/AI-Marketing**). They will give you an idea of the true power in conjoint analysis. Three of them are different versions of a single product optimization simulator, one in PowerPoint, one in (Adobe Acrobat) PDF format, and one in Excel. The other shows responses to different print advertisements, revealing the optimal configuration. We encourage you to follow the instructions in this chapter, and use and explore all of them.

Bonus Chapter 1: Finishing experiments and on to the non-experimental world

This bonus chapter shows the best uses of the other key trade-off methods, MaxDiff and Q-Sort/Case 5, which provide clearly differentiated importance for lists of features, claims or messages. It will give you guidance on when it is most appropriate to use each of these methods, and when you would be better served by either discrete choice modelling or conjoint analysis. It also provides critical contrasts between these methods as a group and those that deal with less structured data – including how to apply and interpret each.

Access this bonus chapter online here:

www.koganpage.com/AI-Marketing

Predictive models 06

Via classifications that grow on trees

This chapter describes the classification tree methods, a remarkable set of approaches that uncover complex relationships in data. Here our focus broadens from predicting shares and understanding variables' relative importances to developing models that boost the odds of reaching a desired outcome. Several illustrations will take the mystery out of these methods and show how they apply. We also discuss several useful extensions of basic classification trees.

Classification trees: understanding an amazing analytical method

Now that we have absorbed a great many facts about predicting what happens when you change the features of a product (or service or message), it is time for something completely different. As a reminder, through Chapters 4 and 5 (and bonus online Chapter 1) we have seen highly powerful means of understanding variables' effects, and other methods that diagnose variables' importances. Discrete choice and conjoint provide remarkable power in answering **what/if**-type questions, and the MaxDiff and Q-Sort/Case 5 methods clearly delineate relative importances.

Here we shift from focusing on these areas, expanding to methods that also can work to improve the odds of an outcome. Market share and odds are closely related concerns. Improving the odds of an outcome is something different. The goals of doing that include reducing uncertainty and waste. Also, as we will see, these investigations can provide insights that lead to further analyses, and finally propel changes.

Classification trees, the subject of this chapter, are the first set of methods that can be turned towards increasing the likelihood of an outcome.

Other methods that are pressed into service in this way include the Bayesian networks explained in Chapter 7, and the ensembles and neural networks in Bonus online Chapter 2. Many other methods exist.

Classification trees started as more of a promise than a solution. Many years ago (in the 1980s, to be exact, which practically counts as ancient history) precursors of today's methods were dismissed as weak and inadequate. Since then, the procedures and computers have developed. Now classification trees have become a powerful and well-studied set of predictive methods.

In the last few chapters, we kept the analytical details discretely tucked away, doubtless to the relief of many. We will mention now that discrete choice modelling and conjoint use variants of either **regression**, **multinomial logit** or **mother logit**. These last two are regression-like methods that solve problems where the target variable is a set of **categories**. (The distinct choices we are trying to predict are the categories.) There are several related methods that could be used, but understanding the distinctions does not help understand the uses and output of these methods. The fine details are best left to the experts.

A highly visual approach

With classification trees, the analytical method itself is key. Seeing how the analysis progresses is important in understanding the results. The Bayes Nets we discuss in Chapter 7 also are highly visually oriented. Each of these methods is quite different from all that have gone before.

In this chapter we will mostly discuss the classification tree method called **CHAID**. There are a host of other, closely related methods with different names, most notably **CART** (also called **C&RT** and **CRT**). We will talk about how CHAID and CART (and the others) compare and contrast after we review some applications.

Seeing how trees work, step by step

Splitting and resplitting

CHAID and related methods split the data into groups, seeking to find some group (or groups) with more of some desired characteristic. Then it splits each of these groups again. It continues splitting until it reaches some stopping point you specify. We can think of it as something like a sifter that works in stages, with each stage refining the selected group more finely.

For instance, seeking buyers of a product, we might use a variable such as **number of children at home** to find groups buying more and buying less. Looking at all possible numbers of children at home, from zero to 14, we might then find the biggest difference between those with five or more children at home and those with fewer than five children. Classification trees zero in on the best ways to find differences of this kind.

Once these methods split the data, they then return to the smaller subgroups formed and split those again – and if possible, again. Each split produces still smaller groups. Some of those groups will have a great deal of the desired characteristic. Suppose we go back to families with five or more children. We might then find that those living in the suburbs within this group are still more likely to be buyers. This may sound abstract, so let's take a look at how this actually works.

Combatting Kardboard Krunchies

The example deals solely with behaviour and demographics. It starts with a database, which contains household characteristics and data about purchases of breakfast foods. The client, **SoggyOs**, has grown concerned about inroads made by their dread competitor, **Kardboard Krunchies**. These two brands, together with **Sorghum Sweeties**, dominate the cellulose-enriched, overly sweetened breakfast-like substance product category. (For those of you who have not been out of doors much, these are fictionalized brand names. Also, the outcome has been slightly disguised, as you will see.)

SoggyOs, Inc. had amassed information about purchasers of their category from scanner data at a large grocery chain. They collected information on some 14,552 households that bought products in their specific category. Some 20 per cent purchased Kardboard Krunchies.

Because this was scanner data and the store had a so-called **loyalty programme**, they knew the address of each purchaser. (The purchaser scanned a tag or held up their smartphone next to a scanning device with each purchase.)

SoggyOs, Inc. then merged the purchase with information about the purchaser's household demographics. An amazing amount of such information is available to be added, or **appended**, to the data of any individual whose address is known (at least in the United States, and nearly as much so in the UK). Hundreds of demographic and product-usage items are available. The days of privacy are long behind us.

Among the demographic characteristics appended to households in this database, we find items such as the type of town in which they live, reported

Figure 6.1 The database 'population'

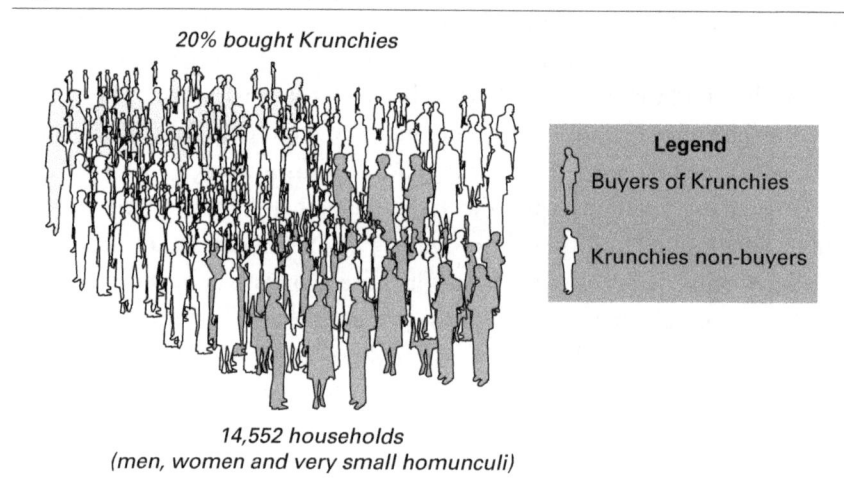

20% bought Krunchies

Legend
Buyers of Krunchies
Krunchies non-buyers

14,552 households
(men, women and very small homunculi)

household incomes, education levels and the presence and ages of children – and so on. In total, there are 46 demographic characteristics for each household in the database. Figure 6.1 depicts the incidence of Krunchies buyers in this population.

The classification tree procedure (CHAID) will examine all these demographic characteristics, first seeking the one that can best split the sample into smaller groups that differ as much as possible in likelihood of buying Kardboard Krunchies. The CHAID software in question can split the sample into 2–15 groups.

Examining all factors, CHAID found the strongest difference lay in contrasting those who **live in suburban areas** in one group versus those **living in either cities or rural areas** in a second group. Some 22 per cent of those in

Figure 6.2 The tree's first split

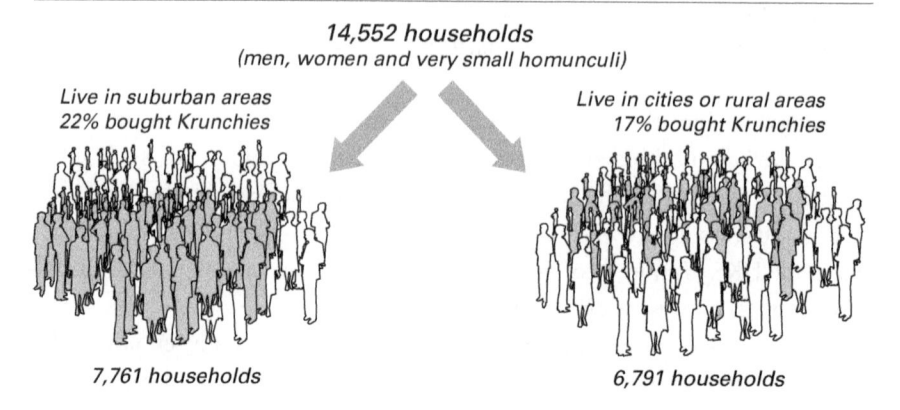

14,552 households
(men, women and very small homunculi)

Live in suburban areas
22% bought Krunchies

Live in cities or rural areas
17% bought Krunchies

7,761 households

6,791 households

the suburbs buy the competitive product, versus 17 per cent in the other two areas combined. That is, the suburban group is 1.3 times as likely as the other to be buyers of this breakfast substance. We see this division in Figure 6.2.

Trees and artificial intelligence

The procedure did something quite advanced here, which may not be immediately apparent. It found that we needed to combine the study participants in **two geographies into one group** to get the strongest contrast in incidences.

For the CHAID procedure to select this variable as the strongest differentiator, it needed to examine splitting the population based on this variable in four different ways. (Another way of dividing would have been combining people in cities and suburbs into one group versus those in rural areas, another combining people in the suburbs and rural areas versus those in cities, and the last simply splitting the three geographies into three groups.)

Sifting through four ways of grouping people to determine which is best may not seem that impressive, but recall that the procedure simultaneously looked at all 45 other demographic characteristics – and at all the ways in which those could be used to divide the population. Here is our historically

Figure 6.3 Resplitting the first subgroup

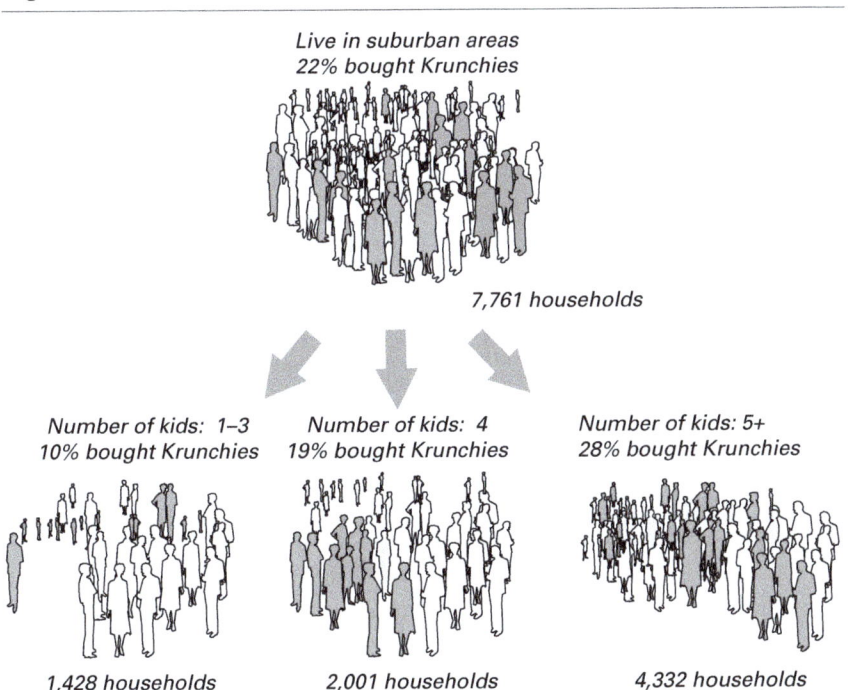

Live in suburban areas
22% bought Krunchies

7,761 households

Number of kids: 1–3
10% bought Krunchies

Number of kids: 4
19% bought Krunchies

Number of kids: 5+
28% bought Krunchies

1,428 households

2,001 households

4,332 households

earliest brush with genuine artificial intelligence (AI). The analytical methods CHAID uses for figuring out how to split a sample are so advanced that they were first presented at an AI conference.

What the program does next adds more value (and complexity) to the findings. It returns to the first group split from the total, the one with 7,761 households that we see in Figure 6.2. It then searches all the remaining demographic characteristics specifically within that group to find the one that will lead to a subgroup with a still higher incidence of Krunchies buyers.

Figure 6.3 shows what the procedure found. This is a three-way split of the group living in the suburbs, based on number of children at home.

We see a very strong contrast among these three smaller groups: some 28 per cent of suburbanites with 5+ children bought Krunchies, which is nearly three times as high as the incidence among suburbanites with 1–3 children (only 10 per cent bought this substance in this group). Here we see an **interaction** between two demographic characteristics.

An **interaction** between variables means that the effects of two (or more) together differ from the sums of each individual effect. More specifically, in this example, the percentage buying Krunchies among those who live in the suburbs **and** who have 5+ children is higher than what we would expect, either among people who just live in the suburbs, or among people who just have 5+ children. We must have **specific values of both variables combining** to see this high a percentage of SoggyOs eaters.

In this instance, the variables work together to lead to this unexpectedly strong outcome. This is one time when we can use the once-popular term **synergistic** and mean it.

Interactions

The effect of two or more variables working together to produce an outcome that is different from what we would expect based on the effects of the variables separately. This effect can be larger, or **synergistic**, or smaller or anti-synergistic (not nearly as good a buzzword).

CHAID is amazingly good at finding interactions. The word **CHAID** is an acronym of chi-squared automatic interaction detector. Classification trees may be unique in that interactions are unmistakable in their output. Interactions do not automatically appear in nearly all other statistical procedures. Also, most other procedures do not tell you if you are missing an important interaction.

Clearly, if you want to understand effects on some outcome, you should understand if two or more variables combine to act in an unexpected way. CHAID has unique problem-solving abilities in revealing and displaying these patterns.

What precisely does this have to do with a tree? The common display that CHAID produces looks tree-like. Let's examine again the splits we just laid out, this time in the standard tree format (see Figure 6.4).

Perhaps not apparent in Figure 6.4 is the remarkable analysis the program performed in dividing the suburban group based on the number of children at home. This is the three-way division we just discussed.

We can see that the group with five or more children at home is the largest of the three (4,332 households), and that it still was not divided into smaller groups having different numbers of children. (Households were recorded as having up to an awe-inspiring 14 children. The mind boggles.)

This choice of grouping was based on complex statistical testing. All families with five or more children have the same statistical likelihood of eating Krunchies. That is, those with five children have the same likelihood as those with six, or those with seven or those with eight – and so on.

The classification tree program was instructed to separate people into groups only where it found statistically significant differences, while it searched through all possible ways of dividing the sample to find the one way that was the strongest. This group of 4,332 was large enough to divide further, but no differences existed that could lead to a further division.

Figure 6.4 Splitting of groups shown as a classification tree

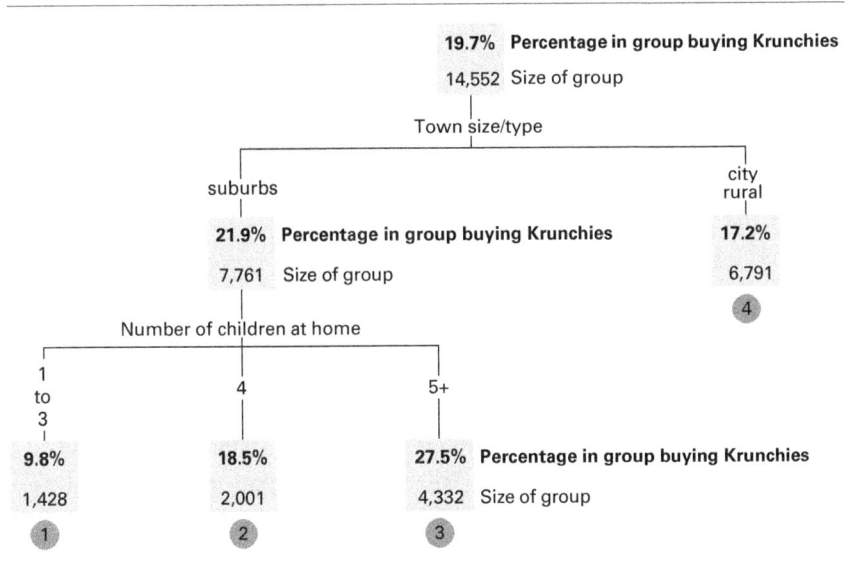

```
                        19.7%  Percentage in group buying Krunchies
                        14,552 Size of group
                              |
                        Town size/type
              ┌───────────────┴───────────────┐
          suburbs                           city
                                            rural
         21.9%  Percentage in group         17.2%
                buying Krunchies
         7,761  Size of group               6,791
                                              (4)
     Number of children at home
     ┌──────────┼──────────┐
    1 to 3      4         5+
    9.8%      18.5%      27.5%  Percentage in group buying Krunchies
    1,428     2,001      4,332  Size of group
     (1)       (2)        (3)
```

This contrast found by the program (based on number of children at home) is very strong statistically. There is only a 0.00001 per cent chance that the three groups have the same incidence of buying Krunchies. This is far beyond the lowest acceptable threshold (a 5 per cent chance of the groups being the same). If you feel in need of a refresher on statistical significance, please check back to Chapter 2.

The full analysis would continue past this point, continuing to use other characteristics to grow the tree. This would go until we ran out of demographic characteristics that led to further significant differences, or until we decided that the groups were too small to split further.

We will say a fond farewell to Krunchies by noting again that a very high 27.5 per cent of all suburban families with five or more children buy this fine product. This led to an insight that warranted further exploration.

Namely, SoggyOs, Inc. asked, 'Could a larger-size package help attract this group?' SoggyOs pursued this finding, investigated the appeal of this idea using a discrete choice model and came up with an optimal new product. This is their highly popular economy gunny-sack size. (US cereal buyers may notice that many brands now offer, if not exactly this, a massive multi-large-box special. There definitely is appeal in having heaps of one's favourite cereal-like substance at home.)

Optimal recoding

Classification trees' ability to split a variable in the best possible way, picking the breaking points and the number of groups, is a remarkable analytical strength. This is called **optimal recoding**. It has particular value when dealing with **categorical** variables.

As a reminder, a categorical variable is one where the numeric codes hold places for non-numerical values. In our example, town type/size was a categorical variable. The program held the values of 1, 2 and 3 for this variable, corresponding respectively to city, suburban and urban.

Optimal recoding

Optimal recoding is classification trees' unique ability to split the codes in a variable in the best possible way to predict an outcome variable. Codes are automatically arranged into groups and the best splitting points found. This involves very complex testing, sophisticated enough to be classified as artificial intelligence.

Strong, yet weak

Clearly, everything in a classification tree depends heavily on which variable gets chosen first. The variable with the strongest statistical significance will get the nod, unless you tell the program to do otherwise. Yet, while this variable could be the best at that specific point, it might not work best from the point of view of making a good overall model. Trees do not look forward to see what might happen if another variable were chosen.

Technically, trees are an example of a **greedy algorithm**. This is a method that makes a choice at each given point and then deals with whatever outcomes arise later.

We often find that many variables would pass the test of significance at any given spot in a tree diagram. Therefore, any one of them could be chosen as a predictor there. The differences in significance between the 'best' variable and the next few best – or even the next 20 or more – can be vanishingly small.

The best predictor could be significant at something like the 10^{-16} level (that is 16 zeros after the decimal point, or to write this out just once, 0.0000000000000000). The next few on the list might be significant at better than the 10^{-14} level, so the differences in statistical significance are microscopic. Yet putting in different variables at any point can lead to very different trees below.

What can we do to guard against this problem? Random forests can provide some guidance.

Random forests

This method runs many hundreds of classification trees, in each tree swapping out people and variables at random. Then all the trees 'vote' on a final outcome. An excellent reading of true variable importances comes from observing how classification levels change as variables and people are moved into and out of many models. The analysis also provides diagnostics showing how variables' importances shift as more trees are added. Eventually, after running a few hundred alternative models, we reach stable estimates.

'Random forests' adds to the list of horrible names beloved of maths and science types (think of SCSI – pronounced 'scuzzy' – drives, box and whisker plots, and p/p plots, for instance). However, random forests illustrate a key finding from machine learning. That is, the average of many weak estimates typically is better than any of the individual estimates. This is important enough to call out separately.

Any approach that uses many models, getting an average of estimates, is called an ensemble method. With ensembles, we have ventured deep into machine learning.

> **Ensembles: many models boost accuracy**
>
> The average of many indifferent or weak models typically performs better than any of the individual models. This is a key insight from machine learning. Random forests are an example of ensemble learning.

In our example below, we will run a forest with 500 tree models. Having 500 trees is powerful, but poses a problem. We cannot see what this method is doing. Unlike a model based on a single tree, where we can see how variables split, this method gives us importances but otherwise remains opaque. We cannot glance across all the many analyses and intuit what has happened.

In the example, we therefore used variables that were among those with the highest importance (across the many different trees) as candidate variables, and built one final classification tree model. This one model, based on 'assured winners', was then used to guide decision making.

A case study: let's take a cruise

Imperial Admiral Cruise Lines found itself sitting atop a large database of people who might take one of their fanciest cruises. (This is a fictionalized name – please do not look for them in the hope of booking a trip.) The family running this august enterprise had recently married into the one that ran the mighty **German Königlich Luxus Boot-Unternehmen** (KLBU) fleet. And together, they had just bought the bankrupt **Platinum Nigerian Prince Line**.

Having records of who had travelled on all these lines, they wanted to put this data to good use. They were interested in selling their most luxurious cruise, the **Admiral Deluxe Imperial Royal Diamond Special Plus** Cruise (or as they affectionately called it, the Big-Tips Cruise), and wanted to find those in their databases most likely to indulge in this extravagance.

Here, they were hoping to improve their odds by finding people like those who had already taken such a cruise. They had a plethora of household demographics and buying characteristics to work with, literally a list with hundreds of items that they had bought from various external vendors and merged into their data.

Predictive Models Via Classifications that Grow on Trees

They also had information on travel on their own line and the KLBU. This included the number travelling, last destination, number of cruises, number of times a trip was upgraded, and more. (Unfortunately, data from the Platinum Nigerian Prince Line proved to be sketchy and so most of it was discarded.)

They reasoned that those who were most likely to have taken such a cruise, based on these characteristics – but had not done so – would be the most promising upcoming customers. Therefore, Imperial Admiral Cruise Lines was hoping to improve the odds of finding a customer by appealing to select groups.

However, the odds that they were hoping to improve started with a vanishingly small baseline. Only 0.6 per cent of those in their database had ever taken the plunge and bought their most expensive offering. Even increasing this tenfold would give them only a 6 per cent likelihood of finding a buyer.

Figure 6.5 Importances from random forests

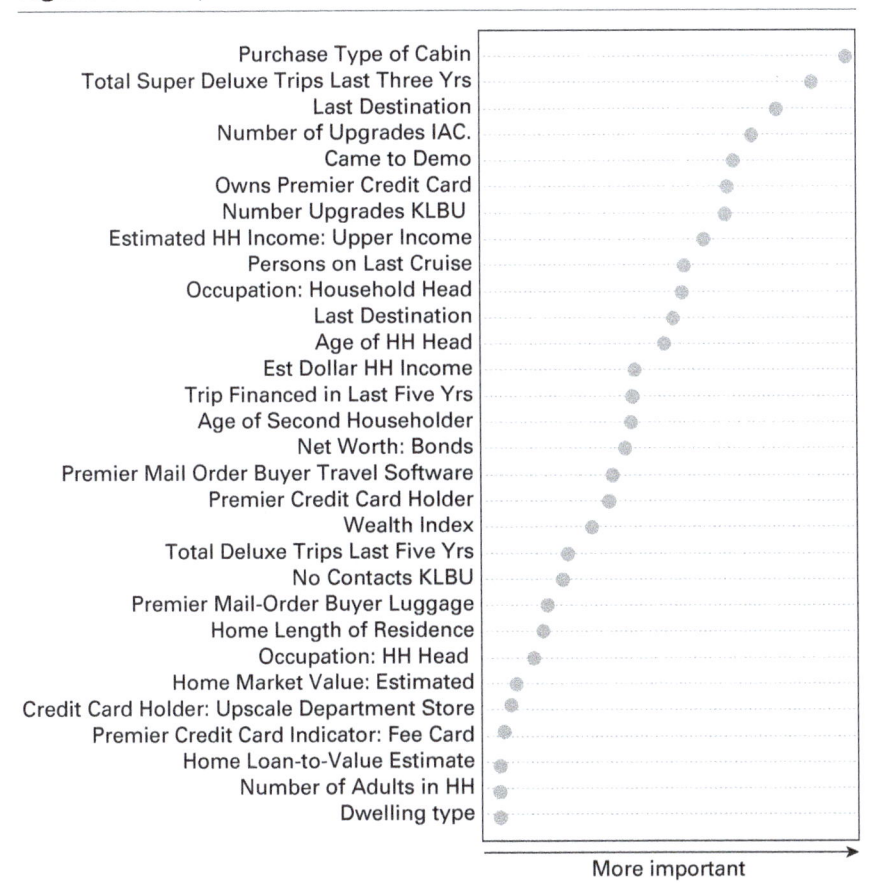

Slender as this may seem, this would still be 10 times better than doing nothing. Much like the US advertisers of medications for Crohn's disease mentioned in online bonus Chapter 1, they were willing to pursue low odds. The best they likely could do would be finding a population where nearly all would not be good prospects, even though the odds of finding a prospect there would be far better than average.

The most important variables from random forests

Several hundred variables were put into a random forests analysis. It built 500 trees, randomly swapping people and predictor variables into and out of the analysis. Figure 6.5 shows the 30 most important variables and their relative importances. Variables from this list were used in constructing a classification tree. Note that this study took place a number of years ago, and at that time, buying by mail order was a more robust business. Variables relating to buying by mail order appear on the list.

Constructing the tree

Elements appearing in each spot in the tree

We should first explain what you will see in the tree diagram. These displays vary in the information they show. There does not appear to be a default layout. Your author favours a display highlighting just the information needed, eschewing fancy graphs and flourishes. As you will see when we reveal the entire tree (in Figure 6.11), even an unadorned tree can be visually imposing.

Figure 6.6 explains what you will see at each point, or **node**, in the tree. The large, bold-faced number is the percentage of people in that group who have ever taken an Admiral Deluxe Imperial Royal Diamond Special Plus (fondly recalled as the Big-Tips) cruise. This percentage is the target or dependent variable in the analysis. In the figure, some 2.3 per cent of those in the group shown have taken this type of trip.

The two smaller numbers inside the node show how many people are in this group (12,003) and the percentage of the total sample that this group comprises (3.5 per cent). Please do not confuse the **incidence** of Big-Tips cruise-goers in the group (the very large number, or 2.3) with how large the group is (the small number in the corner, or 3.5 per cent).

Above the node, you will see information about the variable on which the sample is split at that point, and the statistical significance of the difference

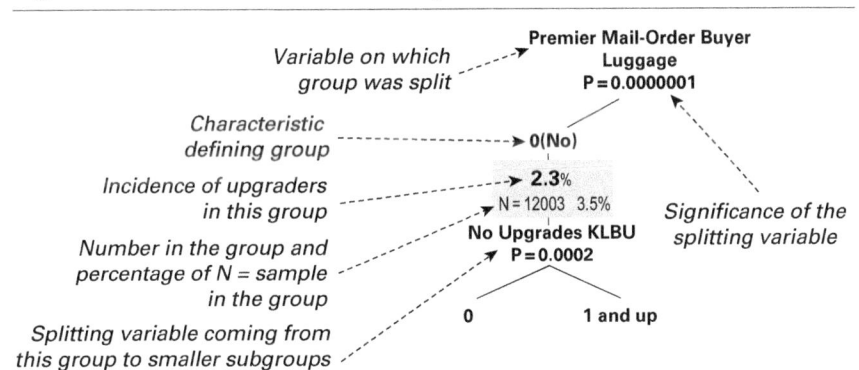

Figure 6.6 The elements in a tree diagram

```
                                    Premier Mail-Order Buyer
        Variable on which  ------>       Luggage
         group was split               P = 0.0000001

        Characteristic
        defining group    ------>  0(No)
                                     |
        Incidence of upgraders ---> 2.3%
               in this group     N = 12003  3.5%          Significance of the
        Number in the group and           No Upgrades KLBU   splitting variable
        percentage of N = sample           P = 0.0002
                 in the group
        Splitting variable coming from        0       1 and up
   this group to smaller subgroups
           and its significance level
```

between the split-off groups. Please recall that we are looking for a number of 0.05 or less to pass the test. In this instance, we have a much smaller value of P=0.0000001.

This group comes from another that has already been split out of the total sample, so it has two variables or characteristics that define it. Only the most recent splitting variable appears directly above. (That is, they have not bought premium luggage by mail order.) You would need to trace further up the tree to find the other characteristic.

Below the node, we see the variable leading to the next split, upgrades on the companion KLBU Line. The procedure found the best difference was between those who had no upgrades and all others who had ever upgraded.

To the whole tree: our first split of the sample

The first split is based on how many times customers upgraded a trip with Imperial Admiral Cruise Lines. Some debate arose about using this as a predictor, because the Admiral Deluxe Imperial Royal Diamond Special Plus (aka Big-Tips) trip itself could have been chosen due to upgrading. The data was probed somewhat more, and it was discovered that nearly all of the upgrades went to expensive, but still lesser, cruises – such as the popular Regal Super Extra Gold Deluxe package.

Figure 6.7 shows us how this first split looked. Note that this is a four-way division of the total sample. The largest group has done no upgrades. This is nearly three-quarters of the database. Only some 0.3 per cent of this group have taken IAG's most extravagant cruise.

Those who have upgraded once make up the next group. They are nearly at the average, with some 0.7 per cent having taken the plunge on a Big-Tips cruise.

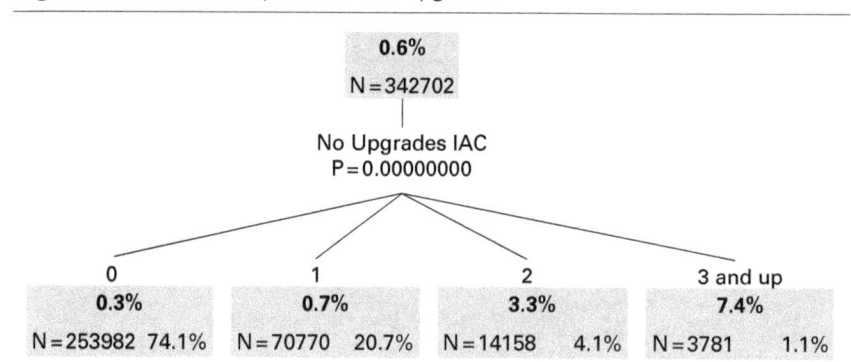

Figure 6.7 The first split, based on upgrades

```
                    0.6%
                  N = 342702
                      |
                No Upgrades IAC
                 P = 0.00000000
       ┌──────────┬──────────┬──────────┐
       0          1          2         3 and up
      0.3%       0.7%       3.3%        7.4%
  N=253982 74.1% N=70770 20.7% N=14158 4.1% N=3781 1.1%
```

Two smaller groups are far more likely to have taken such a voyage. This level reaches 3.4 per cent among the 14,158 who upgraded twice. Among the smallest of all groups, those who upgraded three or more times, some 7.7 per cent have taken this super-luxury journey.

It may seem that 7.7 per cent is not very good odds. This is true in the absolute, but it is 12.8 times as high as the average, and over 25 times as much as those who never upgraded. Therefore, this is a substantial improvement over not having even this much of a tree analysis.

This is a very powerful difference, and so the split is highly significant (shown by the notation P = 0.0000000, where **P** stands for 'probability'). This means that we have a near-zero chance that the averages in the groups are in fact the same, even the two groups where the levels are 0.3 per cent and 0.7 per cent. The artificial intelligence behind the splitting methods in the tree analysis allows us to be extremely confident that such seemingly similar groups are in fact not the same.

Onward to our first section of the tree

We will return to those who had no upgrades. They are not promising prospects, but perhaps some other characteristic of a subset of this group will reveal a more likely subgroup among them.

The tree will reach a set of final, or **terminal**, nodes. These nodes will get numbered so that we can refer to them more easily.

As we see in Figure 6.8, the first split is based on the last destination. This seems to make sense because IAG cruises to certain regions cost more than to others. This split divides the group with no upgrades into two nearly equal parts. However, one of those groups is four times as likely as the other to have taken the expensive trip. This group consists of those who last disembarked in Scotland and Portugal, and the 141 hearty souls who took the one and only adventure tour around Siberia.

Figure 6.8 The first section of the tree

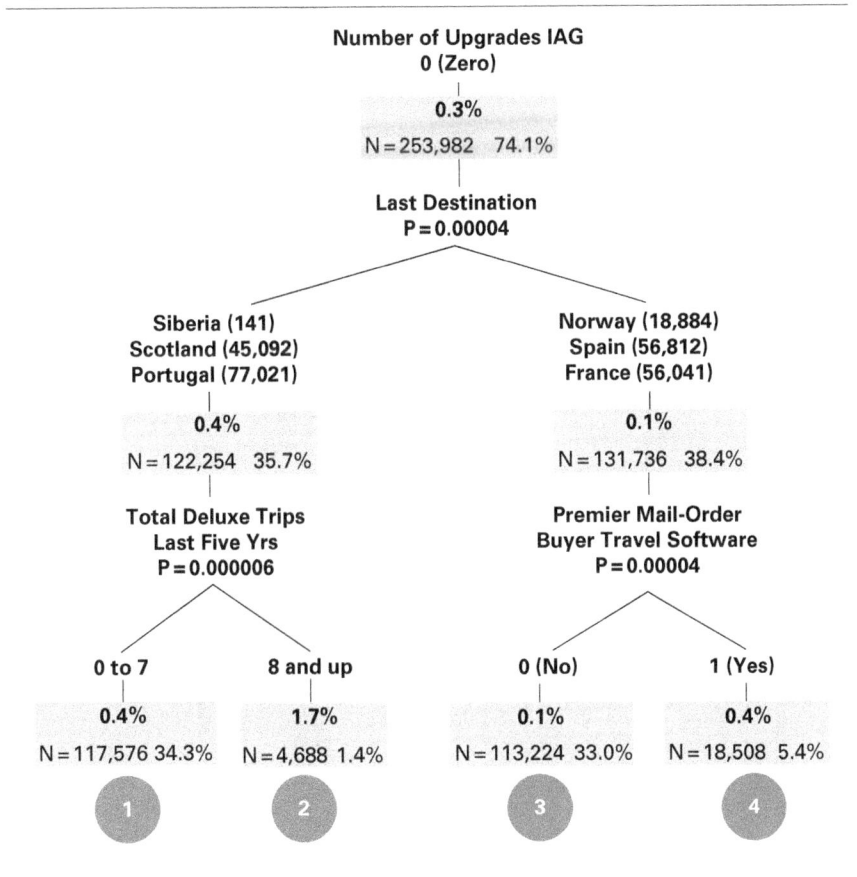

```
                    Number of Upgrades IAG
                           0 (Zero)
                              |
                             0.3%
                     N = 253,982   74.1%
                              |
                       Last Destination
                         P = 0.00004
                     ╱                ╲
          Siberia (141)            Norway (18,884)
          Scotland (45,092)        Spain (56,812)
          Portugal (77,021)        France (56,041)
                 |                         |
                0.4%                      0.1%
          N = 122,254  35.7%       N = 131,736  38.4%
                 |                         |
          Total Deluxe Trips       Premier Mail-Order
            Last Five Yrs          Buyer Travel Software
            P = 0.000006             P = 0.00004
            ╱         ╲               ╱         ╲
       0 to 7      8 and up        0 (No)      1 (Yes)
          |           |              |            |
        0.4%        1.7%           0.1%         0.4%
   N=117,576   N=4,688        N=113,224    N=18,508
    34.3%       1.4%            33.0%        5.4%
     (1)         (2)              (3)          (4)
```

The other group took the less expensive voyages around Norway, Spain and France. A mere 0.1 per cent of them took the super-deluxe trip.

Going back to the group on the left, a variable was found that could isolate a small subgroup with above-average likelihood of taking the big trip. This was those who also had taken eight or more luxury trips of any kind in the last five years. The correct way to define this terminal group, marked with a large '2', would be as follows:

Upgrades on IAG = 0 AND last destination = Scotland, Portugal or Siberia AND took eight or more luxury cruises in the last five years

You must have **all three of these** together to define this group. No one or two of them alone or in combination leads to a subgroup with this high an incidence of people who took the big trip.

Terminal group 1, which makes up most of the group above it, took seven or fewer luxury trips. They remain at 0.4 per cent incidence.

Figure 6.9 Splitting variables for those upgrading once

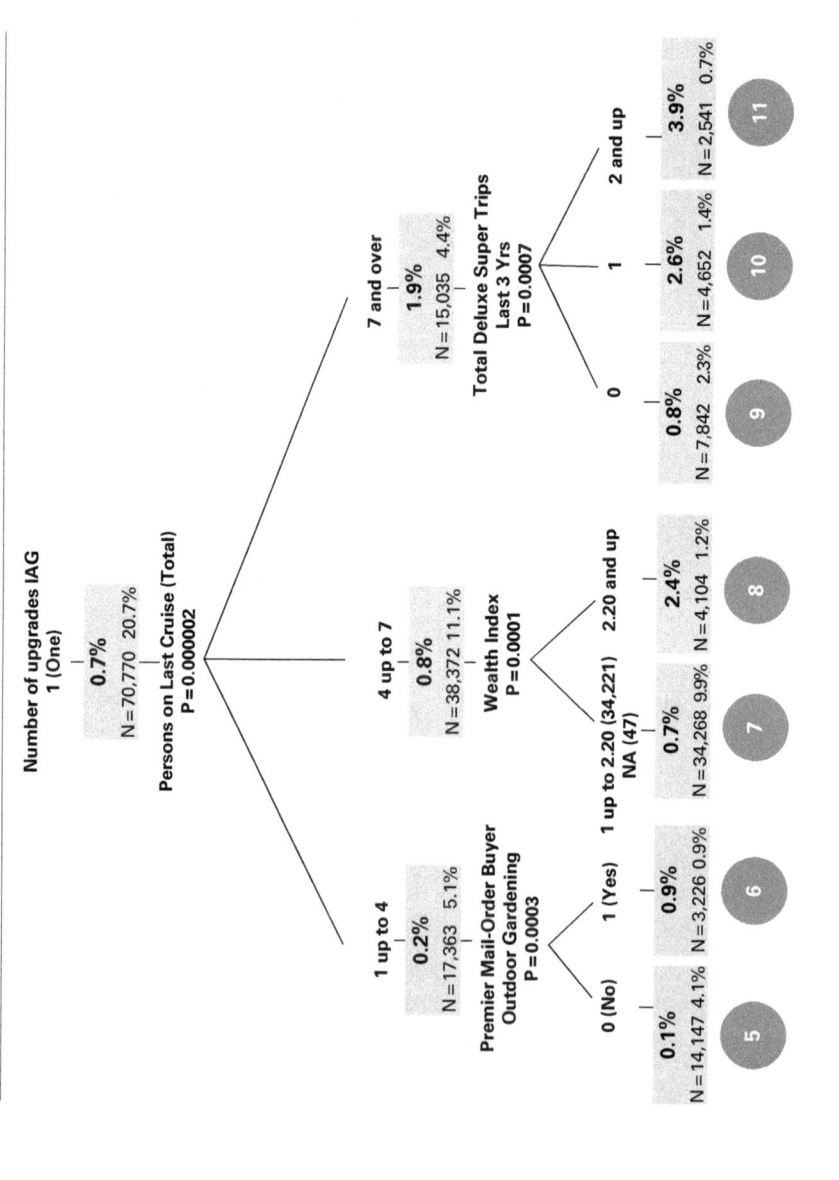

Rounding out this branch of the tree, the next split within the group who went to Norway, France or Spain does not lead to a subgroup with above-average incidence people who took the Big-Tips cruise. Terminal group 3 has a 0.1 per cent likelihood and terminal group 4 remains at 0.4 per cent. The most sharply differentiating characteristic found here was whether a person was a mail-order buyer of travel software.

Moving to the upgraders

Those who upgraded once make up about 21 per cent of the database. But with nearly 71,000 in this group, there was room for the tree to branch several times. This is the most complex portion of the diagram, with seven terminal groups or nodes, as you can see in Figure 6.9.

Four variables work together to define these groups. One of these, the so-called **wealth index**, was calculated by an external database provider. Since it is appended to all the people in the database, the meaning of this is not important, just the score at which a difference was found.

The way this variable splits, points out that CHAID can handle both **categorical** and **continuous** predictor variables. It will find the best place at which to split off groups with either kind of data.

Two of the groups are well below average in incidence of super-luxury trip buyers. The first is terminal group 5, defined as: upgraded once AND had 1–4 persons on the last trip AND not a premier mail-order buyer for outdoor gardening. Only 0.1 per cent in this group took the super-deluxe cruise.

The other is terminal group 7, with an incidence of only 0.3 per cent. A small number of people with no data (47 to be exact) are mixed in with those having lower wealth index scores.

Missing values are not a problem

This admixture of data and missing responses points out one additional strength of CHAID. **Missing values** can be handled just as any other response. You must ask the program to do this. If you do, these responses are put into the group of codes where they best boost contrasts in responses to the dependent variable.

CHAID can even be used to **impute** or estimate what missing values might be. Since these missing responses are grouped with the responses that have statistically identical levels of the target variable, this can be a very sensible way of estimating what those missing values could be.

Our first groups with high incidences of super-luxury buyers

Two of the terminal groups (group 7 and group 9) have about average incidence of people who took the Big-Tips cruise. But the remaining three groups (8, 10 and 11) have incidences of super-luxury buyers that are well above average. Group 11 is the richest in this select group, reaching some 3.9 per cent. This is some 6.5 times more than the average. This group is described as follows:

> Number of upgrades = 1 AND persons on the last cruise 7 and over AND total super-deluxe trips in the last 3 years = 2 and up

The best of slender odds: those most likely

We find the groups with the highest likelihood of taking the super-deluxe voyage in the last section of the tree, those upgrading two or more times. Figure 6.10 shows this comprises two branches. Those who upgraded three

Figure 6.10 Mostly the best prospects, those upgrading more than once

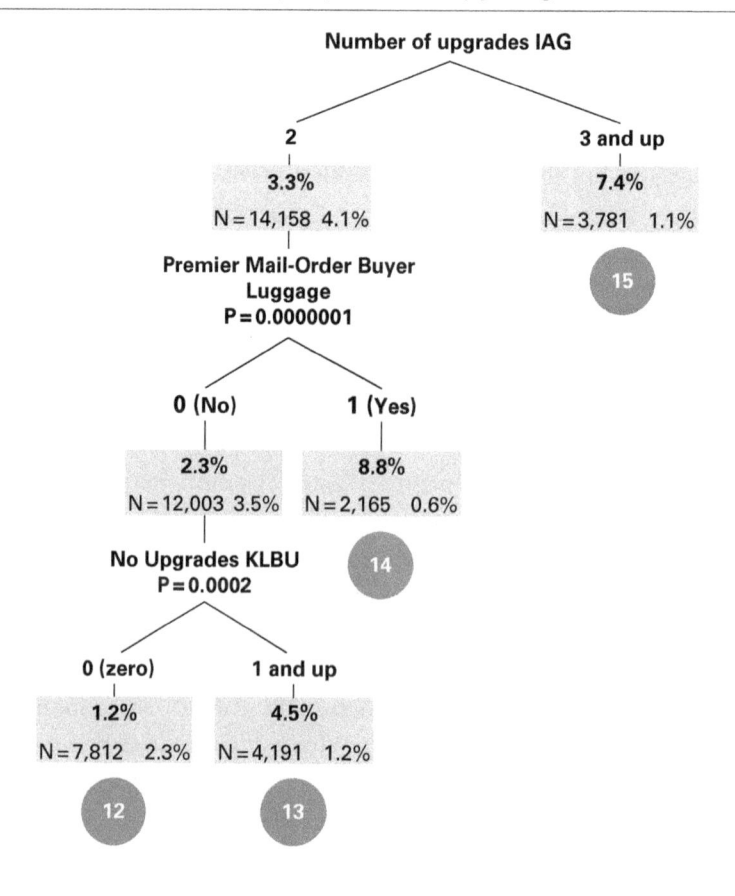

```
                    Number of upgrades IAG
                   /                      \
                  2                      3 and up
                3.3%                       7.4%
           N=14,158  4.1%              N=3,781  1.1%
                 |                          |
        Premier Mail-Order Buyer           (15)
              Luggage
           P = 0.0000001
           /           \
        0 (No)        1 (Yes)
         2.3%          8.8%
    N=12,003  3.5%   N=2,165  0.6%
         |                |
   No Upgrades KLBU     (14)
      P = 0.0002
      /         \
   0 (zero)   1 and up
    1.2%        4.5%
 N=7,812 2.3%  N=4,191  1.2%
    |              |
   (12)          (13)
```

Figure 6.11 The whole classification tree

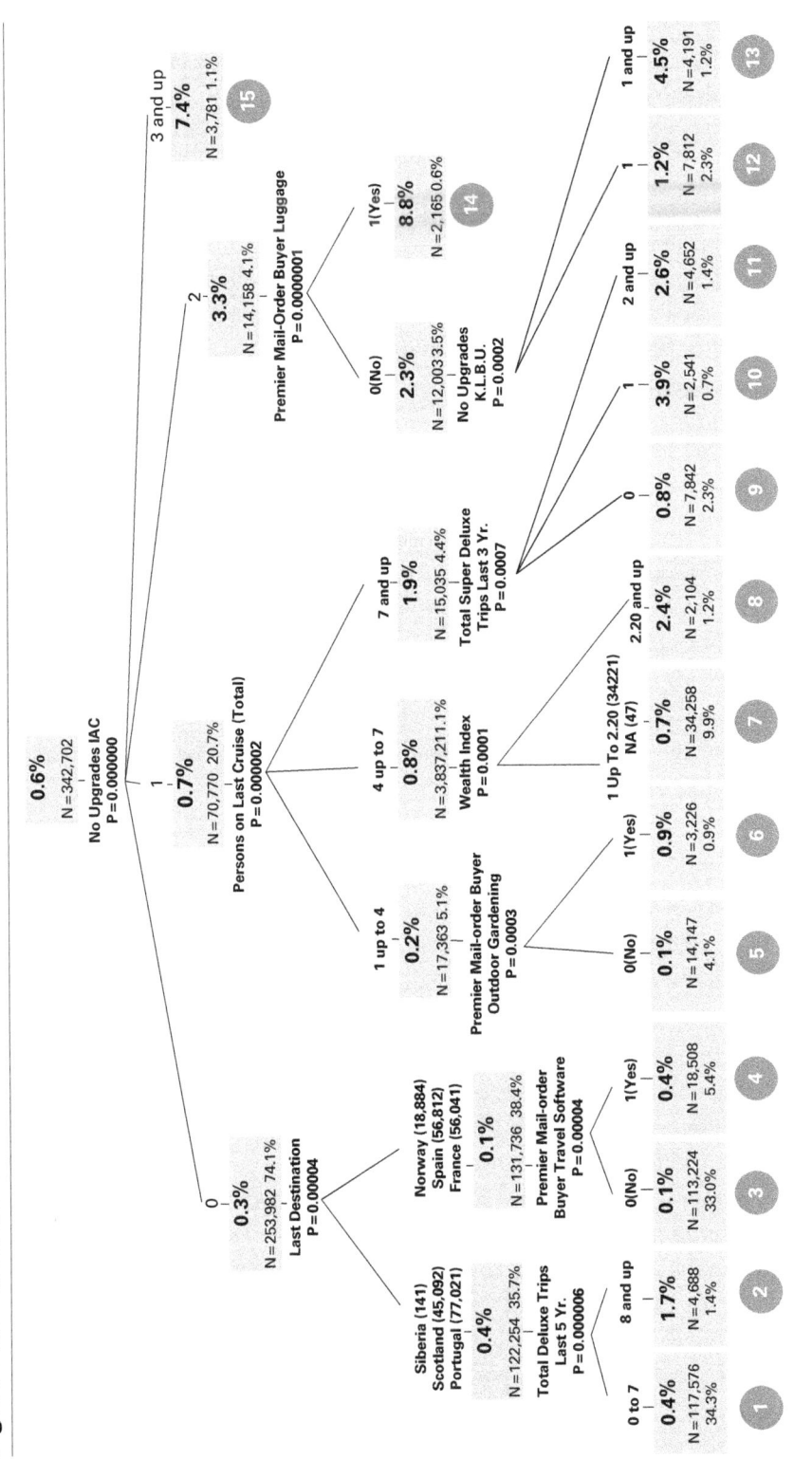

times or more stand alone, with an incidence of 7.4 per cent (in terminal node 15). No further splits were possible once this group was isolated. It is the only group described fully by a single characteristic.

The incidence of super-luxury travellers in this group is some 12.3 times the average of 0.6 per cent. The odds are still low, but clearly far better than just picking at random.

The group with the highest incidence of all falls under those who upgraded twice. This group (number 14) is defined by one further characteristic, namely that they were mail-order buyers of premier luggage. In this group, some 8.8 per cent took the really big cruise. This comes to some 14.8 times the overall average, a truly sizeable increase.

The entire tree diagram

Figure 6.11 puts all the pieces together. This is not a particularly large tree, but even at this size the display is visually imposing. The tree has a great deal of valuable information, but looking at it in this form, it is easy to miss much of what is shown.

Two forms of additional displays will help make the information in the tree more accessible. These are the **classification rules** and a very handy chart called variously a **gains analysis**, a **lift analysis** or a **leverage analysis**. Let's discuss what each does.

Classification rules and trees

Classification trees do not generate equations like (for instance) a regression, which have variables and their weights (or coefficients). You may be familiar with a formulation from regression something like this:

$$\text{Variable } y = 0.4*A + 0.6*B + 0.7*C + 81$$

Rather, classification trees lead to a set of simple 'if-then' statements, or **classification rules**. In Table 6.1 you will see the rules describing the first four groups in the tree. The rule numbers correspond to the numbers in the tree diagram. Typically, we use rules describing only the very ends of the tree, or the **terminal nodes**. Groups or nodes inside the tree lead to only a partial description of any group formed.

Rules like these are all we need to describe the output, or **create a model**. This model is what we would use to score another data set. In this example, everyone in the data set got a probability of taking the big cruise based on the model. Then those most likely to buy into this could be approached with appeals to consider this enriching (and possibly bankrupting) experience.

Table 6.1 The first four classification rules

RULE 1 IF	Total Deluxe Trips Last 5 Yrs = 0 to 7
	AND Last Cruise Destination = Siberia, Scotland or Portugal
	AND No. Upgrades IAC = 0
THEN	Took the Big-Tips Cruise = 0.4%
RULE 2 IF	Total Deluxe Trips Last 5 Yrs = 8 and up
	AND Last Cruise Destination = Siberia, Scotland or Portugal
	AND No. Upgrades IAC = 0
THEN	Took the Big-Tips Cruise = 1.7%
RULE 3 IF	Premier Mail-Order Buyer Travel Software = 0 (No)
	AND Last Cruise Destination = Norway, Spain or France
	AND No. Upgrades IAC = 0
THEN	Took the Big-Tips Cruise = 0.1%
RULE 4 IF	Premier Mail-Order Buyer Travel Software = 1 (Yes)
	AND Last Cruise Destination = Norway, Spain or France
	AND No. Upgrades IAC = 0
THEN	Took the Big-Tips Cruise = 0.4%

NOTE the numbering of the rules follows the numbering of the ending nodes on the tree diagram

> **Classification rules**
>
> A classification tree leads to a set of simple **if-then** statements describing the combinations of predictor variables that lead to different values of the target variable. They typically describe just the ending boxes or nodes in the tree. These rules can be used to assign values to another data set.

These rules are extremely simple and so very easy to program into a database. This great simplicity of the model, with its absence of equations or other calculations, is a highly appealing feature of classification trees.

This tree requires 15 rules, one for each terminal node. We also used only 10 predictor variables. This tree has done a tremendous amount to clarify the data with a highly compact model. Recall that this database ran into the hundreds of thousands. Everyone was classified into a group, and only one group.

More formally, the model is **mutually exclusive and completely exhaustive**. This kind of jargon can become catching in certain environments.

At one client company, people were sitting in a meeting and talking about a model being something that sounded like 'me-see'. At first their sanity seemed in doubt. It then emerged they were indeed talking about the initials for **mutually exclusive and completely exhaustive,** or MECE. However, we are still not sure about their sanity.

In any event, this ability (to capture and characterize everyone in a group with so few variables) is a tremendous strength of classification tree methods. With some audiences it may pose some difficulties. They may not believe that you can reveal so much about a data set with so few predictors, and may even question why their favourite item was not included.

The ultimate in detail: the gains analysis

We can learn still more about the finer points of the classification tree from a **gains analysis.** This may also be called a **lift** or **leverage** analysis. It lists the terminal nodes of the tree in order, from highest incidence to lowest. It also provides other details about them. Table 6.2 shows a portion of a gains analysis. The full analysis for this tree would have 15 sections (one for each terminal node). We will show and discuss the first five.

The portion of the chart to the right, under '**A**', is more intuitive. This first shows where the node falls in the tree, how large the group is, and the incidence of super-luxury buyers in the group.

One number that is less apparent is added, namely the **lift** or **leverage**. This is an indexed value, showing how the incidence of super-luxury buyers in this group compares to the overall average. The overall average is set to 100. Therefore, the index for the first group of 1,480 means that the incidence of these buyers in this group is 14.80 times as high as the average.

The portion of Table 6.2 under '**B**' is somewhat more complex. This shows **cumulative** figures. Cumulative figures are the weighted average of all groups down to and including the one on that line of the table. So, for instance, cumulative figures for the third group are a weighted average of the values for groups 1, 2 and 3. (The third group is defined as: No. upgrades KLBU = 1 and up AND premier mail-order buyer of luggage = 0 (No) AND no. upgrades IAC = 2.)

Cumulative figures are valuable because they help decide on a cut-off point for targeting. When you use a gains chart to target, you would tag a number of groups in the database. The simplicity of the if-then rules coming from the classification tree makes it easy to specify that any of a dozen or more conditions be met. Some classification tree programs even generate the rules in database (SQL) language automatically.

Table 6.2 Gains chart showing the five groups with the highest index values

Group characteristics (Group characteristics work together. Only the second group is defined by one characteristic)	Position in tree	Individual group statistics			Cumulative statistics		
		Group as % of total	Incidence of buyers	Lift or leverage (Index: 100 = average)	Groups as cumulative % of total	Cumulative incidence of buyers	Cumulative Lift
Premier Mail-Order Buyer: Luggage: 1 (Yes) AND No. Upgrades IAC: 2	14	0.7%	**8.8%**	1,480		**8.8%**	1,480
No. Upgrades IAC: 3 and up	15	1.2%	**7.4%**	1,233	1.9%	**7.9%**	1,331
No Upgrades KLBU: 1 and up AND Premier Mail-Order Buyer: Luggage: 0 (No) AND No. Upgrades IAC: 2	13	1.3%	**4.5%**	750	3.2%	**6.5%**	1,096
No. Upgrades IAC: 1 AND Persons on Last Cruise (Total): 16 and up AND No. Upgrades IAC: 1	11	0.8%	**3.9%**	650	4.0%	**6.0%**	1,009
No. Upgrades IAC: 2 and up AND Persons on Last Cruise (Total): 7 and up AND No. Upgrades IAC: 1	10	1.5%	**2.6%**	433	5.4%	**5.1%**	855

A — Individual group statistics
B — Cumulative statistics

Figure 6.12 The gains chart simplified

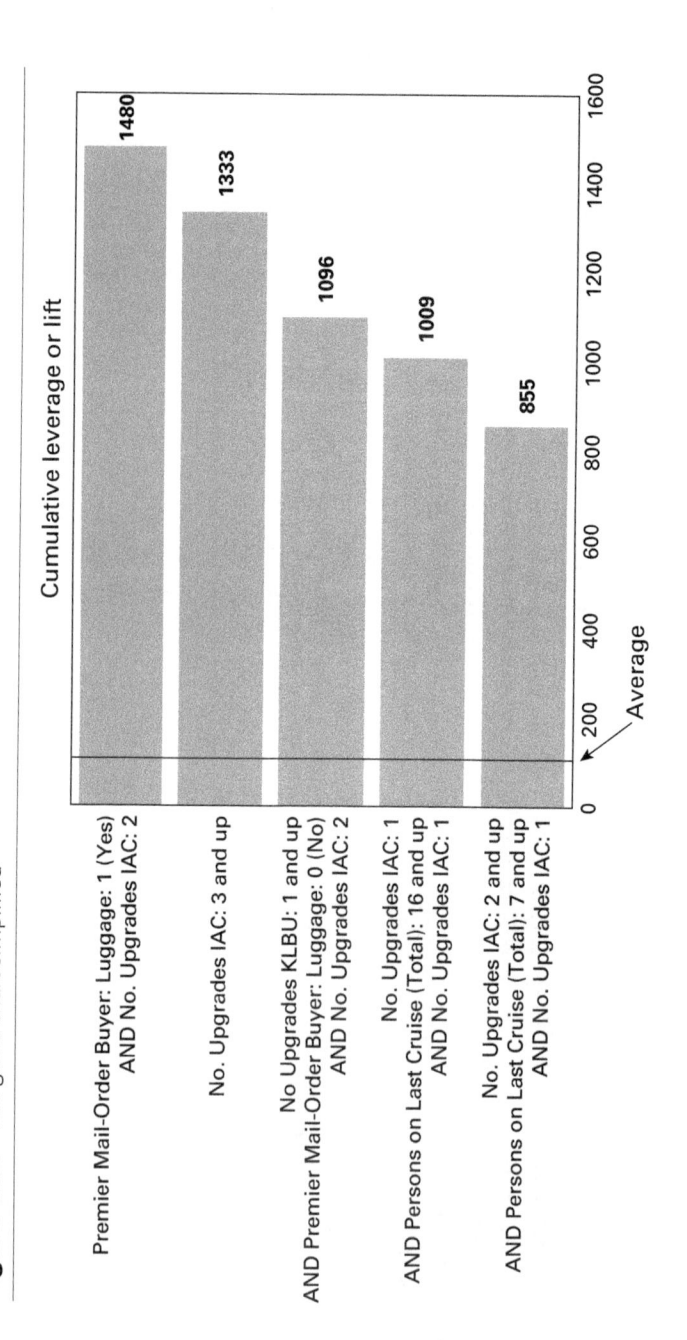

Still more statistics could appear in the diagram, such as the percentage of all luxury buyers in each groups and actual counts of people. However, as many details as we have shown in this chart often seems perplexing, especially to harassed management people. Sometimes, then, a simpler display can help get the message across more easily. One such chart, which we could subtitle 'Gains for management', appears in Figure 6.12.

We included another six groups in the actual targeting exercise. That amounted to some 20 per cent of the total sample, and some 70 per cent of the luxury buyers. (Cumulative incidence for these 11 groups was 350.) This represents a terrific gain in efficiency versus not having the model.

One way to calculate efficiency would be taking the increased incidence of buyers, as shown by the cumulative gain (350), and taking into account that you are skipping 80 per cent of the total database. That is, efficiency would be 3.5/0.2, or some 17.5 times as efficient in finding luxury buyers as not having the model.

So while the odds are still not high, they are far better than they could be without the model. Using classification trees greatly increased the odds of finding likely prospects, and so increased certainty and decreased waste.

Still, while the trees have guided IAG to those who might take such a trip, they do not reveal **which features or messages** might be most appealing. Those investigations would need to be done using the trade-off methods we discussed in Chapters 4, 5 and online bonus Chapter 1.

Growing trees: automated or guided?

In the example, we could have made the tree larger, or have grown it further. We elected to stop at 15 terminal groups because adding more splits provided no additional information useful in directing tactics. That is, we **guided** the growth of the tree.

You either can let classification trees run automatically or (with some programs) guide what the procedure does. Some programs run only automatically, which in your author's opinion is a strong disadvantage if you want to do anything more than **optimal recoding** of variables.

The 'greediness' of tree methods that we discussed earlier is one main reason that automation can be a serious problem. That is, tree programs will automatically choose the one variable that looks 'best' at each spot in the tree, even if that variable would not lead to the best overall result when adding other variables later.

In fact, we encounter this issue with nearly all methods that try to build models by adding variables. It is worse with trees because choosing the wrong variable can lead to no further growth in the tree. This can become a serious problem because trees typically do not contain many variables.

Sometimes the 'best' variable or even the next 'best' will cause the tree to stop growing because no further statistically significant variables can be found below it. However, some other statistically significant variable could lead to further growth, and to further valuable information about what influences an overall outcome.

Recommendations on tree growing

Typically results are excellent if you let the program pick automatically first and then go back and check any spots that seem problematic – for instance, a place where a large group was left undivided. The most complete classification tree programs let you look at a list of possible variables that could split the sample at each point in the tree (all of these variables passing your chosen test of statistical significance). You then can explore how the tree grows when you swap the program's first choice for another variable.

No matter which program you use, you will need to set the acceptable significance level, and the smallest group you will allow when the program does splitting. If you do not set a minimum, the program may even split off **a single person** into his or her own group. And of course, the minimum size you select will influence how the tree grows.

All these factors lead to the conclusion that we may never reach a **demonstrably optimal tree**. Small fluctuations in the data – for instance, dropping one person with questionable responses – might lead to very different-looking trees being selected as the best possible by a computer program.

Still, while this is a caution, it should not be a deterrent to using this remarkable method. The goal should always be to create a model that has **the most useful information** and that still has **strong predictive power**. Squeezing the last possible drop out of a score showing the goodness of prediction should not be your aim. Scores are valuable things, but real-world applicability is more important. Sacrificing a point or two of a score for a more useful model makes a great deal of sense.

CHAID and CART (and CRT, C&RT, QUEST, J48 and others)

Before we get to our next new method, we need to clear up some terminology about trees. As you have noticed, we have been talking here about a specific type of classification tree analysis, called **CHAID**.

AID, a notoriously inaccurate method, came first. Over the last few decades, a healthy host of related methods have been developed. CHAID was the first method to solve the problem of comparing significance when using variables that have different numbers of categories – as it turns out, a fiendishly difficult problem.

Over the years many alternatives to CHAID have been proposed. Again venturing out onto a metaphorical limb, we will say that they all do basically the same things, but with different restrictions and rules. At one time, there were fierce partisans of various methods. Now that classification trees are no longer the latest word in predictive models, the rancorous language seems to have subsided.

Perhaps the disputes also have quieted because there now are so many variations of classification tree methods, well over 40. The most widely used along with **CHAID** is called **CART** (also called **CRT** and **C&RT** because strangely the word CART was allowed a trademark).

CART and its relatives, such as **QUEST**, do only two-way splits while CHAID can split more finely. Some users still prefer CART, but for the purpose of performing optimal recoding, CHAID appears to be more efficient. All the groups you need can be formed at once, rather than in a series of two-way splits.

You may also encounter such programs as **AC2, J48, C4.5** (free) and **C5** (not free). We have discussed one outgrowth of classification trees, **random forests**. Next we discuss another, **boosted decision stumps**.

Decision stumps rescue a theoretical model

A **decision stump**, aside from being another unlovely term, is simply a one-level tree. These can be used for **optimal recoding**, as in the example shown in Figure 6.13, where a decision stump links a large regression-based model to market share.

Regression-based models can become highly complex, with some extensions of regression actually creating new variables by combining related ones. These combined variables then act on the target or dependent variable.

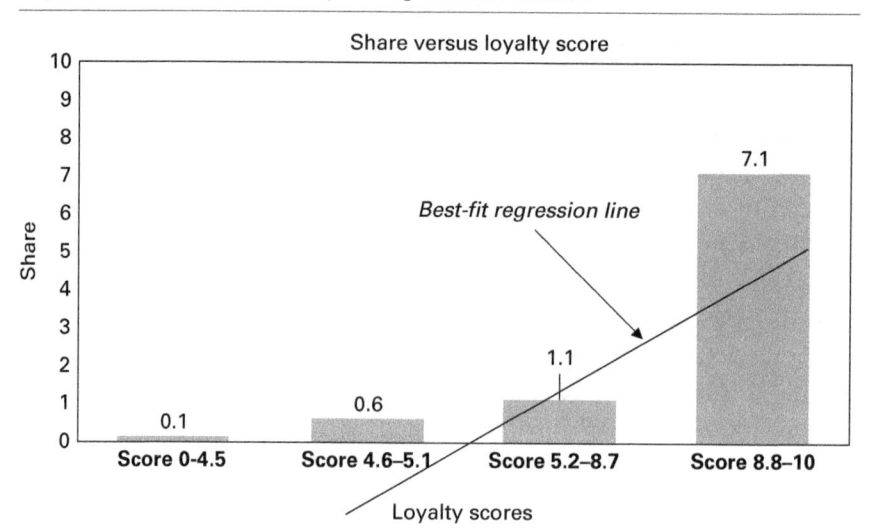

Figure 6.13 Decision stump linking scores and share

Share versus loyalty score

Score 0-4.5	Score 4.6–5.1	Score 5.2–8.7	Score 8.8–10
0.1	0.6	1.1	7.1

Best-fit regression line

Loyalty scores

They also can influence each other. (The best-known of these methods are **structural equation models** and **partial least squares** path models.) The new, combined variables are considered to be underlying ideas or themes that the actual variables indirectly measure.

Here a large number of variables were envisioned as combining into a **loyalty score**. However, while the loyalty score itself was predicted accurately by the individual variables, the model did not link well with market share. This happened because regression expects relationships among variables to fall into a straight line. Share and the score did have a strong relationship, but it was not at all linear. A decision stump revealed how they related.

As you can see in Figure 6.13, share jumps abruptly once the loyalty score goes over 8.7. (This score was a weighted average of many other variables, and so could be any value between 0 and 10.) The classification tree program found the best places to split the score variable, **using optimal recoding**.

The best-fit regression line misses this relationship. It even falls below a predicted value of zero for share when the score is about 5.2.

Boosted decision stumps

This application gives us another, distinctive way to determine variables' importances. It uses a process of building single-level trees repeatedly. Its approach differs from that of random forests, which reruns larger trees while randomly swapping predictor variables and cases (people) in and out of each model.

Figure 6.14 Output from boosting

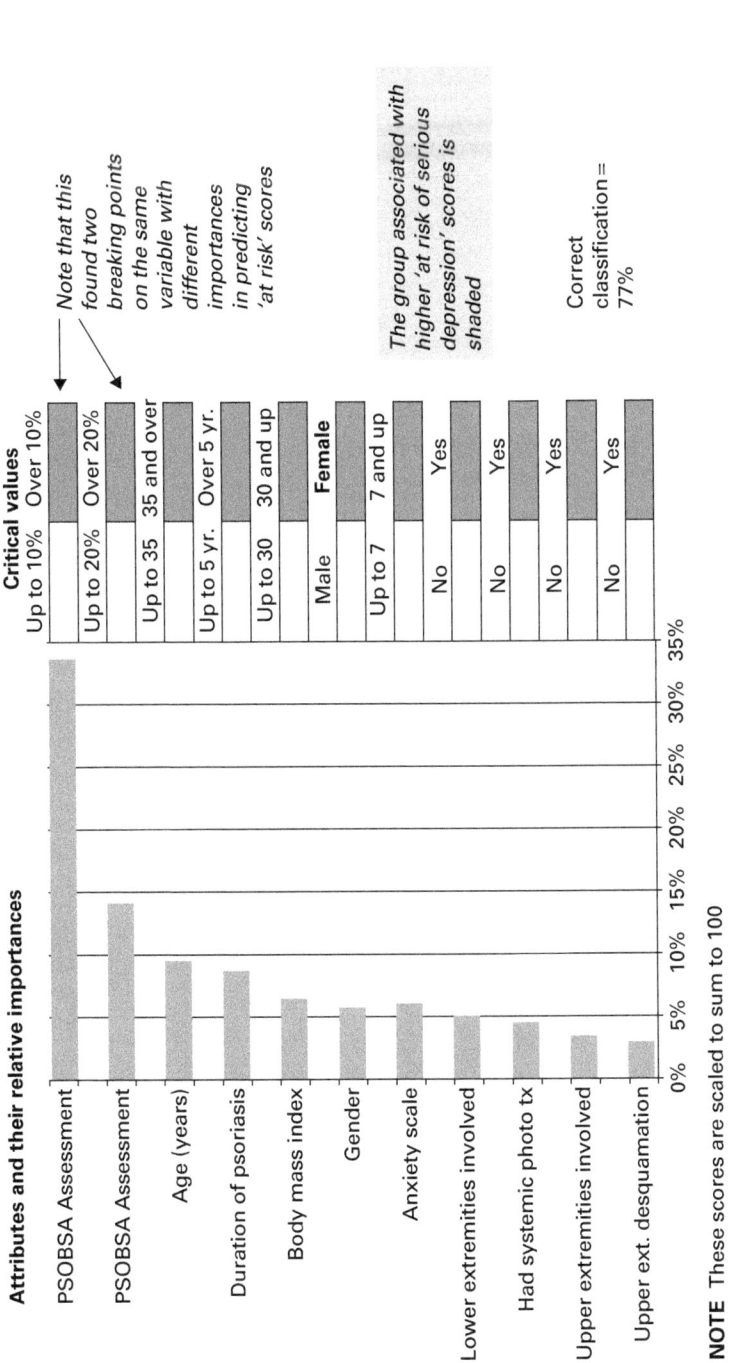

Attributes and their relative importances

Attribute		Critical values	
		Up to 10%	Over 10%
PSOBSA Assessment		Up to 20%	Over 20%
PSOBSA Assessment		Up to 35	35 and over
Age (years)		Up to 5 yr.	Over 5 yr.
Duration of psoriasis		Up to 30	30 and up
Body mass index		Male	**Female**
Gender		Up to 7	7 and up
Anxiety scale		No	Yes
Lower extremities involved		No	Yes
Had systemic photo tx		No	Yes
Upper extremities involved		No	Yes
Upper ext. desquamation			

0%   5%   10%   15%   20%   25%   30%   35%

Note that this found two breaking points on the same variable with different importances in predicting 'at risk' scores

The group associated with higher 'at risk of serious depression' scores is shaded

Correct classification = 77%

NOTE These scores are scaled to sum to 100

Rather, **boosting decision stumps** runs a first model, a single-level tree, and then **learns** from that model. The procedure marks which cases are predicted correctly and which are not. The correct cases are marked as the **easy** ones and the incorrect cases as **hard**. The procedure then puts more weight or emphasis on the hard cases, and tries to fit a model that captures them better.

It will redo this as many times as you request. Each time, it focuses most on the hard cases, trying to predict those people who were incorrectly classified the last time. **Boosting** is another type of **ensemble model**.

Figure 6.14 shows an output from a run of boosted decision stumps. These importances followed a classification tree model showing the linkages between the nature of psoriasis and depression. The model used measurements of the extent and location of the affected skin areas for about 6,900 patients. These patients also took an internationally normed test designed to measure serious depression.

The tree model led to a simple set of if-then rules, with each rule corresponding to a different probability of severe depression. It was easy to use, since it was based on measurements that doctors would take in any event as a part of treatment. It could even be scored using a pencil and paper.

A question arose about how important the variables in the model were, and for this boosting was used. The specific method is called **AdaBoost.M1**, which specifically is made to use with classification trees.

We asked the method to run boosting 40 times, and the importances that appear in Figure 6.14 emerged from the analysis. As you can see in the figure, two values of the same predictor were the most important. This one predictor is percentage of body surface area with psoriasis (PSOBSA). One critical threshold is over 10 per cent of body surface area and the other is over 20 per cent. Few other methods match this ability to isolate two values of the same variable as important.

This model proved to be valuable because psoriasis patients often conceal how depressed they feel, even from their doctors. The classification tree model gave doctors a simple way to determine which patients might be most at risk. The boosting gave them a few features to watch with particular extra attention.

Summary: applications and cautions

Classification trees remain pre-eminent for teasing out and seeing **interactions** – the ways in which variables' influence on a target variable is stronger or weaker than expected when they work in combination. When two variables work together to produce an effect that is stronger than we would expect based on the ways that each behaves separately, we can actually say for once that these effects are **synergistic** – and mean it.

Other analytical methods allow variables to interact as part of their normal operation, in particular the **Bayes Nets** we discuss in Chapter 7. But nowhere are these patterns as apparent as they are in a classification tree analysis.

These methods are so effective at finding interactions that they make a good first step before other methods of analysis, such as regression-based models. The important interactions that classification trees find can be entered into the regression, improving results.

We mainly discussed the **CHAID** method, which can produce many-way splits. This is particularly efficient to find the best way to split a large categorical variable that holds many codes. Another type of classification tree method, exemplified in **CART** (or C&RT or CRT), produces only two-way splits and so makes **optimal recoding** somewhat more cumbersome.

Trees do not produce equations like regressions. Classification tree models typically are small, with few variables and few **classification rules**. Rules are simple **if-then statements** that describe how the variables work together to lead to an outcome. This simplicity, even with very large data sets, is a salient strength of these methods. We typically can explain everything important quickly and efficiently. Some audiences may find this hard to believe though, so this could require some advance explanation.

Classification tree methods do not produce a **truly definitive model**. Small fluctuations in the data or small changes in the way you choose to set minimum acceptable group sizes, for instance, can lead to very different-looking trees. If you allow the software to do all the choosing in shaping the tree, you might get a result that is not best suited to your strategic or tactical needs.

Some programs claim to find the best possible model automatically, but you alone know what you really need. Therefore, you are best served by a program that allows you to modify the model to fit your objectives.

We explained two **ensemble methods** based on trees. Ensembles run many models and either average or take votes. One of the key findings of machine learning is that the average of many indifferent or weak models typically works better than any of the individual models.

Random forests help understand the importance of variables. They build hundreds of classification trees with random swapping of people and predictors into the model each time. They can help you focus in on the truly important variables, as we did in the IAG Cruise Lines example. **Adaptive boosting** is another approach that can provide an excellent reading of variables' importances. Which of these approaches you use would depend on which most clearly shows the information you need to meet the goals of your project.

However, another method, **Bayes Nets**, arguably provides the ultimate in seeing how variables relate and understanding variables' importances. We discuss Bayes Nets in Chapter 7.

Remarkable predictive models with Bayes Nets

07

In this chapter we will learn about the remarkable set of methods called **Bayes Nets** or Bayesian networks. We will show how they readily see patterns in the real world that completely elude us. We also illustrate how they automatically learn data structures, fitting variables together into natural groupings. We review some of their many other abilities, including the ways they can trim groups of variables, determine the true importances of predictors, and generally make sense of data. Using numerous illustrations, this chapter demonstrates the remarkable properties of these methods.

What are Bayes Nets and how do they compare with other methods?

Now that we have assimilated a great deal about trade-off methods, classification trees and ensembles, we head in another direction entirely: exploring **Bayes Nets** or Bayesian networks.

Bayes Nets have remarkable properties allowing them to surpass many other methods in showing useful patterns in data. They can even solve some problems that elude other methods entirely. They will repay learning a new way to think about data.

Comparing to the regression standard

Bayes Nets can tackle many of the same problems that have traditionally been addressed with various **regression**-based models. Nearly everyone who has sat (or suffered) through a statistics class has heard about regression. Many people believe that they know these methods and their uses, and some in fact do understand them.

So that everyone is on an even footing, let's review a few basic properties of **regressions**. One basic idea behind them is that we can **add the effects** of variables to predict the values of some target variable. This target could be, for instance, a scaled rating or the level of use of a product or service. The types of regression we typically use all work based on seeking **straight-lines relationships**. Hence, the designation you will sometimes see: **linear additive models**.

Regressions are based on the patterns of **correlations** among variables. As a reminder, while **correlation** has been taken to mean many things, with regression it means a simple summary measure of how closely two variables fall into a straight-line relationship.

Some extensions to regression deal with curved lines for the target variable, but you are not likely to encounter these outside scientific settings. Even if the line is curved, regression seeks the best fit to that line, as it does with the straight line in Figure 7.1.

A regression generates an **equation** that we can think of as something like a recipe for making a cake. A regression equation would look like this:

$$Y \text{ (the value of the target variable)} = 0.5 * A + 0.7 * B + 81$$

In an equation like this, you add ingredients in certain proportions, and perhaps add another number at the end (the constant). These values together then forecast the target variable. In Figure 7.1, the straight line represents the regression's best estimate of the values of the target variable, based on

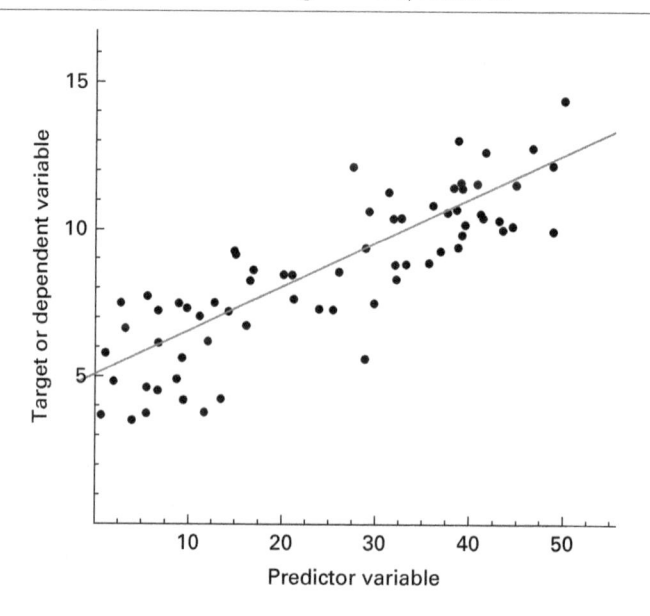

Figure 7.1 A regression line showing the best prediction

values of one predictor. The dots show the actual values of the target variable (shown as distances across) versus the predictor variable (shown as distances up and down).

Regression-based methods have had a long, distinguished history of working well in many settings. They are among the most venerable and most tested of all analytical methods. Still, at times regressions perform indifferently, poorly or even not at all.

Regular regressions do not work with target variables that are **categorical** (such as predicting the group to which a person belongs, or in which region a person lives). You also must break down categorical predictors into sets of yes/no variables. Most commonly this is done via a process called **dummy coding**.

We did not talk much about the methods underlying **discrete choice modelling** – these are complex and not critical to understanding the output. However, they are based on relatives of **regression** that can use a categorical target variable. Specifically, these are variants of **multinomial logit** or the more inclusive **mother logit**.

Regressions are great for experiments

Regression-related methods are a perfect match for an **experiment**. That is, you have all the variables that you want to measure and none extra. Regression expects that. Also, in an experiment, all the predictor variables have zero or near-zero correlations. This allows the regression to measure each variable's effects precisely. With this careful set-up, you really can measure the effect of a variable if all other variables remain constant.

Some trouble in the real world

However, regressions may run into trouble with messier, real-world data. When predictor variables are related to each other, the coefficients of the variables can shift or even reverse signs (going from positive to negative or vice versa). Variables that are too closely related can get squeezed out of the final model altogether.

Regression will not alert you to situations in which variables interact, or combine to produce a result different from what we would expect from each variable separately. You may recall that in Chapter 6 we saw that large families living in the suburbs bought more Kardboard Krunchies than we would expect either from large families overall or from those living in the suburbs overall. That was an interaction. While it appeared in a classification tree, it would not emerge spontaneously from a regression.

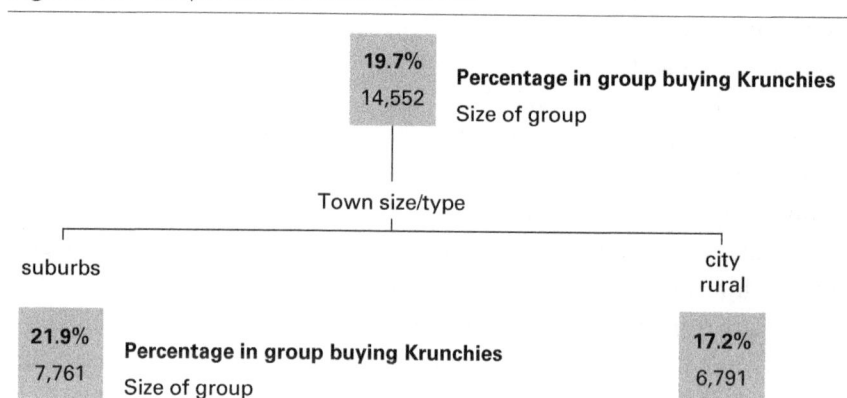

Figure 7.2 A split from a classification tree

```
                    19.7%     Percentage in group buying Krunchies
                    14,552    Size of group
                         |
                  Town size/type
        ┌────────────────┴────────────────┐
     suburbs                            city
                                        rural
     21.9%   Percentage in group buying Krunchies     17.2%
     7,761   Size of group                            6,791
```

Reviewing trees

Classification trees take a radically different approach from regressions, allowing them to tease out different patterns in the data. All tree methods handle categorical, ordinal and continuous variables equally well. They can break apart continuous or large categorical variables in the best way to lead to a strong prediction. This is called **optimal recoding**.

Tree methods even can handle missing values in data as another type of response, as we saw in Chapter 6. They do all this in addition to their unparalleled ability to show how variables interact.

As a reminder, **classification trees** work by **splitting** the sample into contrasting groups and resplitting those groups again and again, seeking to find small subgroups that differ as much as possible in levels of some target variable. (This target could be, for instance, preference ratings or levels of use.) We can see a single split in a tree in Figure 7.2. This comes from the first example in Chapter 6.

Classification trees do not generate equations. Rather, they produce a set of simple **if-then rules**. You might say, for instance:

> IF type of town = suburbs AND number of kids = five or more THEN likelihood of buying Kardboard Krunchies = 27.5 per cent

Now, on to networks

You may well be wondering what kind of predictive model could differ from both this type of splitting routine and from regressions. And so we come to **Bayes Nets**.

The first clue to the nature of this method comes in the term **network**. All the variables connect and all influence the target **and** each other. A network can be as simple as two variables that relate to each other, or it can contain thousands of variables, as in research into how genes interact, for instance.

Soon we will get to a small (but still mind-bending) example showing how remarkably these networks perform. First, though, we will pause to reassure you that they are very solid methods, with extensive use in airplane guidance systems, public safety, running nuclear power plants, cancer research, the genetic research we mentioned just above – and even national defence.

We have seen an example online showing how a Bayes Net is used to determine whether to launch a surface-to-air missile. We actually can say that these networks have been battle-tested. The social sciences and marketing sciences have been a little late to the party. Catching up now seems like the right thing to do.

What do these networks actually do?

These networks can solve a vast and even bewildering array of problems. Applications range from brainstorming to highly sophisticated modelling and forecasting systems. Here are some uses:

- automatically finding meaningful patterns among variables;
- getting accurate measures of variables' strengths;
- screening large numbers of variables quickly, for data mining;
- developing models of cause and effect (in the right circumstances);
- incorporating expert judgement into data-driven models;
- solving problems in **conditional probability**.

We will show several examples of networks in action following our small introductory model. One example will link survey responses to actual marketplace behaviour with high predictive accuracy. Another will support and extend a theoretical model. A third will show how accurate readings of variables' importances helped to guide decisions and strategy.

What makes a Bayesian network Bayesian?

Everything Bayesian refers back to the work of Reverend Thomas Bayes, who lived an apparently quiet life in Tunbridge Wells, England, in the 18th century. He published two books in the 1730s, but never anything he called 'Bayes Theorem'.

Bayes's formulation itself is simple. Any reasonably literate person can easily understand it in its entirety, once we step aside from the nearly blinding formula often used to represent it. Starting from Bayes's straightforward assertion and arriving at many of the types of analyses that bear his name likely would have caused the good reverend to take on a strange hue. This perhaps is the inevitable price of progress.

We can formulate Bayes's idea in a variety of ways. Let's start with this more practical formulation:

> We start with **prior** (existing) information or beliefs that we can then update or modify by using information that we get from data we observe. This updating gives us a new and more accurate **posterior** estimate. From this posterior estimate, we draw conclusions.

That's really all there is to it. However, it is usual to encounter this headache-inducing representation:

$$P(Bi|A) = P(A|Bi)P(Bi)/\Sigma i\{P(Bi)P(A|Bi)\}$$

Most of us likely would prefer the simple descriptive paragraph.

The ground rules for networks

Diagrams of variables are key. Bayesian networks are graphically based methods. As they are based on **graph theory** and on **probability theory**, they fall under the heading of **graphical analytical methods**. Grasping their workings fully requires both a diagram and the calculations that underlie it.

Bayes Nets in fact are called **directed acyclic diagrams** (DAGs) because all the variables connect, and all must point somewhere. None can point back to itself, or form a **cyclic** structure.

A Bayes Net may look familiar if you are one of the lucky few having experience with **structural equation models** (SEMs) or with **partial least squares** (PLS) path models. Variables are connected with arrows, as in those types of models. You can see pathways among the variables, and finally these lead to a target variable.

Arrows matter, but not as you might think

The arrows have a specific meaning in Bayes Net diagrams; however, this is not entirely intuitive. We can say that a variable at the start of an arrow **leads to** another variable, or **explains** another variable. In highly specific conditions we even can say that the starting variable **causes** the variable at the end. However, if we change the variable at the end of an arrow, the

Figure 7.3 Relationships in networks

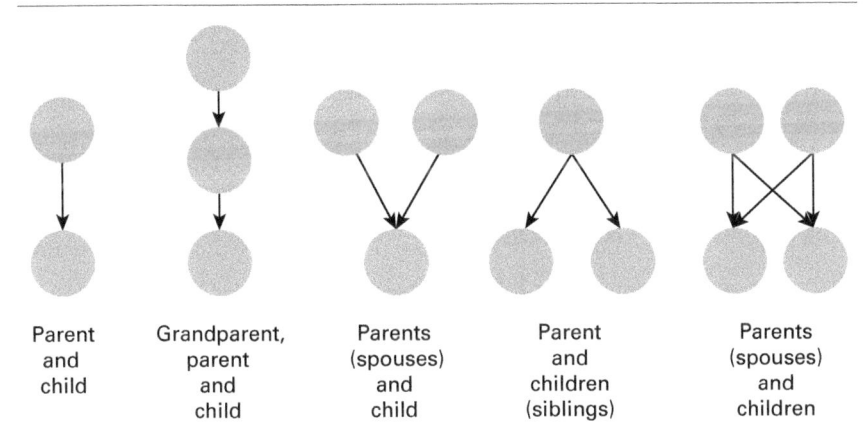

| Parent and child | Grandparent, parent and child | Parents (spouses) and child | Parent and children (siblings) | Parents (spouses) and children |

variable at the starting point will change as well. So **effects run in both directions** in a network.

Dealing with the data we typically encounter, connected variables in a network almost always have an equal chance of being the cause and being the effect. Strong influences go both ways. It is very rare indeed that we can prove one variable in fact **causes** another, dealing with the messiness inherent in behaviour, opinions and beliefs.

Terms and phrases: it's all in the family

There is, of course, some terminology to learn. Fortunately, this part largely goes down easily, being (for statistics) warm and fuzzy. Some of the relationships are (shown in Figure 7.3):

- The variable at the start of an arrow is called a **parent**.
- The variable at the end is called a **child** of the parent.
- Children can have several parents and parents can have several children.
- If there are two or more parents, they are called **spouses**.
- A parent of a parent is a **grandparent**, and so on.
- Variables are **dependent** only if they are directly connected:
  - Children and parents are dependent on each other.
  - Children are independent of grandparents and other variables further away.

Whether variables are **dependent** on each other becomes important when screening variables for inclusion in a model. One powerful screening technique involves including only those variables that are **dependent on the target variable** (its parents and children) and any other **co-parents** of the children. This quickly eliminates less important variables where there are many – as in data-mining applications. This set of variables has a name also: the **Markov blanket**.

> ### Everything is connected
>
> Changes move through the whole network. Understanding this is critical. In whichever way the arrows between variables point, **all variables in a network change when one changes**. Networks **convey information across all the connected variables**.

Network construction ranges from simple to complex

When we are attempting to understand relationships among variables, the way we fit the network together is of prime importance. Networks **can learn structures from the data**, building themselves automatically. This is something akin to a classification tree constructing itself on autopilot. However, networks are far less prone to taking on different shapes based on small changes in the data.

There are many ways that you can choose for a network to assemble itself. The simplest methods fit all the variables directly to the target variable. This is very much like a standard regression – all the predictor variables are put into the mix and each one connects only to the target variable, and not to another predictor.

At their most complex, networks have many branches and result from countless attempts to develop a best model. They test and retest how variables best fit together to predict the values in the target. These methods ensure that the network does not seize upon a connection that is good 'locally' (where a variable is being added) but not good for the overall network.

You also can put a network together yourself. If you do not violate any basic construction rules, it will return answers about variables' effects based on the way you have assembled everything. There are various intermediary strategies as well, such as letting the network form an initial shape and then modifying it based on your understanding of the questions you need to answer.

About conditional probability

We need to explain **conditional probability**. This idea appears in many discussions of Bayes Nets. A probability that is **conditional** is no more than what we just described: it is an estimate of probability that takes into account some information from an earlier estimate or item of information.

That is, we understand how one or more variables will change based on what is happening to another variable or variables. In the simplest terms, this means all changes in variables consider all values in all other variables.

The workings of conditional probability may be difficult to grasp, but let's try in the small example we have been promising. This is called the three-door let's-make-a-deal or Monty Hall problem. The answer is surprising!

Let's make a deal

Some may have seen the long-running television show *Let's Make a Deal*, and some may recall its inimitable former host, Monty Hall. Although he went off the air many years ago, shows with him can still be found by the curious, lurking in dark crannies of the web.

The show poses a challenge to contestants. They need to pick which of three doors has a prize behind it – with an added wrinkle. The contestant first picks whichever of the doors feels right to her/him. The host **never** opens that door to reveal whether it has the prize, though. Rather, he opens another door that does **not** have the prize behind it. Then he asks, 'Will you stay with your door or will you switch to the other unopened door?'

Now we ask you to consider this: if you were advising the contestant, would you tell her/him to switch or to stay? Alternatively, do you think it makes any difference? Nearly everyone says there should be no difference. And nearly everyone is **wrong**.

In fact, this very problem and its solution appeared in a magazine column by Marilyn vos Savant, billed as the world's smartest person. Whether Ms Savant is in fact smartest, she got this answer right. **You are better off switching, by a factor of 2 to 1.**

This correct answer seems somehow impossible to nearly everyone. Some 10,000 people wrote to Ms Savant, saying she was mistaken. About 1,000 of them had PhD degrees. Let's now vindicate her.

Solving the problem is simple using a Bayes Net

You can struggle with standard statistics to get the right answer. You can, for instance, find code on the web for using standard statistics to run 10,000 simulations to address this question. Your answer will be nearly correct. A basic Bayes Net taking about three minutes to construct can solve this problem exactly.

Recall that we can make a network ourselves by linking variables. Here, we will form a tiny network by joining three events: the door you choose, the door that is opened and the winning door.

The simplest representation of a Bayes Net looks like connected shapes. This is what appears in Figure 7.4. We know that the winning door can be any of the three, and the door you choose can be any of the three. However, the door that the sneaky game-show host opens depends on **both** the door you have chosen and the winning door.

You can see this diagrammed in Figure 7.4. There, an arrow goes from **the door you choose** to **the door opened**. Another arrow goes from **the winning door** to **the door opened**. The direction of those arrows matters this time, because **the door opened** depends on, or is **conditional** upon, the other two choices.

Each of these three spots is called a **node**. We gain explanatory power by seeing what is inside them. Each **node** actually holds a table corresponding to what is happening with the three doors.

First we set up the node showing the odds of your opening each door. This is one-third for each door. Then we set up the node showing odds of each door winning. That is also one-third apiece. Here at last we encounter something that is simplicity itself, as we can see in Figure 7.5.

Now we set up the last and most complicated of the nodes. Once we have made the first two nodes and connected them to the third, the table describing this node automatically appears in the software, ready to fill. As we mentioned, in Bayes Nets, seeing what you are doing is key.

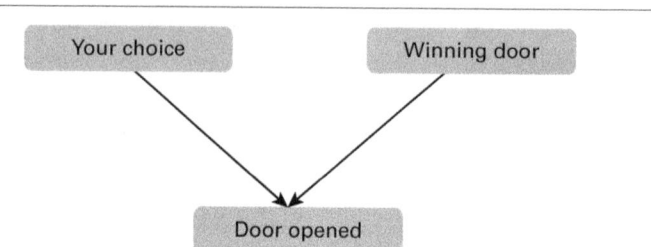

Figure 7.4 The network for the three-door problem

Figure 7.5 Inside the first two nodes of the network

Node: Your_Choice		
Chance ▼	% Probability ▼	
Door 1	**Door 2**	**Door 3**
33.333	33.333	33.333

Node: Winning_door		
Chance ▼	% Probability ▼	
Door 1	**Door 2**	**Door 3**
33.333	33.333	33.334

Figure 7.6 Part of the third node – when you choose Door 1

	Node Selection: **Door opened** ▼	Rename		
Your choice	Winning door	Open 1	Open 2	Open 3
	Door 1	0.000	50.000	50.000
Door 1	Door 2	0.000	0.000	100.000
	Door 3	0.000	100.000	0.000

A   D

B
C

Because this table is more complicated, we will take it in parts, starting in Figure 7.6. This shows what happens if you choose Door 1. Above letter **A**, you see that Door 1 NEVER gets opened if you pick it – it doesn't matter which door is the winner. This is a basic rule of the game.

If you pick Door 1 and it is the winner, you can see (on the first row of the table in Figure 7.6) that the chances of opening Door 2 or Door 3 are 50 per cent each. That row is next to letter **B**.

So far so good. Now, if you choose Door 1 and the winning door is 2, the host **must** open Door 3 or reveal the prize. So here the odds for the other doors are not the same at all – in fact, they are zero versus 100 per cent. You can see this on the row near letter **C**.

Finally, very much the same condition holds if you chose Door 1 and the winner is 3. The host **must** open Door 2. The probability that he or she will do so is 100 per cent. We see this above letter **D**.

Once we have filled in the correct values for Door 1, it becomes relatively simple to fill in the correct values for Door 2 and Door 3. The entire table for the third node appears in Figure 7.7. We have added some heavily outlined boxes to separate the sections of the table corresponding to each door you might have chosen. Otherwise, all we did was fill in the

Figure 7.7 All of the third node

Your choice	Winning door	Open 1	Open 2	Open 3
Door 1	Door 1	0.000	50.000	50.000
Door 1	Door 2	0.000	0.000	100.000
Door 1	Door 3	0.000	100.000	0.000
Door 2	Door 1	0.000	0.000	100.000
Door 2	Door 2	50.000	0.000	50.000
Door 2	Door 3	100.000	0.000	0.000
Door 3	Door 1	0.000	100.000	0.000
Door 3	Door 2	100.000	0.000	0.000
Door 3	Door 3	50.000	50.000	0.000

Node Selection: Door opened ▼   Rename

NOTE Outlines are added here for clarity of reading

correct numbers. Again, the network created the blank table itself once we connected the three nodes together.

Now for the surprising answer

Maybe this is a good time to take a deep breath. As you can see in Figure 7.8, **you should switch doors.**

We have included four possible outcomes, starting with you choosing either Door 1 or Door 2. These results should lead all (or nearly all) readers to believe that precisely the same thing will happen if you start by choosing Door 3.

We made the network run each time by simply clicking twice. First we clicked on **the door you chose**, which went to 100 per cent. Then we clicked on **the door the host opened**, which also went to 100 per cent.

Looking under letter **A**, we see what happens if you start by choosing Door 1 and the host opens Door 2. The odds appear automatically in the **winning door** node. The chances of the prize being behind your door are actually 33.3 per cent. For the other door, Door 3, the odds are 66.7 per cent.

Under letter **B**, we see what happens if you start with Door 1 and the host opens Door 3. The odds for Door 2 then are 66.7 per cent and for your door 33.3 per cent.

Just to confirm that this is not a fluke related solely to Door 1, we show what would happen if you started with Door 2. Over letter **C**, you see the

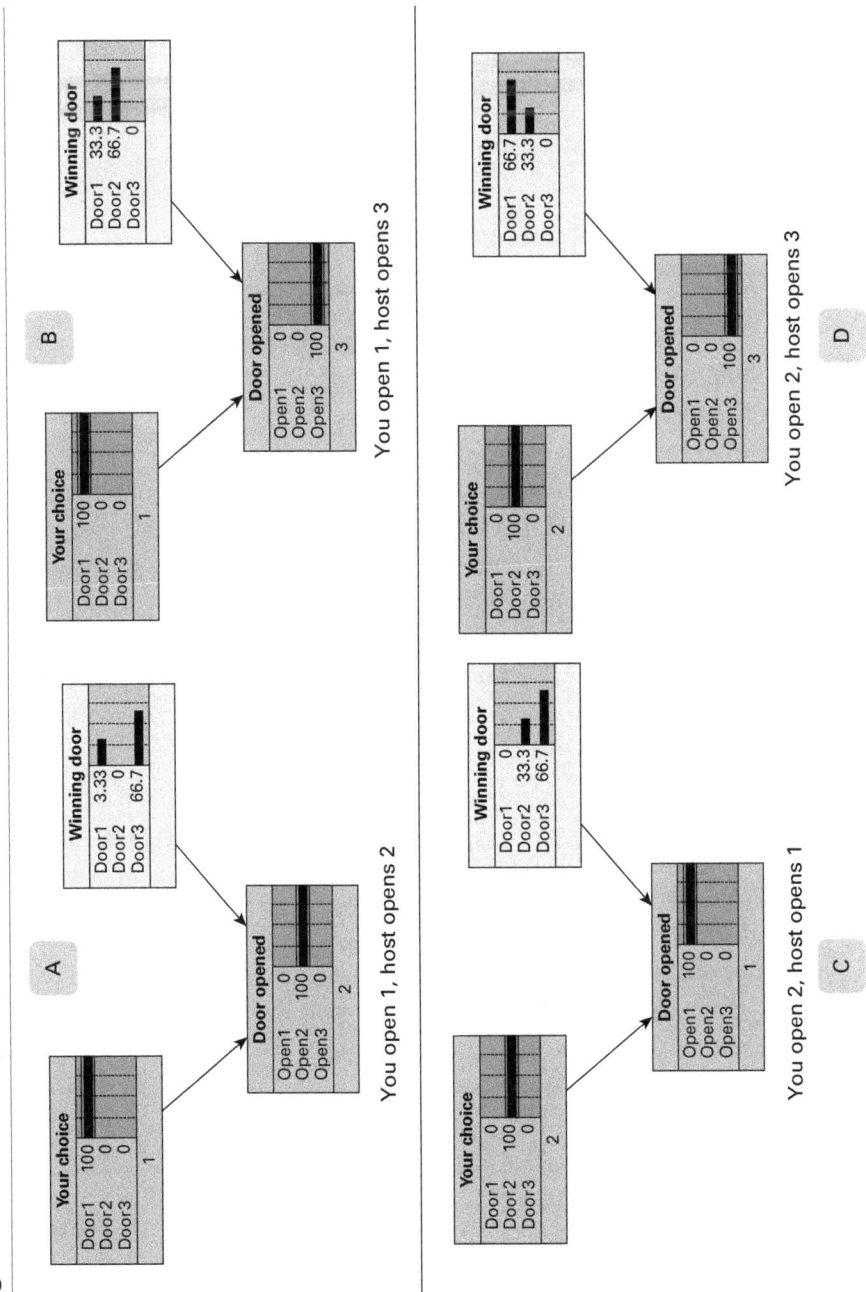

Figure 7.8 How likely the prize is to hide behind each door

result if the host follows by opening Door 1. Odds for the other door are again 66.7 per cent. And finally, if the host opens Door 3, the odds for the door you did not pick are again 66.7 per cent.

Again, this also underlines a key property of networks. If you change a variable, any variable connected to it changes. We see that **door opened** has an arrow pointing to it from **winning door**. Yet when we change **door opened**, the variable leading to it also changes.

Why is the correct answer so different from what we expect?

This happens because what the host does actually **depends on**, or is conditional upon, your choice and the winning door. We do not think in terms of this kind of **conditional probability**.

Here we come upon an issue with Bayesian networks. We have just neatly and simply unravelled a problem that likely eluded most of us. And yet, the answer seems strange until it is explained – and perhaps even afterwards.

As an expert on this subject (Eliezer Yudkowsky) points out, solving problems of this type poses difficulties for novice students and trained professionals alike. We have an approach that is truly powerful and that easily reaches answers we cannot guess intuitively. This method learns patterns in the data that we cannot see or guess. With that in mind, let's discuss in more detail how Bayes Nets work.

More about networks compared with regressions

Bayes Nets look at the whole pattern of scores or responses in the variables they analyse. For instance, comparing two variables that we will call **A** and **N**, this method creates a chart, or matrix, that shows how the scores relate. We can see this in Figure 7.9. In this chart, each box represents how often scores coincide. At the top right, for instance, we see that 33 people gave a score of 10 on variable A and 10 on variable N, that 44 gave a score of 9 on variable A and 10 on variable N, and so on. The darkened boxes are where the scores on the two variables align most often.

Bayes Nets will pick up the basically S-shaped relationship that you can see in those highlighted boxes in Figure 7.9. Regression, on the other hand, seeks how well the relationship between the two variables falls into a straight line, which we have superimposed. You can see that this is not accurate. For instance, it does not fit a higher score on variable A than 8 out of 10.

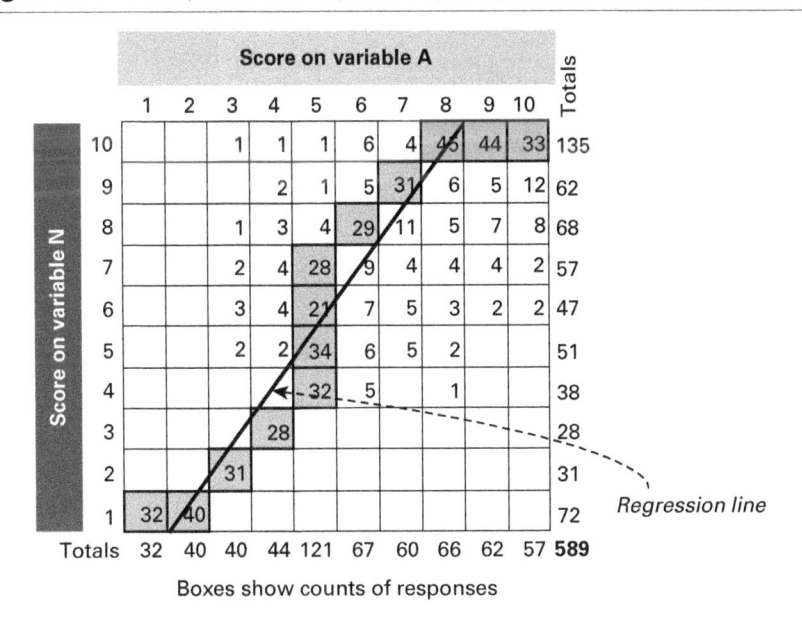

Figure 7.9 S-shaped relationship found by a Bayes Net, but not a regression

	Score on variable A										Totals
Score on variable N	1	2	3	4	5	6	7	8	9	10	
10			1	1	1	6	4	45	44	33	135
9				2	1	5	31	6	5	12	62
8			1	3	4	29	11	5	7	8	68
7			2	4	28	9	4	4	4	2	57
6			3	4	21	7	5	3	2	2	47
5			2	2	34	6	5	2			51
4				32	5		1				38
3			28							28	28
2		31								31	31
1	32	40								72	72
Totals	32	40	40	44	121	67	60	66	62	57	**589**

Regression line

Boxes show counts of responses

Networks take a more comprehensive view

The straight line is key, as regressions rely on **correlations**. A correlation is a **single number** describing how well pairs of variables conform to a straight line. As a reminder, correlation can range from 1, where the two variables change together in a perfect straight-line pattern, down to –1, where the two variables have a perfect inverse relationship (one rises exactly as the other falls in value).

Correlations provide a less detailed understanding of how variables relate than the whole pattern captured by Bayes Nets. And many times the Bayes Net will also provide a more accurate model.

Bayes Nets versus classification trees

Classification trees take a step towards looking at the whole distributions of variables. But they do this in a different and more restricted way than Bayes Nets. Classification trees seek to split apart the scores in the target variable based on scores in the predictors. One way to express this is that classification trees look for **situational relationships,** as in saying, 'when variable N is like this, THEN variable A is like that'.

The **splitting** done by classification trees leads to relatively few variables getting chosen as predictors. As we discussed in Chapter 6, the tree forms subgroups that become smaller at each step. Finally, the groups become too small to split further. This compactness has advantages and disadvantages. Variables that you might want to consider could get left out of the model.

Differences in dynamic predictions: networks take the more realistic view

We have said this before, but it is worth underlining: in networks, when one variable changes, all the other variables change as well. Any given variable has the most influence on variables with which it is closely connected. Still, effects from changes travel through the network like ripples going across a pond. Another, more formal, way to say this is that **information propagates across the network**.

The way networks account for changes differs strongly from the assumptions of regression-based models. Measuring any variable's effect in a regression assumes that **all other variables remain the same**. This is a particularly unrealistic view when dealing with data such as opinions, beliefs or purchasing patterns, as these all tend to be highly interrelated.

Indeed, some authorities on regression (for instance Leland Wilkinson), bemoan the tendency of regression-based models to fail in real-world applications, in particular setting policy. In the real world, when we change one factor, many other factors change along with it – leading to the downfall of some precise-looking forecasts that regression delivers.

> **Realism in Bayes Nets**
>
> **Bayes Nets** gain in realism by taking into account how every variable must change if any one changes. This sometimes is referred to as **information propagating through a network**. Networks also take into account the entire patterns or distributions of all variables. This is much more realistic than regression. There, effects from changing one variable assume all other variables remain the same. And in regression all relationships are based on correlations, a one-measure summary of how well variables fit a straight line. Classification trees see different patterns, but all relationships are restricted to certain values of each variable, as in 'when variable N is like this, THEN variable A is like that'. Bayes Nets look at the entire pattern in each variable.

Drivers, causes and what works

Bayes Nets ultimately lead us to rethink what happens when we model the effects of variables. Many of us have become accustomed to talking about the independent variables as 'predicting' or 'driving' the independent. It seems doubtful that this preferred terminology will ever change. Still, in a regression, the independent or predictor variables actually **explain** some part of the target variable's behaviour.

This may seem puzzling (this is becoming a refrain), but each independent variable accounts for (or explains) some of the **variance** or **pattern** in the dependent variable. You can see this clearly when you think again about a regression equation.

In the equation, you multiply the score in each variable by some amount, add up everything (and maybe add some unchanging number) – and you have the predicted score for the target variable. Each predictor variable actually is **a part of the target's score**.

Nonetheless, the phrase **driver analysis** likely is with us for the long term. This is common but not learned usage. 'Driver analysis' apparently is not covered in texts on statistics. With Bayes Nets, you may encounter more accurate terminology for what happens to a target variable when you change another variable. This is **sensitivity of the target to changes in another variable**. If you see that, and it seems confusing, just think of **drivers**.

Our first example: Bayes Nets linking survey questions and behaviour

We will start with a relatively simple example of Bayes Nets showing a predictive relationship between responses to survey questions and behaviour. In this example, Bayes Nets address an important set of questions:

- what the relative effects are of several variables on the dependent variable;
- how strongly changing each variable affects the dependent;
- the ways these variables relate to each other and to the dependent.

The predictor variables were heavily weeded in this example. As mentioned, Bayes Nets can cut out variables having little direct relationship to the target variable. They can, for instance, restrict the predictors to those in the **Markov blanket** that we mentioned earlier. (Mr Markov and his blanket could be the subject of another whole discussion, but we will have to skip this here.)

Now on to the actual network

This example comes from a survey done among professionals using an information technology (or IT) product. It involved a very long questionnaire. We will leap past the variable screening phase, to the point where we have just seven key variables. Figure 7.10 shows how these variables relate to each other and to the target variable, which is **the percentage of services each corporate customer signed up to use again.**

Before we describe how the variables relate to each other, please recall that this network assembled itself. That is, the Bayes Net routine sought out the strongest patterns of relationships in the data, then created a diagram of how the variables relate. This arrangement definitely passes the test of common sense.

Figure 7.10 A simple network linking share and ratings

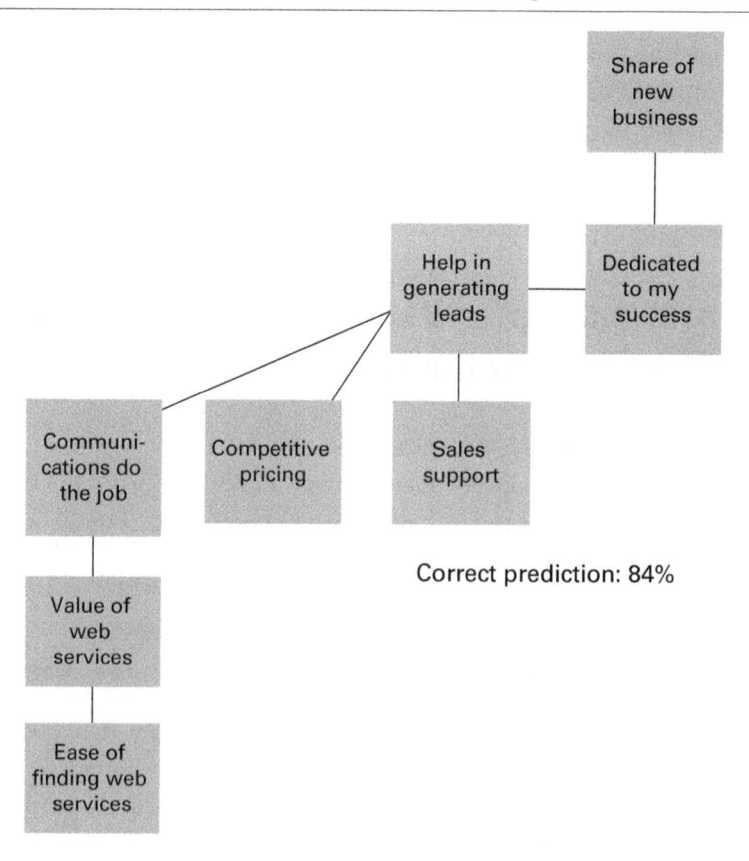

Correct prediction: 84%

Starting at the top in Figure 7.10, you can see that all predictor variables other than **gives me a competitive advantage** ultimately converge on that one. This means that all the other variables **explain** something about the way in which this company is seen as giving such an advantage.

This variable is directly explained by **help in generating leads**. Three variables link directly to this latter variable. These are ratings for **sales support, pricing** and **effective communications**.

Additionally, **value of web services** supports **effective communications**. In turn, **value of web services** is supported by **ease of finding web services**.

The network configuration, as a reminder, also will determine the importances of the variables and sensitivity of the dependent variable to changes in the independents. **Correct prediction levels**, which we discuss soon, are high. So we can have confidence that we have an accurate picture. The sensible-seeming arrangement of the network gives us more assurance that effects are measured accurately.

Figure 7.11 shows the **absolute** and **indexed** sizes of effects from changing each predictor variable. This **absolute effects** chart shows, for instance, that changing **gives me a competitive advantage** has 45 per cent of the effect possible if we could somehow directly change the target variable.

These absolute effects can be hard to compare, so the other chart in Figure 7.11 shows them **indexed**. The average index is set to 100. This chart shows, for instance, that **gives me a competitive advantage** has 1.94 times the effect of each variable on average (seen in its index of 194).

The unindexed values are similar to the **Beta values** or **coefficients** from a regression. However, networks develop a fuller understanding of effects. Changes in a predictor variable actually can have varying levels of impact for different values of the target variable. We could make another chart allowing us to see this.

While we will skip this second chart in this short example, it would indeed show that effects on the target variable vary, depending on the values of the predictor variable and the target variable. That is, over some ranges of the values of each, the target variable changes more. This is another level of information beyond what we can see in a simple regression coefficient.

There is still more that we can learn. Inside the more comprehensive programs creating Bayes Nets, the network diagram itself is dynamic. We can change a variable and observe how every other variable changes as a result. Some programs also allow you to make stand-alone simulator programs. These are similar to the simulators for discrete choice modelling and conjoint analysis discussed in Chapters 4 and 5.

Figure 7.11 Effects relative to the target and indexed versus the average

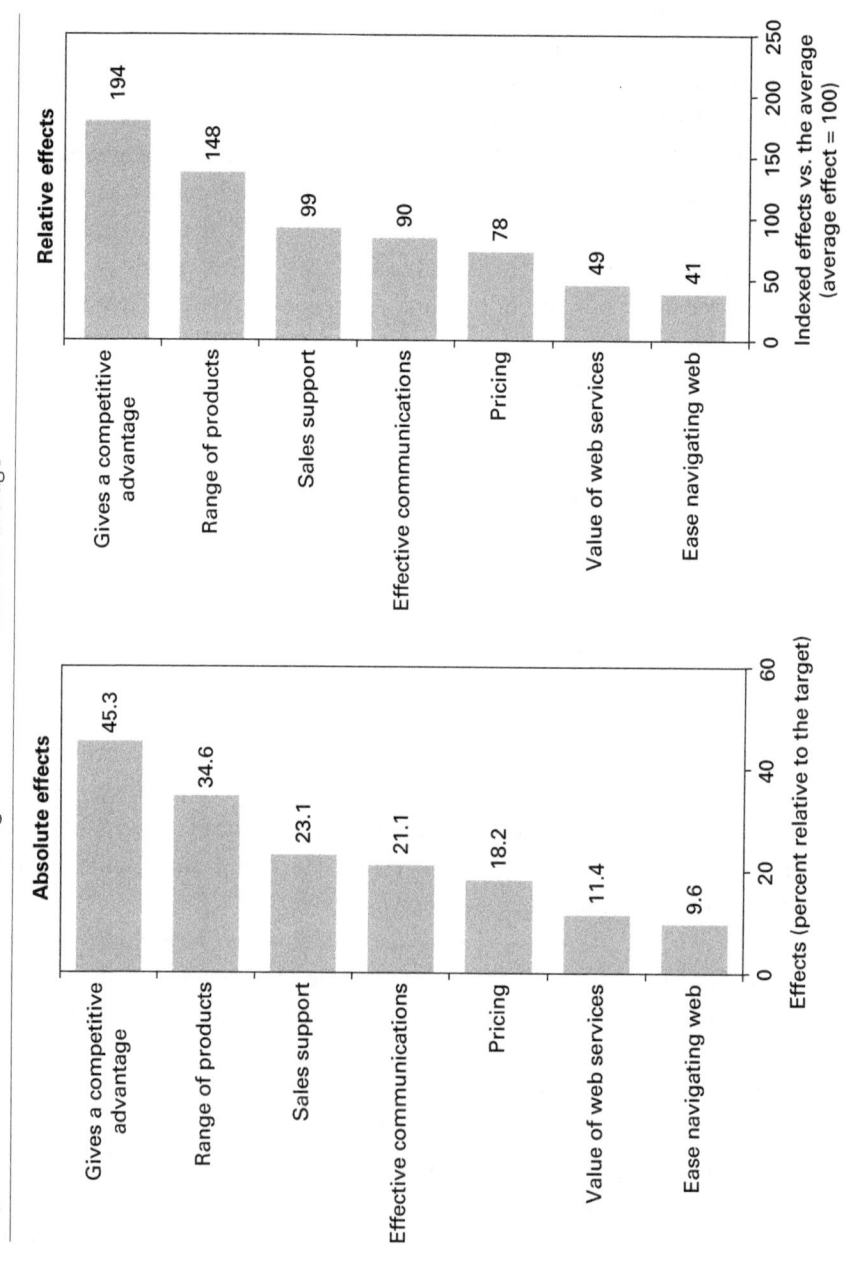

Information moving across the network

Variables that are closely connected (such as parent nodes and children nodes) have strong influences on each other. The further the variables are from each other in the diagram, the less impact they tend to have on each other. However, all changes propagate through the whole network.

As a reminder, this whole-network understanding of the data makes any prediction of real-world effects much more realistic than the estimates from a regression-based model. In regressions, we must assume that all other variables remain the same if we change any one variable.

How the model performed

Correct prediction levels were very strong indeed for fitting questionnaire questions to behaviour. The level of correct prediction for the target variable (percentage of business signed for) was 84 per cent. This was using a stringent form of **testing** or **validation** of results, called **cross-folded validation** (more on **validation** follows). Without any validation, predictions were a stellar 93 per cent correct.

Those of us who have tried to fit questionnaire questions to actual behaviour know that this almost invariably has poor results when using regression-based models. Networks do not always do as well as this one. Still, they have usually outperformed regression-based models on overall measures of model fit with a behavioural target variable, such as actual use levels or purchases.

In this case, the best regression-based model emerged from a very complex variant of regression called a **partial least squares** (PLS) path model. This created intermediary variables that grouped items, and even so turned in a paltry 11 per cent correct prediction of share.

What precisely is validation?

We discussed **validation** in Chapter 2, but a refresher could be useful. Validation is not a new idea, but the notion that you should use it regularly has gained support as data sets have become larger and models have grown more complex.

With validation, you build the model on part of the data, **holding aside** the rest of it. You then try out the model on the portion of the data that you held aside. When you try the model on this **hold-out sample**, predictive accuracy usually comes in at a lower level than when you simply look at the how the model performed where it was made.

Even the best predictive modelling technique will fit some random bumps and fluctuations that are found only in the data set on which a model was built. Trying out the model elsewhere, even on another part of the same data that you set aside, gives you some safeguards against **overfitting**. Overfitting builds a model using seeming patterns in your data that you will not find in the outside world.

> **Model validation**
>
> This is holding aside some of the data when you build a predictive model, then trying out the model on that portion of the data. This aims to give you a better reading of how well the model will perform in the outside world, when it is actually applied. It helps avoid **overfitting** your predictive model to features that are peculiar to just your data set.

Why is it good to validate? As mentioned in Chapter 2, larger data sets often lead to many effects seeming to be meaningful, simply because you have so much data. Statistical tests start to break down, because with enough data everything seems significant.

When you have a massive data set, it is entirely feasible to put some of it to one side and have ample amounts left for building a complex model. So validation often is a prudent step in assessing how well predictive models actually will perform.

Bayes Nets confirm a theoretical model, mostly

Many theoretical models postulate that a person must process information in certain ways, or that certain psychological changes must take place, before that person takes action. We know now that action can arise without much thought – and many more cynical observers always suspected as much.

However, models postulating complex pathways to behaviour still have enormous influence. They could be called stepwise, or more formally **hierarchical**. We can find such models going back at least to the turn of the 19th century. The so-called **AIDA** model, by the gratifyingly named E St Elmo Lewis, dates back to 1898. **AIDA** stands for Attention, Interest, Desire, Action.

Figure 7.12 A classic hierarchical model

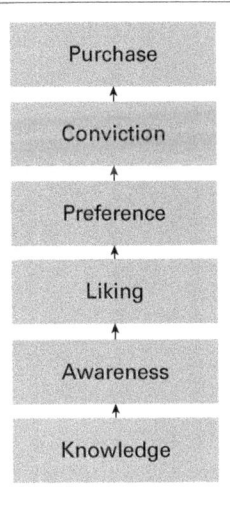

```
Purchase
   ↑
Conviction
   ↑
Preference
   ↑
 Liking
   ↑
Awareness
   ↑
Knowledge
```

Perhaps the most influential of these hierarchies appeared in 1961, posited in a brief article by Lavidge and Steiner, called 'A model for predictive measurements of advertising effectiveness'. They postulated six stages, building from awareness to purchase. The idea was that you needed to pass through and complete one stage to move to the next – something like climbing the rungs of a ladder. Their model appears in Figure 7.12.

Once you are alerted to the existence of hierarchical models, you will notice them in many places. The Lavidge and Steiner model itself appears in many slightly altered forms, some without attribution. Many of the measurement strategies that organizations routinely follow, such as keeping track of how many are aware of their products, reflect belief in a hierarchical model.

These models also have had great importance due to analytical limitations. For years, it was almost impossible to link behaviours with questions about awareness, liking or preference. This problem arose because regression models expect linear relationships, and many times the relationship between share or sales and ratings is not linear. We saw this in the loyalty score example in Chapter 6.

Going the next step with Bayes Nets

The model in Figure 7.13 is based on a study of commercial brokers done by a firm that provided services to them. The survey asked many questions about how well the firm performed, and how their customers perceived them and felt about them. They also asked for self-reported estimates of the

Figure 7.13 Bayes Nets discover a hierarchy

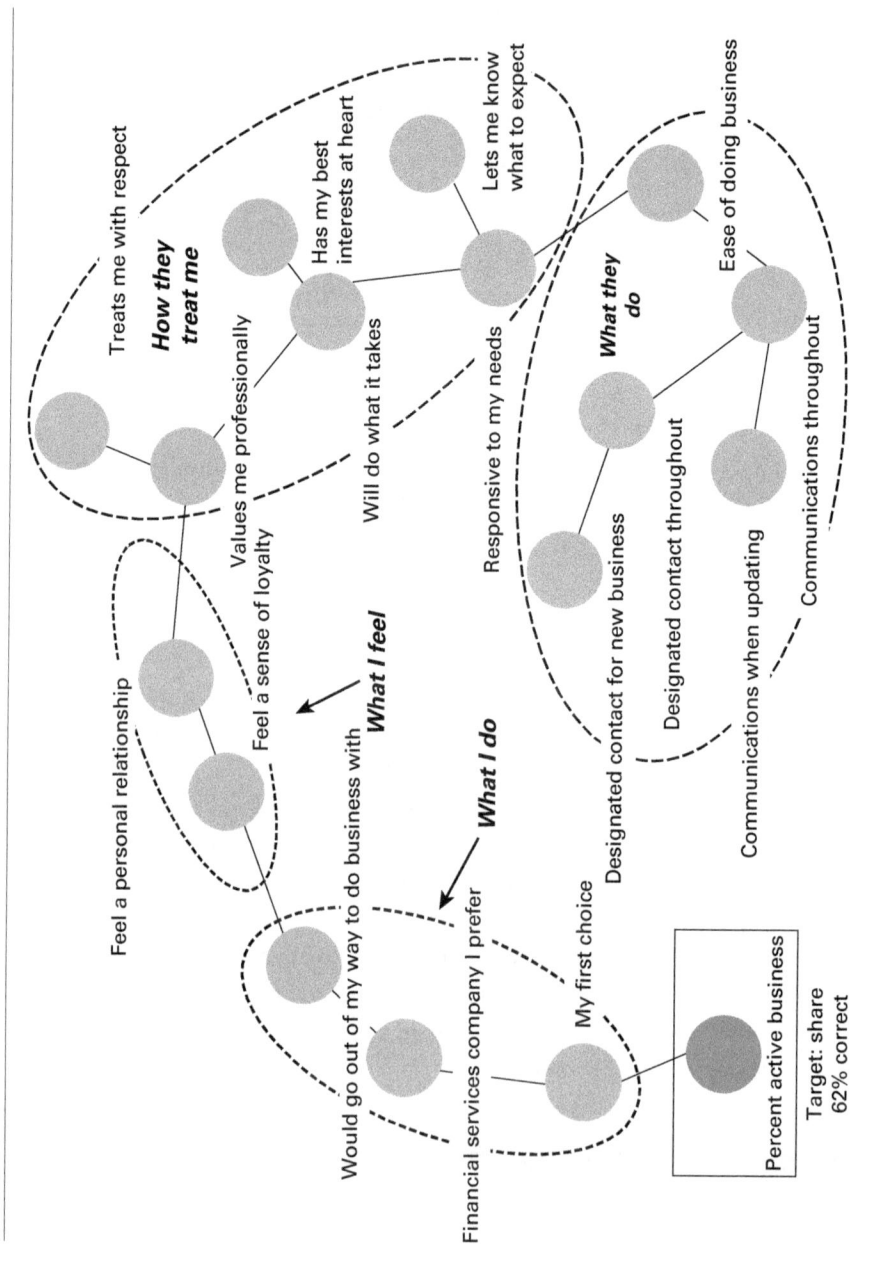

study sponsor's share of business. (This diagram is part of a much larger model with many other variables.)

Figure 7.13 shows how Bayes Nets extended and refined a model that was tried first with a complex form of regression. This specific type of regression is called a **partial least squares** (PLS) path model.

PLS path models group similar variables together, and those grouped variables then influence the dependent variable, and sometimes each other. These grouped variables (the so-called **latent variables**) actually are created in the analysis, then added to the ones that were directly measured.

You need to figure out what these latent variables represent and name them. Those of you who are familiar with factor analysis will recognize these latent variables as being something like the factors created by that method.

PLS path models overcome one salient problem of regular regressions, namely dealing with variables that are highly correlated. Regular regression cannot adequately handle highly correlated variables. Some of them will get squeezed out of the model, and readings of the strengths of the others typically get distorted.

The underlying theory being explored

The PLS model was based on a theoretical hierarchical model. It was built by hand, slowly and painstakingly. This model postulated that the client's actions were part of **satisfaction**, while the customer's feelings were part of **relationship**. Together, these were supposed to predict **loyalty**, which in turn would predict **share**.

Loyalty was conceived as a weighted average of the variables in the two groups labelled in Figure 7.13 as 'what I feel' and 'what I do'. The original model finally tried to link **loyalty** to **share**. While that model did well predicting what went into its view of loyalty, it predicted share with only 18 per cent accuracy.

This was a clearly unacceptable level, but it was the best that could be managed. Recall that the PLS path model was constructed in many steps and with many stops and starts. Elements were added and subtracted to theorized groups. Combinations that proved to be impossible had to be scrapped and tried again, and again.

Letting the data speak with a Bayes Net

Because of the poor PLS path model results, a Bayes Net was tried as an alternative. It was allowed to learn patterns in the data, and the result appears in Figure 7.13. The network shows a clear hierarchy. However, this differs markedly from two chains of variables, one related to **satisfaction** and one related to **relationship**.

The Bayes Net determined patterns in the data where effects ran in a different sequence. This is the hierarchy that appeared, going from actions to the target variable (share):

What they do (objectively) → How they treat me → How I feel → What I do → Share

The Bayes Net reached 62 per cent correct prediction, with cross-validation. The model seems entirely sensible. It supports parts of the postulated model. The various feelings proposed to make up **loyalty** do fall together, and they lead directly to share. The other variables support or explain this **loyalty** group.

However, the reality otherwise differs from the initial theory. **Actions** do not form a group working separately from **relationship** to influence **loyalty**, and then **share**. Rather, how **actions** are viewed by customers informs or explains their **feelings**, which in turn explains how **they act**, which in explains **share**. This is what the diagram shows. The strong prediction of share by this model argues that this is plausible.

What next?

Variables' importances also come from this analysis. While we will skip the entire chart here, several types of specific actions emerged as important in affecting feelings and shares. Among these were several that appeared in Figure 7.13 and a few we did not have room to show. These included:

- designated contact throughout;
- communications when updating;
- designated contact for new business;
- voice menu system;
- dedicated person for problem resolution.

Knowing the importance of these items could possibly provide enough information to guide decisions. Ultimately, the client decided to test the specific ways that these areas could be improved using the conjoint-based service optimization that we discussed in Chapter 5.

Here we see both the strength and the weakness of this analytical method when used with survey-based rating questions. The method is powerful enough to give a precise relationship between changes in ratings and changes in share. However, the limitations of standard survey ratings make it difficult to move from knowing **which changes** must be made to knowing precisely **how changes** must be made.

What is important to buyers of children's apparel

A major manufacturer of children's apparel ran large semi-annual surveys in which they measured reactions to their products and competitors' offerings. They asked numerous questions related to awareness, shopping, use patterns, and ratings of the products in many areas, such as value for money and appropriateness for the child. They also asked shoppers to estimate what percentage of their spending went to each of many brands.

They had many thousands of answers and wanted to learn more about what specifically drove levels of purchasing. After exploring a few alternative methods without much success, including regression-based models and classification trees, they tried Bayes Nets. The results were highly informative.

The specifics of the analysis

Children's apparel is actually not a single market. Based on the age of the child, up to 13, expectations and needs vary sharply. This manufacturer saw children as falling into these age groups:

- infants (age up to two);
- toddlers (age 2–4);
- early school age (age 4–8);
- pre-teens (age 8–13).

Parents with children in each age cohort were analysed separately. There were some 9,000 cases in total, or about 2,250 in each age group. In all, some 46 variables were measured and analysed. You can see the importances of these as determined by Bayes Nets, disguised in Figure 7.14. (This disguising is a necessary evil using real data.)

Strong differences emerged, most markedly in the importance of the variable **a brand I trust**. This has exceptionally low importance for parents of infants. This perhaps should be expected, as for many parents at that time all brands are new.

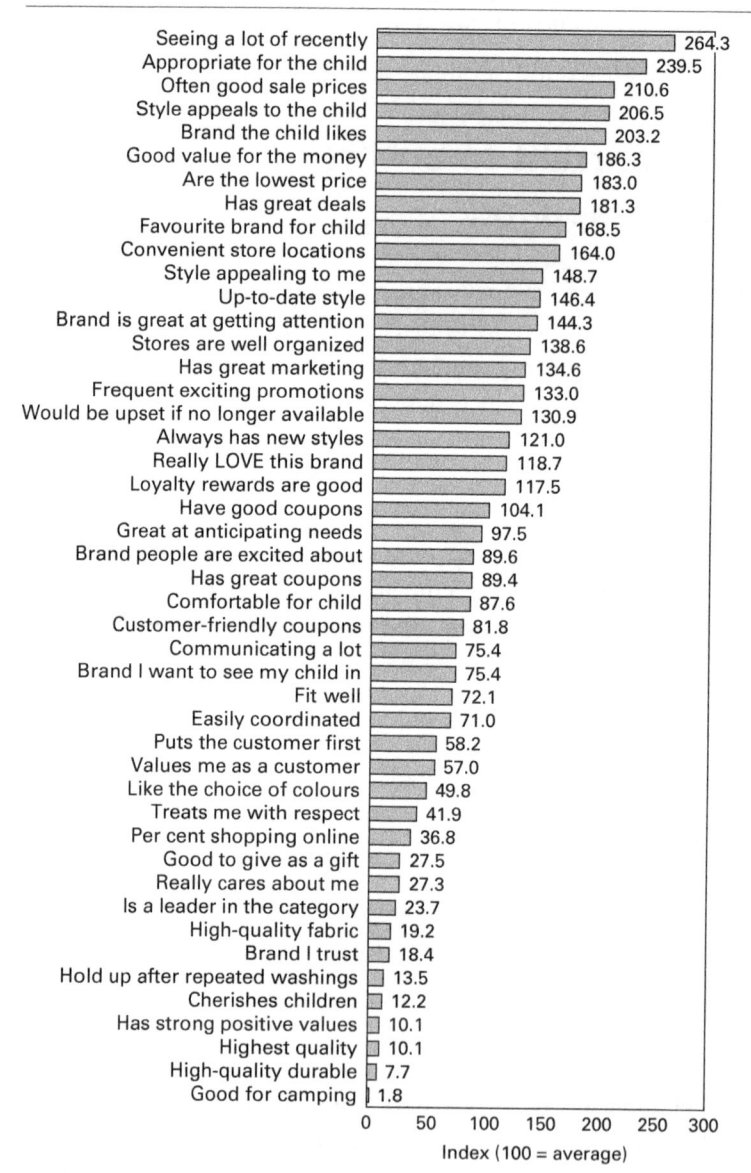

Artificial Intelligence Marketing and Predicting Consumer Choice

Figure 7.14 Importances for 46 (disguised) attributes

Attribute	Index (100 = average)
Seeing a lot of recently	264.3
Appropriate for the child	239.5
Often good sale prices	210.6
Style appeals to the child	206.5
Brand the child likes	203.2
Good value for the money	186.3
Are the lowest price	183.0
Has great deals	181.3
Favourite brand for child	168.5
Convenient store locations	164.0
Style appealing to me	148.7
Up-to-date style	146.4
Brand is great at getting attention	144.3
Stores are well organized	138.6
Has great marketing	134.6
Frequent exciting promotions	133.0
Would be upset if no longer available	130.9
Always has new styles	121.0
Really LOVE this brand	118.7
Loyalty rewards are good	117.5
Have good coupons	104.1
Great at anticipating needs	97.5
Brand people are excited about	89.6
Has great coupons	89.4
Comfortable for child	87.6
Customer-friendly coupons	81.8
Communicating a lot	75.4
Brand I want to see my child in	75.4
Fit well	72.1
Easily coordinated	71.0
Puts the customer first	58.2
Values me as a customer	57.0
Like the choice of colours	49.8
Treats me with respect	41.9
Per cent shopping online	36.8
Good to give as a gift	27.5
Really cares about me	27.3
Is a leader in the category	23.7
High-quality fabric	19.2
Brand I trust	18.4
Hold up after repeated washings	13.5
Cherishes children	12.2
Has strong positive values	10.1
Highest quality	10.1
High-quality durable	7.7
Good for camping	1.8

Importance rose to about average among the next age cohort, the toddlers, then skyrocketed for children aged 4–8. For that group, it actually is one of the three most important attributes out of the entire long list.

However, for the pre-teens, the importance of **brand I trust** plummeted to a very low level, as low as for infants. This posed a seeming mystery, but soon patterns in other ratings explained what had happened.

Remarkable Predictive Models with Bayes Nets 225

Figure 7.15 shows the pattern in ratings for **brand I trust**. The other chart in this figure offers an explanation of what happened. Three related concerns become highly important among parents of pre-teens: **a style appealing to me, a brand or style the child likes**, and **clothing appropriate for a child this age**.

We see here a sad story of parent–child relationships. Among families with pre-teens, everything else gets subsumed by an argument over the question of, 'You are thinking of going out wearing WHAT?'

Here is a critical learning for creating messages about the benefits of this manufacturer's fine products. By all means, for parents of early-school

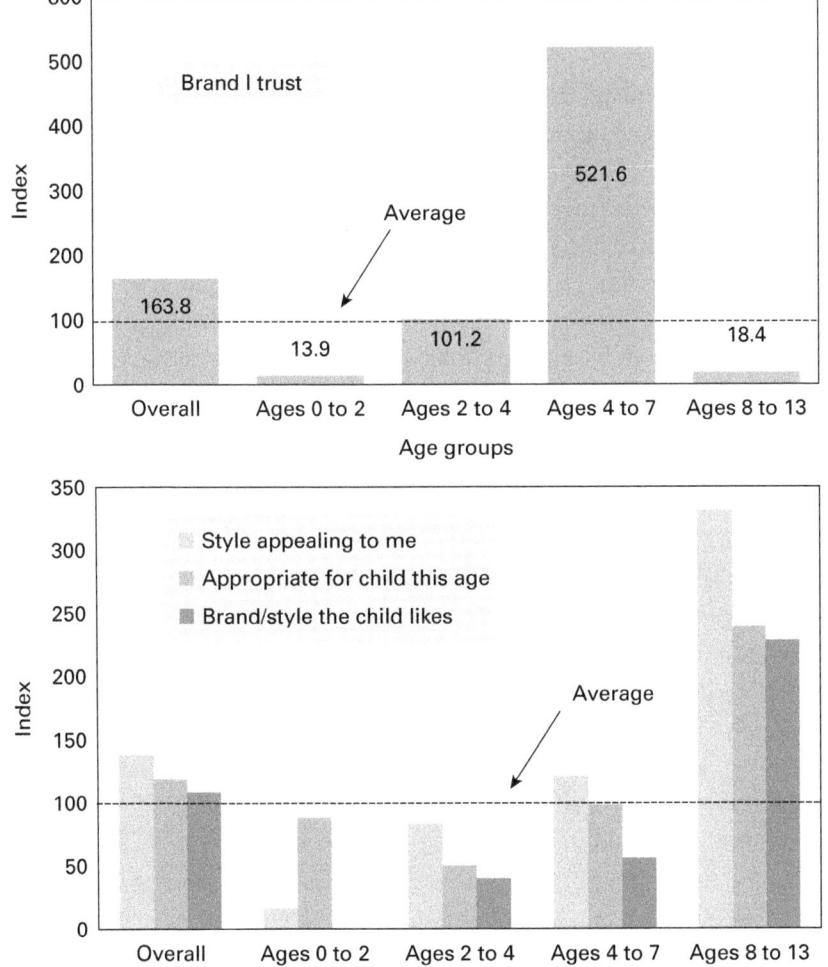

Figure 7.15 Importance of trust and fashion by age of child

children, stress how this is a brand that families can trust. For pre-teens, stress how parents will find the clothing acceptable (all right, not heart-stopping) and their children will not simply say, 'I can't even…' (this last locution was current for 'no way' when the book went to press, but by the time you read this, who knows?).

The manufacturer did this analysis after a segmentation study, and so was particularly interested in what was important in affecting share of wallet for their target segment, called **Savvy Sylvia**. This company's management really believed in the validity of the segments found, and the target segment was a loadstone for their efforts. For the hard-working analyst involved, it was strange but gratifying to hear the whole company asking 'What would Sylvia do?'

Running your own Bayes Nets

Software unfortunately is a confusing terrain, even more so than for classification trees. Some programs are free, although they follow the general rule that free software is harder to use and more limited in what it can do than programs you buy. You can spend a great, great amount on some Bayesian Network software. But you may not have to, because there are some very powerful choices among the more reasonably priced options.

As with any software, it is best to start with a curated list online (that is, a list with a person's name attached). Then try as many programs as seem reasonably likely contenders. Because Bayes Nets operate differently from other methods, even if you use regular statistical software, there will be at least some learning. Ultimately, only you know what will work best for your needs.

Summary and conclusions

Bayes Nets or Bayesian Networks are a remarkable set of methods with strong predictive powers. As we saw in the first example, they can sail with aplomb through problems that are extremely difficult with traditional statistics – and that completely baffle nearly all of us.

They typically do better than more traditional methods, such as regressions, in several areas. In particular, they excel in getting an accurate fix on variables' importances, while including all variables of interest in a predictive model. Networks take into account all the interrelations of all variables when estimating importances, unlike regressions, which assume that when one variable is changed all others remain constant.

Like classification trees, Bayes Nets give us insight into how variables interact, but the understanding in Bayes Nets extends to a holistic view of the ways in which all variables in a model fit together. Classification trees' view of interactions is **situational**, that is, any variable beyond the first one in the model will have an effect **only if** the other variables have specific values. Bayes Nets models see patterns across all values in all variables.

Bayes Nets also are more comprehensive than classification trees, in that trees tend to produce simple models with relatively few predictors. You can enter a great many variables into a Bayes Nets model, and it will include and evaluate all of them. Even with this comprehensive view, Bayes Nets run quickly, just as classification trees do.

New, different and worth getting to know

Bayes Nets are newer methods that use analytical approaches quite different from more traditional methods. They can solve problems easily that may entirely elude other analytical procedures. However, they require some new terminology and their unfamiliarity may make some audiences less willing to accept them.

Bayesian Networks definitely are **machine learning** methods. They fall under the heading of **graphical analytical methods**. Diagrams are key to understanding their workings. You can get a great deal out of networks – such as variables' relative importances and effects – without ever looking at the network itself. However, those with the patience to examine the structure of the network will develop a fuller understanding of whether the outcome makes sense.

Bayes Nets do not involve **equations** (as regressions do) or sets of **if-then rules** (as classification trees do). At times, you might encounter someone who needs to see equations, and for that person, networks might not provide a satisfying answer.

To see the effects of changing more than one variable at a time, you need to go back to the network diagram itself, in those programs that dynamically allow you to interact with the network diagram. Some software programs allow you to construct a stand-alone simulator. These simulators are similar to the ones that we encountered for discrete choice modelling and conjoint analysis in Chapters 4 and 5.

In a network, even with a single variable being changed, effects can vary depending on the values of the target variable and the predictor variable. Effects from changing several variables at once requires taking many factors into account and certainly are nothing we could see intuitively – even though the network will handle as many changes as you want with aplomb.

We have covered new material and new concepts in this chapter. Using Bayes Nets requires still more in terms of hands-on experience and learning about the details of the software you choose. They almost always merit the effort. Still, like any method, Bayes Nets are not guaranteed to develop useful output every time.

At times, the questions being analysed themselves limit how much you can extract from the analysis. For instance, in the example with the brokerage, the most important variables affecting share emerged clearly. However, the ratings analysed were broad. They showed **what** needed to change, but not **how** to make the changes. For that, another approach was needed, namely, the conjoint-based service optimization discussed in Chapter 5.

Overall, Bayes Nets are among the most powerful of analytical methods, typically producing very strong predictive models that often can address your informational and strategic needs. Any learning that they require definitely will be more than repaid.

Bonus Chapter 2: Artificial intelligence, ensembles and neural nets

This bonus online chapter explains the promise and pitfalls of the one method most closely associated with artificial intelligence: neural networks. We discuss the practical applications and limitations of this approach, including how it performed versus other methods with actual data. We help you navigate through the morass of terminology, hype and conflicting claims about this evolving field. The chapter also reviews ensembles, including one method with strong predictive performance and an interesting name: decorate. Finally, it reviews some of the more basic questions raised by the quest for increasingly autonomous machines.

Access this bonus chapter online here:

www.koganpage.com/AI-Marketing

Putting it together

08

What to use when

If we take a broad definition of **artificial intelligence**, then we see that it actually has been working alongside us for many years. Those who did not skip directly to this chapter may have noticed this. This also assumes that this topic has not become totally blurred for readers who have got this far (and thank you for persevering).

All the way back in the Preface, we mentioned what some people working at the epicentre of artificial intelligence, Alphabet (formerly Google), had to say when asked to define this term. As a refresher, here are some answers:

'I would definitely interview someone else.'

'I'm not sure. I haven't done anything with AI.'

'I don't know anything about it.'

'It's machine learning.'

'I work at Yahoo…'

In Chapter 1, we hazarded a definition of artificial intelligence. So you do not have to page back, here it is again. Broadly, **artificial intelligence** means anything a machine does to respond to its environment to maximize its chances of success. Since we are not discussing cars that drive themselves or machines that otherwise amble around in the outside world, the environment of our machines, computers, is data. We set their goal as detecting complex relationships we cannot, to aid in our making better decisions.

We can find this type of artificial intelligence in many places. For instance, we encounter this in the way the computer takes many alternative views of a problem, as in **ensembles** such as **boosting, random forests** or **decorate**. We see it in the way that the computer learns from thousands of passes through the data, as in the **hierarchical Bayesian analysis** that we use to extend the power of **discrete choice modelling, conjoint analysis** and **maximum difference scaling**.

In a different way, we find **computer learning** in solutions that completely escape us, as in **Bayes Nets** and how they use **conditional probabilities**. This method finds underlying relationships and solves problems that entirely baffle us.

One of the earliest applications of artificial intelligence is found in the highly sophisticated testing done by **classification trees**. One of the most current, and most rapidly expanding, applications is in the complex learning done by **neural networks**.

The tasks the methods do

Our discussion has been organized by method. We explained a particular approach, then explained what it could accomplish. This chapter takes an alternative view, starting with the type of problem, then reviewing the methods that can address it.

First, what older methods can do

We explained one more traditional method, **Q-Sort/Case 5**, which can give you a clear hierarchy of importances for long lists of items. We included this approach because it nicely complements **Maximum Difference Scaling** (**MaxDiff**), which gets much of its power from the machine learning method, **Hierarchical Bayesian analysis**.

Many other long-established methods solve key problems. For instance, **clustering** neatly handles the problem of **finding groups** in data. **Discriminant analysis** can determine differences among groups. It also can assign new people into groups. Clustering has been applied since at least the 1950s, discriminant analysis since the 1930s. Newer, high-tech alternatives to these methods exist, but we did not have the space to discuss them.

Several other methods use advanced concepts and plenty of calculations but do not involve machine learning. Among these, we find mapping methods such as **correspondence analysis, MD-PREF** and **bi-plots**. They serve the important function of visually revealing relationships among groups or among brands. Comparisons of many groups would be addressed by many methods in the **analysis of variance** (**ANOVA**) family. Some of these reach hair-raising levels of complexity.

A complete tool-kit for solving problems and addressing tactical and strategic issues therefore needs to include a mix of the cutting-edge and the old. Now let's go on to what can be accomplished with the newer methods we have been discussing.

Finding and characterizing groups

Chapter 6 showed how **classification trees** greatly boosted the odds of finding a group. This method not only locates groups, but characterizes them. It also can determine what characterizes different levels of consumption or spending.

Classification trees provide simple **if-then rules** that are easy to program into a database. Using these, new people (outside the data set being examined) can be assigned to groups or assigned different probabilities of acting. The **gains analysis** (or **lift** or **leverage analysis**) provides a straightforward roadmap to locating best prospects.

Classification trees can be supplemented with **random forests**. This **ensemble** method, also discussed in Chapter 6, runs hundreds of trees, randomly swapping predictors and cases (people) into and out of each run. Based on these hundreds of trees, it develops importances for each variable. Unfortunately, like all ensembles, its workings are opaque.

In the example in Chapter 6, we used **random forests** to zero in on a list of definitely important predictors. We then used those predictors to construct a single classification tree that could be studied, evaluated and applied.

Boosting also can extend insights from classification trees. In Chapter 6 we showed how a boosting method, **AdaBoost.MI**, added to a model developed using classification trees. This model showed which psoriasis patients were most at risk of severe depression. Boosting highlighted two values of one predictor that warranted particular attention.

Finding what is most valuable in a list of items

Determining what is most valuable in a list of items has many applications. For instance, it can help you decide which of many possible incentives (or, as they are called, 'free gifts') have the most appeal. This also can help prioritize corporate message elements or claims.

The first online bonus chapter (available at www.koganpage.com/ AI-Marketing) shows how **Maximum Difference Scaling (MaxDiff)** and **Q-Sort/Case 5** provide a substantially clearer picture of importances or levels of appeal than direct scaled ratings. Both methods provide **ratio-level** readings. You can say, for instance, 'Free gift N is twice as appealing as Free Gift T'.

The power of MaxDiff is greatly enhanced by **Hierarchical Bayesian analysis**. Thanks to this machine learning method, MaxDiff can provide individual-level data. The Q-Sort method relies on an older form of analysis, and provides importances only for groups.

While the **Q-Sort** method is lower tech, it can prioritize many more items. In practice, **MaxDiff** starts to become overly burdensome for people participating in a survey with about 35 items. Q-Sort/Case 5 results have been reported with up to 100 items.

Determining the effects of variables (aka 'drivers')

Bayes Nets remain one of the best methods for determining the effects of variables on an outcome, such as share or intent to buy. They work remarkably well with non-experimental data, such as questionnaire questions, demographics and other characteristics.

They have many features that make them a superior method. Among these, Bayes Nets measure effects taking all variables into account. This differs entirely from methods in the regression family. There, measuring the effects of changing any variable must assume that all other variables remain constant. (That rarely happens in the real world. We typically find a web of interconnected relationships and effects.)

Bayes Nets also look at the whole pattern of scores in all variables. A regression-related model is based on correlations. A correlation is a simple one-number summary of how well two variables fall into a straight line. Bayes Nets also take a more comprehensive view than classification trees. Trees describe specific situations, as in 'variable T has this effect IF (and only if) variable R has this value'.

Bayes Nets also provide ratio-level importances, as do MaxDiff and Q-Sort/Case 5. However, Bayes Nets go beyond these methods, also providing the absolute strengths of effects. Networks will show the precise amount of influence over each range of the predictor variable and the target variable. It can reveal effects that are either straight-line or that change in non-linear ways.

As we showed in Chapter 7, Bayes Nets allow you to see the patterns of connections among variables. You then can check these to see if they make sense. You should accept an analysis only if it provides a reasonable-looking network diagram. This almost always happens.

Random forests and **boosting** also return variables' importances. However, Bayes Nets usually have higher predictive accuracy, and they take a more comprehensive view of the data. Therefore, they typically are a better choice for determining variables' importances. In those few instances where the performance of a Bayes Net is indifferent, you could check these other methods as an alternative way to find importances.

Optimizing complex messages, advertisements or single products

Conjoint analysis has worked well in applications like these. Conjoint analysis, in particular the traditional **full-profile** method, has the advantage of asking for an evaluation of a whole product or message. This ensures that elements or features are evaluated in a realistic context. However, if you want to determine how products would fare in a competitive environment, **discrete choice modelling** is a superior method. Chapters 4 and 5 explain the reasons.

Experimental designs underlie conjoint analyses. These ensure that there is no relationship in the way features (or attributes) vary from one evaluated product description (or profile) to another. This complete lack of relationship in the way profiles vary ensures that effects arising from changing any attribute are measured purely and precisely.

Conjoint analysis is an established method, going back at least to the 1970s in an older form. It can be extended considerably by the use of the machine learning method, **Hierarchical Bayesian (HB) analysis**. Complex products and services with many features and many variations of those features now can be investigated. Before HB analysis, this was not possible.

Conjoint analysis leads to **market simulator programs**. They show the effects of changing features in any of hundreds or thousands of ways and return results in real time. These are easy to use and can run under popular programs such as Microsoft Excel and Microsoft PowerPoint.

Determining responses to alternative new products in a competitive marketplace

Discrete choice modelling remains the best method for determining the effects of varying a product, introducing a new product, and/or eliminating products in a competitive marketplace. Like conjoint analysis, discrete choice modelling uses designed experiments. Any effects from varying the features of a product or service are measured precisely.

Also like conjoint analysis, discrete choice modelling gains considerable power from the use of HB analysis. With HB analysis, you can measure effects in complex situations where many products or services change in many ways.

Discrete choice modelling goes beyond conjoint in taking a whole-marketplace perspective. Consumers participating in a well-designed discrete choice study see the main choices they would have in the actual market. They do what they would do in real life – make a decision.

This method has the most realism of any method for forecasting what will happen in a changing marketplace – assuming it is set up well. Unfortunately, though, there are far too many poorly thought out and poorly designed studies. It is important to set the context for the decision with reasonable accuracy. Recent research shows how much consumers rely on this context when making decisions. It also is critical to think of all reasonable contingencies. You need to consider both how your fine product might change and what competitors might be doing at the same time, or in response to your actions.

You also need to build in adjustments to go from the **share of preference** found in simulations, to estimate **market share**. Most commonly, you need to adjust for how aware consumers are of each product and how widely each is distributed.

If you succeed with all the hard thinking involved, these studies can have remarkable predictive power. Market simulators and market simulations can do exceptionally well at forecasting what consumers will choose in a real and changing marketplace.

Finding complex relationships and structures in data

Bayes Nets and **classification trees** come closest to the elusive goal of machine learning spontaneously showing 'patterns' in the data. Bayes Nets take a holistic view, looking at how all variables fit together into a network of relationships and effects. Classification trees reveal **interactions** more clearly than any other method.

An **interaction** occurs when two or more variables together produce an effect that we would not expect from the individual variables. In our example in Chapter 6, for instance, we saw that families with five or more children who lived in the suburbs bought more cardboard-like cereal than either families of that size or all suburbanites. Both characteristics worked together to lead to high levels of purchasing.

Bayes Nets include all the variables that you are examining. They all connect into a network. You will get strengths of relationships to the target variable and connections for all of them. **Classification trees** are sparser. In our cruise line example in Chapter 6, for instance, only 10 variables clearly differentiated levels of purchasing among over 340,000 people in a database. Both methods reveal structures that we could not otherwise understand.

Now about neural networks

Neural networks are being touted as the future of artificial intelligence. And with swaths of data and ample training, they have done remarkable things. For all their promised strength in finding patterns, though, they remain largely mute about what they are doing.

In Bonus Online Chapter 2 (available at **www.koganpage.com/ AI-Marketing**) we use neural networks to try to predict share. As you will see, the diagram that the network provided was basically unintelligible, as were the reported variable strengths in the hidden layers.

It also did poorly at prediction, substantially worse than the other methods we discuss. Even with 1,800 cases and 70 variables, we might not have had enough data for the neural network to function well.

We also saw problems with **overfitting** of the model to the data, traditionally a weak spot with this method. New implementations are being developed all the time, and so some of these limitations may well be overcome. For now, these networks would not be a first choice in many cases. If you have a lot of data, and can do a lot of training, you might want to try them.

Thinking about thinking

Wanting computers to do more of the heavy lifting has been a long-held wish. It goes far back, at least to the earliest days of machine learning. Around 1959, an article about teaching computers to play chequers hoped for the happy day when we would not need to do so much programming of every step. More work for the computer, rather than us, remains a goal. But what do you want the machine to do?

In an old joke, a computer salesperson tells an executive that a new computer will cut his work by 50 per cent. 'In that case', the executive answers, 'I will take two.'

This may not be the funniest thing you have read, even in the last halfhour, but it underscores an important question. Where do you want to be in control, and where do you cede this control to the computers, and/or the friendly vendors running them? We raise this issue at the end of Bonus Online Chapter 2, and it is worth talking about again here.

Many of the newer methods, like **ensembles**, are basically incomprehensible. **Neural networks** epitomize the class of methods that we cannot fully understand. They are doing something, but precisely what remains entirely, or nearly entirely, out of sight.

You may recall the coefficients from the neural network that we show in Table A2.2. In no way could those be squared with what seemed sensible. The coefficients' sizes looked wrong and their signs – positive or negative – seemed backward about half the time. How would you know that this does not reflect a basic mistake?

You could argue that the proof is in the doing. But then, this network did not do that well. It predicted poorly. It also showed a salient problem with **overfitting** of data – modelling features that were peculiar to that one data set, but that would not be found in the outside world.

Also, what do you do when you cannot precisely judge how well a system is doing? It is easy to tell if a self-driving car is not doing well, for instance. It crashes. But what happens if you are running a system that supposedly learns from the data, and it does a middling job – just like many analyses when dealing with messy, real-world situations? How would you check, for instance, on the performance of an automated recommendation system?

We may well be coming to the time when we set computers loose on data, and they learn by themselves. They might even find out once and for all if there is a connection between the sales of disposable diapers and beer. (If this reference is hazy, we mentioned in Chapter 2 what amounted to an urban legend about somebody serendipitously finding such a relationship, just by having a lot of data.) But no amount of digging through transactions will think up a new strategy for you to follow. Even the most exquisite analysis of historical data cannot give you a single idea for a new product or service. You still need to put in the effort and do the hard thinking.

Computers, and machine learning methods in particular, have been working with us to solve problems for many years. They have provided admirable assistance, zeroing in on predictive relationships that we could never have found without them. You may have noted an obvious authorial bias in favour of methods that keep the details out in the open, where you can test the model against your experience and acumen. These seem to be the unquestionably good uses of machine learning.

How much you want to trust the computer to go off on its own, and even learn in ways that you can barely understand, is becoming an increasingly important decision. Recall that we still (theoretically) have an edge in common sense. Then you need to choose.

BIBLIOGRAPHY

Preface

Cuppy, W (1931) *How to Tell Your Friends from the Apes*, Horace Liveright, New York

Ghosh, P (2016) [accessed 15 August 2016] Machine Learning of the Next Decade: The Promises and the Pitfalls [Online] http://wwwdataversitynet/machine-learning-next-decade-promises-pitfalls (an article identifying regression and clustering as advanced machine-learning methods)

Kantrowitz, A (2016) [accessed 15 August 2016] Can Anyone in This Group of Advanced Programmers Explain the Tech World's Hottest Trend? [Online] https://www.buzzfeed.com/alexkantrowitz/finding-the-meaning-of-artificial-intelligence-at-google-io?utm_term=hr8N7KRmY#obKALmWxk (23/5/2016)

Quote attributed to Edward de Bono [accessed 15 August 2016] Edward de Bono Quotes, *101Sharequotes 2016* [Online] http://101sharequotes.com/quote/edward_de_bono-an-expert-is-someone-who-has-suc-80976

Quote attributed to Niels Bohr by Edward Teller (1954), in Dr Edward Teller's Magnificent Obsession, by R Coughlan, *LIFE Magazine*, 6 September 1954, p 62

Chapter 1

Armstrong, JS, ed (2001) *Principles of Forecasting*, Kluwer, Norwell, MA

Bagozzi, R (1994) *Advanced Methods of Marketing Research*, Blackwell Publishers, Cambridge MA

Chakrapani, C, ed (2002) *Marketing Research: State-of-the-art perspectives*, Southwest Educational Publishing, Mason, OH

Dull, T (2015) [accessed 15 August 2016] Data Lake vs Data Warehouse: A Big Data Cheat Sheet: What Marketers Want to Know (Part 4) [Online] http://www.kdnuggets.com/2015/09/data-lake-vs-data-warehouse-key-differenceshtml

Foreman, JW (2014) *Data Smart: Using data science to transform information into insight*, Wiley, Indianapolis, IN

Gelman, A, *et al* (2013) *Bayesian Data Analysis*, 3rd edn, Chapman & Hall/CRC Texts in Statistical Science, Boca Raton, FL

Green, PE and Carroll, J (1978) *Analyzing Multivariate Data*, Dryden Press, Hinsdale, IL

Grigsby, M (2015) *Marketing Analytics*, Kogan Page, London

Bibliography

Ihaka, R and Gentleman, R (1996) R: a language for data analysis and graphics, *Journal of Computational and Graphical Statistics*, 5 (3), pp 299–314

Inmon, B (1992) *Building the Data Warehouse*, Wiley, Somerset, NJ

Kimball, R and Ross, M (2013) *The Data Warehouse Toolkit*, 3rd edn, Wiley, Somerset, NJ

Kugler, T, *et al* (2008) *Decision Modeling and Behavior in Complex and Uncertain Environments*, Springer, New York

Mayer-Schönberger, V and Cukier, K (2013) *Big Data: A revolution that will transform how we live, work, and think*, John Murray, London (a book that says more data is always better)

McCullagh, P (2002) What is a statistical model? *Annals of Statistics*, 30 (5), pp 1225–310

Nisbet, R, Elder, J and Miner, G (2009) *Handbook of Statistical Analysis and Data Mining Applications*, Academic Press, Boston, MA

Oram, A (1998) [accessed 15 August 2016] The Land Mines of Data Mining [Online] http://www.praxagora.com/andyo/ar/privacy_mineshtml

Provost, F and Fawcett, T (2013) *Data Science for Business: What you need. to know about data mining and data-analytic thinking*, O'Reilly Media, Sebastopol, CA

Rainer, RK (2012) *Introduction to Information Systems: Enabling and transforming business*, 4th edn, Wiley, Somerset, NJ

Russo, E and Schoemaker, P (2002) *Winning Decisions*, Doubleday, New York (a book on making decisions that barely mentions data)

Sapsford, R and Jupp, V (2006) *Data Collection and Analysis*, Sage, New York

Silver, N (2012) *The Signal and the Noise: Why so many predictions fail – but some don't*, Penguin, NY

Stoll, Clifford (2006) quote, in Keeler, M, *Nothing to Hide: Privacy in the 21st century*, iUniverse: Lincoln, NE

Struhl, S (2008) [accessed 15 August 2016] Data Mining Comes of Age: Overcoming the Myths and Misconceptions [online] http://www.hospitalitynet.org/news/4036261.html

Sztandera, L (2014) *Computational Intelligence in Business Analytics: Concepts, methods, and tools for big data applications*, Pearson, Upper Saddle River, NJ

Vriens, M (2012) *The Insights Advantage: Knowing how to win*, iUniverse, Bloomington, IN (a book on decision making that barely mentions data)

Winer, R and Neslin, SA (2014) *The History of Marketing Science*, World Scientific Publishing Co, Singapore

Witten, I, Frank, E and Hall, A (2011) *Data Mining*, 3rd edn, Morgan Kaufmann, Burlington, MA

Woods, Dan (2011) [accessed 15 August 2016] Big Data Requires a Big Architecture, *Forbes* [Online] http://www.forbes.com/sites/ciocentral/2011/07/21/big-data-requires-a-big-new-architecture/#1c5ed8bf1d75

Chapter 2

Armstrong, JS and Collopy, F (1992) Error measures for generalizing about forecasting methods: empirical comparisons, *International Journal of Forecasting*, 8 (1) pp 69–80

Barton, SJ (2010) *Strategic Management Simplified: What every manager needs to know about strategy and how to manage it*, iUniverse Press, Bloomington, Indiana (story about apparel manufacturer Levi's)

Box, GEP and Draper, NR (1987) *Empirical Model Building and Response Surfaces*, John Wiley & Sons, New York

Cohen, J (1988) *Statistical Power Analysis for the Behavioral Sciences*, 2nd edn, Erlbaum Publishers, Mahwah, NJ

DeTurck, D [accessed 15 August 2016] Case Study 1: The 1936 *Literary Digest* Poll [Online] https://www.math.upenn.edu/~deturck/m170/wk4/lecture/case1.html

Dziak, JJ et al (2012) Sensitivity and Specificity of Information Criteria [Online] https://methodology.psu.edu/media/techreports/12-119.pdf

Floridi, L (2010) *Information – A Very Short Introduction*, Oxford University Press, Oxford

Jessen, RJ (1978) *Statistical Survey Techniques*, Wiley, Edison, NJ

Kish, L (1995) *Survey Sampling*, Wiley, Edison, NJ

Marcus, AH and Elias, W (1999) Some useful statistical methods for model validation, *Environmental Health Perspectives*, 106 (Supplement 6), pp 1541–50

McCullagh, P (2002) What is a statistical model? *Annals of Statistics*, 30 (5), pp 1225–310

Sapsford, R and Jupp, V (2006) *Data Collection and Analysis*, Sage, New York

Snedecor, G and Cochran, W (1989) *Statistical Methods*, 8th edn, Iowa State University Press, Ames, Iowa

Spanos, S (2011) Statistical model specification and validation: statistical vs substantive information [Online] http://faculty.chicagobooth.edu/midwest.econometrics/papers/megspanos.pdf

Stevens, JP, Pituch, K and Whittaker, T (1999) *Intermediate Statistics: A modern approach*, 3rd edn, Lawrence Erlbaum, Mahwah, NJ

Thurstone, LL (1935) *Vectors of the Mind*, University of Chicago Press, Chicago, IL

Wilkinson, L, Blank, G and Gruber, C (1995) *Desktop Data Analysis with Systat*, SPSS, Inc., Chicago, IL

Chapter 3

Note: references for discrete choice modelling, conjoint, MaxDiff and Q-Sort/Case 5 are found in the chapters focusing on each method.

Hierarchical Bayesian analysis

Allenby, G, Rossi, P and McCulloch, RE (2005) Hierarchical Bayes model: a practitioner's guide, *Journal of Bayesian Applications in Marketing*, pp 1–4 [Online] http://ssrn.com/abstract=655541

Box, G and Tiao, G (1965) Multiparameter problems from a Bayesian point of view, *Ann. Mathematical Statistics*, **36** (5), pp 1468–82

Gelman, A, Carlin, J, Stern, H and Rubin, D (2004) *Bayesian Data Analysis*, 2nd edn, CRC Press, Boca Raton, Florida

Smith, B (1994) *Bayesian Theory*, John Wiley & Sons, Chichester

Experimental designs

Bingham, D, Sitter, R and Tang B (2009) Orthogonal and nearly orthogonal designs for computer experiments *Biometrika* **96**, pp 51-65

Box, GE; Hunter, JS; Hunter, WG (2005) *Statistics for experimenters: Design, innovation, and discovery*, 2nd edn, Wiley, New York

Cochran, W and Cox, G (1992) *Experimental designs*, 2nd edn, Wiley, New York

Fang, K T, Li R, Sudjianto, A (2006) *Design and modeling for computer experiments*, CRC Press, New York

Lin CD, Bingham, D, Sitter R, Tang, B (2010) A new and flexible method for constructing designs for computer experiments, *Ann. Statistics*, **38**, pp 1460–77

Yang, JY and Liu, MQ (2012) Construction of orthogonal and nearly orthogonal Latin hypercube designs from orthogonal designs, *Statistica Sinica*, **22**, pp 433–42

Chapter 4

Agresti, A (2013) *Categorical Data Analysis*, 3rd edn, John Wiley and Sons, Hoboken, NJ

Baltas, George and Doyle, Peter (2001) Random utility models in marketing research: a survey, *Journal of Business Research*, **51** (2), pp 115–25

Bargh JA, ed (2006) *Social Psychology and the Unconscious: The automaticity of higher mental processes*, Psychology Press, Philadelphia

Ben-Akiva, M and Bierlaire, M (1999) Discrete choice methods and their applications to short-term travel decisions, *Handbook of Transportation Sciences*, pp 7–38, Kluwer, Norwell, MA

Ben-Akiva, M and Lerman, S (1985) *Discrete Choice Analysis: Theory and application to travel demand*, MIT Press, Cambridge, MA

Chu, C (1989) A paired combinatorial logit model for travel demand analysis, *Proceedings of the 5th World Conference on Transportation Research*, Ventura, CA, pp 295–309

Greenwald, AG (1992) New look III: unconscious cognition reclaimed, *American Psychologist*, **47**, pp 766–79

Gustafsson, A, Herrmann, A and Huber, F, eds (2013) *Conjoint Measurement: Methods and applications*, Springer-Verlag, Berlin

Hausman, J and Wise, D (1978) A conditional probit model for qualitative choice: discrete decisions recognizing interdependence and heterogeneous preference, *Econometrica*, **48** (2), pp 403–26

Kahneman, D (2013) *Thinking, Fast and Slow*, Farrar, Strauss & Giroux, New York

Kahneman, D and Tversky A (1979) Prospect theory: an analysis of decision under risk, *Econometrica*, **47** (2), pp 263–91

Luce, MF, Payne, JW and Bettman, JR (1999) Emotional trade-off difficulty and choice, *Journal of Marketing Research*, **36** (2), pp 143–60

Luce, RD (1959) *Individual Choice Behavior*, Wiley, New York

McFadden, D and Train, K (2000) Mixed MNL models for discrete response, *Journal of Applied Econometrics*, **15** (5), pp 447–70

Revelt, D and Train, K (1998) Mixed logit with repeated choices: households' choices of appliance efficiency level, *Review of Economics and Statistics*, **80** (4), pp 647–57

Train, K (1978) A validation test of a disaggregate mode choice model, *Transportation Research*, **12**, pp 167–74

Train, K (2003) *Discrete Choice Methods with Simulation*, Cambridge University Press, MA

Chapter 5

Carroll, J and Green E (1995) Psychometric methods in marketing research: part I, conjoint analysis, *Journal of Marketing Research*, **32**, pp 385–91

Cattin, P and Wittink, D (1982) Commercial use of conjoint analysis: a survey, *Journal of Marketing*, **46**, pp 44–53

Green, P (1984) Hybrid models for conjoint analysis: an expository review, *Journal of Marketing Research*, **21**, pp 155–59

Green, P Carroll, J and Goldberg, S (1981) A general approach to product design optimization via conjoint analysis, *Journal of Marketing*, **43**, pp 17–35

Green, P, Krieger, M and Agarwal M (1991) Adaptive conjoint analysis: some caveats and suggestions, *Journal of Marketing Research*, **28**, pp 215–21

Green, P and Srinivasan, V (1978) Conjoint analysis in consumer research: issues and outlook, *Journal of Consumer Research*, **5**, pp 103–23

Green, P and Wind, Y (1973) *Multiattribute Decisions in Marketing: A measurement approach*, Dryden Press, Hinsdale, IL

Luce, RD (1959) *Individual Choice Behavior* Wiley, New York

Marder, E (1999) The assumptions of choice modelling, *Canadian Journal of Market Research*, **18**, pp 1–10

McCollough, PR (2002) [accessed 15 August 2016] Shortcomings of Adaptive Conjoint [Online] http://www.macroinc.com/english/dont-use-adaptive-conjoint-methods/

McCullough, PR (2002) A Users Guide to Conjoint [Online] http://www.macroinc.com/english/papers/A%20Users%20Guide%20to%20Conjoint%20Analysis.pdf

Morowitz, V (2001) Methods for forecasting from intentions data, in *Principles of Forecasting*, ed J Armstrong, Springer, New York

Orme, B (2009) *Getting Started with Conjoint Analysis*, Research Publishers, Madison, WI

Rao, V (2014) *Applied Conjoint Analysis*, Sprinter-Verlag, Berlin

Chapter 6

Breiman, L, Friedman, J, Olshen, R and Stone, C (1984) *Classification and Regression Trees*, Chapman and Hall, New York

Brodley, CE and Utgoff, PE (1995) Multivariate decision trees, *Machine Learning*, **19**, pp 45–77

Buntine, W (1992) Learning classification trees, *Statistics and Computing*, **2**, pp 63–73

Clark, LA and Pregibon, D (1993) Tree-based models, in *Statistical Models*, ed JM Chambers and TJ Hastie, pp 377–419, Chapman and Hall, New York

Hazewinkel, M, ed (1987) Greedy algorithm, *Encyclopedia of Mathematics, Supplement III*, Springer, Norwell, MA

Hochberg, Y and Tamhane, AC (1987) *Multiple Comparison Procedures*, Wiley, New York

Holte, RC (1993) Very simple classification rules perform well on most commonly used datasets, *Machine Learning*, **11**, pp 63–90

Kass, GV (1980) An exploratory technique for investigating large quantities of categorical data, *Applied Statistics*, **29**, pp 119–27

Lim, T-S, Loh, W-Y and Shih, Y-S (2000) A comparison of prediction accuracy, complexity, and training time of thirty-three old and new classification algorithms, *Machine Learning*, **40**, pp 203–28

Muller, W and Wysotzki, F (1994) Automatic construction of decision trees for classification, *Annals of Operations Research*, **52**, pp 231–47

Quinlan, JR (1989) Unknown attribute values in induction, *Proceedings of the Sixth International Machine Learning Workshop*, pp 164–68

Shi, L and Horvath, S (2006) Unsupervised learning with random forest predictors, *Journal of Computational and Graphical Statistics*, **15** (1), pp 118–38

Steinberg, D and Colla, P (1992) *CART: A supplementary module for Systat,* Systat Inc., Evanston, IL

White, AP and Liu, WZ (1994) Bias in information-based measures in decision tree induction, *Machine Learning,* **15**, pp 321–29

Witten, I and Frank, E (2005) *Data Mining: Practical machine learning tools and techniques,* 2nd edn, Morgan Kaufmann, San Francisco

Chapter 7

Cooper, GF and Herskovits, E (1992) A Bayesian method for the induction of probabilistic networks from data, *Machine Learning,* **9**, pp 309–47

Gill, R (2010) Monty Hall problem, in *International Encyclopedia of Statistical Science,* pp 858–63 Springer-Verlag, Berlin

Heckerman, D (1995) Tutorial on learning with Bayesian networks, in Jordan, M, *Learning in Graphical Models Adaptive Computation and Machine Learning,* MIT, Press, Cambridge, MA

Jensen, FV and Nielsen, TD (2007) *Bayesian Networks and Decision Graphs,* 2nd edn, Springer-Verlag, New York

Kahneman, D, Slovic, P and Tversky, A, eds (1982) *Judgment under Uncertainty: Heuristics and biases,* Cambridge University Press, Cambridge, UK

Korb, KB and Nicholson, A (2010) *Bayesian Artificial Intelligence,* Chapman & Hall (CRC Press), New York

Mackay, D (2003) *Information Theory, Inference and Learning Algorithms,* Cambridge University Press, Cambridge, UK

Pearl, J (1986) Fusion, propagation, and structuring in belief networks, *Artificial Intelligence,* **29** (3), pp 241–88

Pearl, J (1988) *Probabilistic Reasoning in Intelligent Systems: Networks of plausible inference representation and reasoning series,* 2nd edn, Morgan Kaufmann, San Francisco, CA

Pearl, J (200) *Causality: Models, reasoning, and inference,* Cambridge University Press, New York

Russell, S J and Norvig, P (2003) *Artificial Intelligence: A modern approach,* 2nd edn, Prentice Hall, Upper Saddle River, NJ

Solving the Monty Hall Three-Door Problem with Bayes Nets [accessed 15 August 2016] [Online] http://download.hugin.com/webdocs/manuals/Htmlhelp/monty_hall_pane.html

Wilkinson, L, Blank, I and Gruber, P (1999) *Desktop Data Analysis with Systat,* SPSS Inc., Chicago, IL

Witten, I and Frank, E (2005) *Data Mining: Practical machine learning tools and techniques,* 2nd edn, Morgan Kaufmann, San Francisco

Yudkowsky, E (2016) [accessed 15 August 2016] An Intuitive Explanation of Bayes' Theorem [Online] http://yudkowsky.net/rational/bayes

Zhang, N and Poole, D (1994) A simple approach to Bayesian network computations, *Proceedings of the Tenth Biennial Canadian Artificial Intelligence Conference*, AI-94, pp 171–78, Banff, Alberta

Chapter 8

Fisher, RA (1936) The use of multiple measurements in taxonomic problems, *Annals of Eugenics*, 7 (2), pp 179–88

Kantrowitz, A (2016) [accessed 15 August 2016] Can Anyone in This Group of Advanced. Programmers Explain the Tech World's Hottest Trend? [Online] https://www.buzzfeed.com/alexkantrowitz/finding-the-meaning-of-artificial-intelligence-at-google-io?utm_term=hr8N7KRmY#obKALmWxk (23/5/2016)

Lloyd, SP (1957) Least square quantization in PCM, Bell Telephone Laboratories paper; published in journal much later: Lloyd, SP (1982) Least squares quantization in PCM (PDF), *IEEE Transactions on Information Theory*, 28 (2), pp 129–37

Metz, C (2016) [accessed 15 August 2016] AI is Transforming Google Search: The Rest of the Web is Next [Online] http://www.wired.com/2016/02/ai-is-changing-the-technology-behind-google-searches (4/2/2016)

Samuel, AL (1959) Some studies in machine learning using the game of checkers, *IBM Journal of Research and Development*, 3 (3), pp 210–29

Bonus online-only Chapter 1

Maximum Difference Scaling (MaxDiff)

Flynn, TN *et al* (2007) Best–worst scaling: what it can do for health care research and how to do it, *Journal of Health Economics*, 26 (1), pp 171–89

Louviere, JJ *et al* (2015) *Best-Worst Scaling: Theory, methods and applications*, Cambridge University Press, Cambridge

Marley, AA and Louviere, JJ (2005) Some probabilistic models of best, worst, and best–worst choices, *Journal of Mathematical Psychology*, 49 (6), pp 464–80

Q-Sort and Case 5

Block, J (1978) *The Q-Sort Method in Personality Assessment and Psychiatric Research*, Consulting Psychologists Press, Mountain View, CA

Borbinha, J, *et al* (c.2005) [accessed 15 August 2016] Adaptive Q-Sort Matrix Generation: A Simplified Approach [Online] http://www.inesc-id.pt/pt/indicadores/Ficheiros/11389.pdf

Bracken, SS and Fischel, J (2006) Assessment of preschool classroom practices: application of Q-sort methodology, *Early Childhood Research Quarterly*, **21** (4), pp 417–30

Bradley, RA and Terry, ME (1952) Rank analysis of incomplete block designs, I: the method of paired comparisons, *Biometrika*, **39**, pp 324–45

Luce, RD (1959) *Individual Choice Behaviors: A theoretical analysis*, J Wiley, New York

McKeown, BF and Thomas, BD (1988) *Q-Methodology*, Sage Publications, Newbury Park, CA

Michell, J (1997) Quantitative science and the definition of measurement in psychology, *British Journal of Psychology*, **88**, pp 355–83

Rasch, G (1980) *Probabilistic Models for Some Intelligence and Attainment Tests*, University of Chicago Press, Chicago

Thurstone, LL (1927) A law of comparative judgement, *Psychological Review*, **34**, pp 273–86

Thurstone, LL (1929) The measurement of psychological value, in *Essays in Philosophy by Seventeen Doctors of Philosophy of the University of Chicago*, ed T Smith and W Wright, Open Court, Chicago

Thurstone, LL (1959) *The Measurement of Values*, University of Chicago Press, Chicago

Regression

Achen, CH (1973) *Interpreting and Using Regression*, Sage Publications, Beverly Hills

Darlington, RB (1968) Multiple regression in psychological research and practice, *Psychological Bulletin*, **69**, pp 161–82

Gorsuch, RL (1973) Data analysis of correlated independent variables, *Multivariate Behavioral Research*, **8**, pp 89–107

Lorenz, FO (1987) Teaching about influence in simple regression, *Teaching Sociology*, **15**, pp 173–77

Mansfield, ER and Conerly, MD (1987) Diagnostic value of residual and partial residual plots, *The American Statistician*, **41**, pp 107–16

Mauro, R (1990) Understanding l.o.v.e. (left out variables error): a method for estimating the effects of omitted variables, *Psychological Bulletin*, **108**, pp 314–29

Mosteller, F and Tukey, J (1977) *Data Analysis and Regression: A second course in statistics*, Pearson, Upper Saddle River, NJ

Stevens, JP (1984) Outliers and influential data points in regression analysis, *Psychological Bulletin*, **95**, pp 334–44

Wilkinson, L, Blank, G and Gruber, C (1995) *Desktop Data Analysis with Systat*, SPSS Press, Chicago, IL

Wolf, G and Cartwright, B (1974) Rules for coding dummy variables in multiple regression, *Psychological Bulletin*, **81**, pp 173–79

Bonus online-only Chapter 2

Asimov, I (1964) Introduction, *The Rest of the Robots*, Doubleday, New York

Baer, D (2016) [accessed 15 August 2016] The 'Outfielder Problem' Shows How Your Brain Is Not a Computer [Online] http://nymag.com/scienceofus/2016/06/outfielder-problem.html

Bengio, Yoshua *et al* (2006) Neural probabilistic language models, in *Innovations in Machine Learning*, ed DE Holmes and LC Jain, pp 137–86, Springer, New York

Bourzac, K (2016) [accessed 15 August 2016] Bringing Big Neural Networks to Self-Driving Cars, Smartphones, and Drones [Online] http://spectrum.ieee.org/computing/embedded-systems/bringing-big-neural-networks-to-selfdriving-cars-smartphones-and-drones

Cellan-Jones, R (2016) [accessed 15 August 2016] Stephen Hawking Warns Artificial Intelligence Could End Mankind [Online] http://www.bbc.com/news/technology-30290540

Cho, S-J and Kim, J (2003) Bayesian network modeling of hangul characters for on-line: handwriting recognition, *ICDAR Proceedings of the Seventh International Conference on Document Analysis and Recognition (1)*, IEEE Computer Society, Washington, DC

Claburn, T (2016) [accessed 15 August 2016] Many Businesses Using AI Without Realizing It [Online] http://www.informationweek.com/strategic-cio/many-businesses-using-ai-without-realizing-it/d/d-id/1326333 (21/7/2016)

Coffman, V (2013) [accessed 15 August 2016] Why You Should Not Build a Recommendation Engine Online] http://www.datacommunitydc.org/blog/2013/05/recommendation-engines-why-you-shouldnt-build-one

Coldewey, D (2016) [accessed 15 August 2016] Deep Learning Software Knows That a Rose is a Rose is a Rosa Rubiginosa, http://www.techcrunch.com/2016/07/26/deep-learning-software-knows-that-a-rose-is-a-rose-is-a-rosa-rubiginosa

Daugman, JG (2001) Brain metaphor and brain theory, in *Philosophy and the Neurosciences: A reader*, ed W Bechtel, P Mandik, J Mundale and R Stufflebeam, Blackwell, Oxford, UK

Davis, E (2016) [accessed 15 August 2016] Collection of Winograd Schemas [Online] http://www.cs.nyu.edu/faculty/davise/papers/WinogradSchemas/WS.html

Etzioni, 0 (2016) [accessed 15 August 2016] Deep Learning isn't a Dangerous Magic Genie it's Just Math [Online] http://www.wired.com/2016/06/deep-learning-isnt-dangerous-magic-genie-just-math (15/6/2016)

Goodman, J (2016) [accessed 15 August 2016] Say One Sentence and it's Done in the AI-First World [Online] https://www.theguardian.com/media-network/2016/may/20/say-one-sentence-and-its-done-in-the-ai-first-world?CMP=oth_b-aplnews_d-1

Hern, A (2016) [accessed 15 August 2016] Google Says Machine Learning is the Future So I Tried It Myself [Online] https://www.theguardian.com/technology/2016/jun/28/google-says-machine-learning-is-the-future-so-i-tried-it-myself (28/7/2016)

Hinton, G (2010) A practical guide to training restricted Boltzmann machines, *Momentum*, **91**, pp 926–43

Hinton, G, Osindero, S and Teh, Y (2006) A fast learning algorithm for deep belief nets, *Neural Computation*, **18** (7), pp 1527–54

Kahneman, D (2013) *Thinking, Fast and Slow*, Farrar, Strauss & Giroux, New York

Koch, C (2016) [accessed 22 February 2017] How the Computer Beat the Go Master [Online] http://www.scientificamerican.com/article/how-the-computer-beat-the-go-master (29/3/16)

Kosko, B (1993) *Fuzzy Thinking: The new science of fuzzy logic*, Hyperion, New York

Livingston, B (2002) [accessed 22 February 2017] Paul Graham Provides Stunning Answer to Spam E-Mails [Online] http://www.infoworld.com/article/2674702/technology-business/techology-business-paul-graham-provides-stunning-answer-to-spam-e-mails.html

Masnick, M (2012) [accessed 15 August 2016] Why Netflix Never Implemented the Algorithm that Won the Netflix $1 Million Challenge [Online] https://www.techdirt.com/blog/innovation/articles/20120409/03412518422/why-netflix-never-implemented-algorithm-that-won-netflix-1-million-challenges.html

Montaner, M, Lopez, B and de la Rosa, JL (2003) A taxonomy of recommender agents on the internet, *Artificial Intelligence Review*, **19** (4), pp 285–330

Nielsen, M (2016) [accessed 22 February 2017] How the Backpropagation Algorithm Works [Online] http://neuralnetworksanddeeplearning.com/chap2.html

Reese, B (2016) [accessed 15 August 2016] Gigaom Chats: Interfacing With Machines in 2026 [Online] http://www.gigaom.com/2016/08/02/gigaom-chats-interfacing-with-machines-in-2026 (2/8/2016)

Ricci, F, Rokach, L and Shapira, B (2012) Introduction to recommender systems handbook, *Recommender Systems Handbook*, Springer, New York, pp 1–35

Sacks, O (1998) *The Man Who Mistook His Wife For His Hat*, Touchstone, New York

Sahmai, M, Dumais, M, Heckerman, D and Horvitz, E (1998) A Bayesian approach to filtering junk e-mail, AAAI 1998 Workshop on Learning for Text Categorization

Shi, L and Horvath, S (2006) Unsupervised learning with random forest predictors, *Journal of Computational and Graphical Statistics*, **15** (1), pp 118–38

Sonnad, N (2016) [accessed 15 August 2016] Easy questions that computers are terrible at answering [Online] http://qz.com/745104/easy-questions-that-computers-are-terrible-at-answering (2/8/2016)

Bibliography

Spam Bayes source code [Online] http://spambayes.sourceforge.net/

Standage, T (2016) [accessed 15 August 2016] Why Artificial Intelligence is Enjoying a Renaissance [Online] http://www.economist.com/blogs/economist-explains/2016/07/economist-explains (15/7/2016)

Stanford University Deep Learning Tutorial [Online] http://deeplearning.stanford.edu/tutorial/ (by A Ng *et al*)

Tracy, A (2016) [accessed 15 August 2016] Suddenly Everybody is Obsessed with AI – Even if Investors Don't Get It [Online] http://www.vanityfair.com/news/2016/06/silicon-valley-artificial-intelligence-obsession (29/6/2016)

Vanian, J (2016) [accessed 15 August 2016] Artificial Intelligence Still Has a Ways [Sic] To Go Before Machines Can Behave Like Humans [Online] http://fortune.com/2016/05/23/google-baidu-research-artificial-intelligence/?xid=smartnews (23/5/16)

Wakefield, J (2016) [accessed 15 August 2016] Would You Want to Talk to a Machine? [Online] www.bbc.co.uk/news/technology-36225980 (4/8/2016)

Zaknich, A (2003) *Neural Networks for Intelligent Signal Processing*, World Scientific Publishing, Singapore

Zhu, X (2008) Semi-Supervised Learning Literature Survey, Computer Sciences, TR 1530, *University of Wisconsin, Madison, WI* [Online] http://pages.cs.wisc.edu/~jerryzhu/pub/ssl_survey.pdf

INDEX

Note: The index is filed in alphabetical, word-by-word order. Numbers and acronyms within main headings are filed as spelt out. Page locators in *italics* denote information contained within a Figure or Table; locators in roman numerals denote information within the Preface.

A/B web testing 127, 131, 132, 146, 161, 162
AC2 191
acquiescence bias 12, 57, 58
actions 218, 222
AdaBoost.M1 (adaptive boosting) 194, 195–96, 231
adaptive choice-based modelling 120
Adaptive Conjoint Analysis (ACA) 76, 156–57
advertisements 140–44, 152–54
AID model 191
AIDA model 218
Akaike Information Criterion (AIC) 45, 48, 54
allocating purchases (choices) 114, 124–25
American Express (Amex) 91–92, *129*
analysis *see* conjoint analysis; correspondence analysis; discriminant analysis; driver analysis; drug sale analysis; gains analysis; HB analysis (hierarchical Bayesian analysis)
analysis of variance (ANOVA) 230
artificial intelligence, defined 4–5, 229
attributes
  brand as 121–22, 131, 158, 160
  contingent 125
  levels of 59, 69–71, 81–82, 89, 92–94, 95, 101, 128–30, 137–38, 140–41
  sensory 119, 125

base case (reference case) 96, 106, 109, 110, *111, 112, 113*, 116, 117
Bayes, Reverend Thomas 201–02
Bayes Nets (Bayesian Networks) 33, 37, 50, 166, 197, 200–28, 232–35
Bayesian Information Criterion (BIC) 45, 48, 54
best practice 94–97, 122–23
bi-plots 230
bias 11–13, 53
  acquiescence 57, 58
Bohr, Niels xiii
boosted decision stumps 192–94

boosting 192–94, 231, 232
  see also AdaBoost.M1 (adaptive boosting)
Box, George 48
brand 32, 34–35, 93, 121–22, 128, 131, 154–55, 158, 160, 223–26
brand awareness 34–35
brand identity 119

cannibalization 79, 83
cards 62, *68*, 127
CART (C&RT) 166, 191, 195
Case 5 analysis *see* Thurstone's Case 5 method
categorical data 45
categorical variables 53, 166, 172, 181, 195, 199, 200
C4.5/ C5 191
CHAID (chi-squared automatic interaction detector) 166, 168–72, 181, 191, 195
change requirements 28, 51, 92
child variable 203, 217
children's apparel 223–26
Choice-Based-Conjoint (CBC) 93, 120, 156, 157–59, 161–62
Citibank 91, 92, *129*
classification *see* classification rules; classification trees; correct classification
classification rules 184–86, 195
classification trees 38, 165–96, 200, 211–12, 227, 230, 231, 234–35
clustering xi, 230
  see also TwoStep
CME (continuing medical education) 148, 149
communications 19, 131, 132, 161, *214, 215, 216, 220*
  see also messages; telecommunications
competitive advantage 214–15, *216*
competitors (competition) 19
  conjoint analysis 79, 130, 160–61
  discrete choice modelling 83, 90, 91–92, 95–96, 110, 112, 117, 122–23, 131, 233–34
complex networks 204

Index

computers 4, 16, 18, 21, 32, 70, 235–36
   discrete choice modelling 60–61, 89–90
   HB analysis 73–74, 123, 229–30
conditional probabilities 205, 206, 207, 210, 230
conjoint analysis 13, 62, 67, 75–77, 78, 79–80, 81, 83–84, 127–64, 233
   and brand 93
   partial profile 156
   and share of preference 34
constant, the 71, 92, 93, 94, 122, *129*, 137, 198
consumers 5, 22, 89
   see also customer satisfaction; customers
contingent attributes 125
continuing medical education (CME) 148, 149
continuous data 46
continuous predictor variables 181
convergence 73, 101
correct classification 45, 46–47, 53, *193*
correct prediction levels 47, *214*, 215, 217, 222
correlations 43–45, 54, 68–69, 128, 198, 211, 232
   see also zero correlation
correspondence analysis 230
counting 14, 22
cross-folded validation 217
CRT (CART) 166, 191, *195*
cultural skew 12, 58
cumulative figures (statistics) 186, *187*, *188*, 189
current case *108*, 109, *115*, 116, 117
customer lists 16–17
customer satisfaction 10, 11, 23, 62, 150, *151*, 221, 222
customers 15–17, 131, 132, 147–52, 161, 162
   see also customer satisfaction; touchpoints

D-optimal designs 90
DAGs 202
data 6–8, 22, 28–31, 45–46, 48–49, 98
   historical 11–12, *13*, 14, 23, 25, 32–33, 51, 56, 75
   ordinal 200
   patterns in 32–33, 38, 234
   ratio-level 65, 77, 80, 149, 231, 232
   scanner 167
   transaction 14, 25, 32–33, 51
   see also sample errors; data lakes; data mining; data quality; data swamps; data warehouses

data lakes 7
data mining 14, 33, 201, 204
data quality 7, 22
data swamps 7
data warehouses 7, 31, 32
database management 16–17, 167–68, 174, 175, 177, 181, 185, 186
de Bono, Edward xiii
debit cards 91–92
decision stumps 191–94
demographic information 10, 167–72, 174
   see also children's apparel
designed experiments 66–71, 82
dietary fibre market 133–36
direct-mail 79, 83, 137–40, 146
direct measurement 8–9
direct questions 12, 24, 56
directed acyclic diagrams 202
   see also Bayes Nets (Bayesian Networks)
discrete choice modelling 13–14, 52, 60–61, 67, 74, 78–79, 81, 83, 85–126, 233–34
   and attributes 128, *129*
   and share of preference 34
   and surveys 17–18
   and utility 130
discriminant analysis 230
donation generation 8
driver analysis 213
drug sales analysis 19, 49, 86, *87*, 114, 124, 142, *143*, 148–52
dummy coding 199

early school age clothing market 223–24, *225*
efficiency calculation 189
elasticity 99
election data 28–29, 39
engineers 71, 95, 156
ensemble learning (models) 174, 194, 195, 229
enterprise class software 21
envelopes 137, *138*, *139*, 140
errors
   data 28–29
   discrete choice modelling 103–04
   in measurement 71, 94, 104
   in pricing 155
   sample 38–41, 53, 103
   and significance testing 42–43
   Type I 36, 52
   Type II 37
   see also margin of error
estimation optimism 135–36

evaluation 35–36, 45–50
Excel 70, 81, 86–88, 107, 109, 114–17, 136, 152
Excel Ribbon 87, 88, 114–15, 117, 152
expectation setting 50–51, 54
experimental methods 10, 12, 23, 24, 34–35, 52, 55–84, 89–90, 233
    see also conjoint analysis; discrete choice modelling; HB analysis (hierarchical Bayesian analysis); market simulator programs (market simulations); MaxDiff (maximum difference scaling); Q-Sort method; Thurstone's Case 5 method
explained variance 45, 47, 49, 53
exponentiation 107
extrapolation 96, 99
extreme responses 57–58
extreme values 144

farmers 71, 156
focus groups 38, 41–42, 53
font *138*, *139*, 140, *141*, *143*
forecasting 4, 15, 19, 25, 125, 201
    see also discrete choice modelling; market simulator programs (market simulations)
fractional factorial orthogonal designs 69, 82
full profile conjoint analysis 62, 76–77, 79, 81, 127, 133–36, 158, 159, 233

gains analysis 184, 186–89, 231
Gallup, George (Gallup Poll) 29
General Social Survey 37
goals 48, 50–51, 66, 165, 190
'good results' 48–49
grandparent variable 203
graphical analytical methods 202, 227
    see also Bayes Nets (Bayesian Networks)
graphical user interfaces (GUIs) 21
gross revenues 99, 111, 112, *113*, *116*, 117
growth curve 43–44
Gumbel distribution 103–04

Hadoop 7
HB analysis (hierarchical Bayesian analysis) 72–74, 78, 82–83, 98, 101–02, 104, 107, 123–24
headlines 79, *139*, 140, *141*, *143*
hierarchical models 218–19
HIPPO (highest paid person's opinion) 140
historical data (models) 11–12, *13*, 14, 23, 25, 32–33, 51, 56, 75
hold-out samples 49–50, 54, 217

if-then statements (rules) 184–85, 186, 194, 195, 200, 227, 231
implicit views 11–13, 23–24
in-depth interviews 38
inelasticity 99, 112
infant clothing market 223–24, *225*
inflection points 99, *100*
information 6–7, 22, 37
information criteria 45, 48, 53–54
information propagation 212
insurance sector 79, 83, 91, 137, 147, 161, 162
interactions 154–56, 158, 170, 195, 234
interpolation 59, 95, 121, 133
interval-level data 45–46
interviews 9, 10–11, 23, 31, 38, 41, 57, 147
    online (web) 60, 64, *65*, 68, 159

Japan 58
JC Penney 32
J48 20, 191

Kahneman, Daniel 105

latent variables 221
Latin America 58
Lavidge and Steiner model 219
Law of Comparative Judgements, The, see Thurstone's Case 5 method
Let's Make a Deal 205–10
letters 137, *138*, *139*, 140
levels, attribute 59, 69–71, 81–82, 89, 92–94, 95, 101, 128–30, 137–38, 140–41
leverage analysis (lift analysis) see gains analysis
linear additive models 198
linear regression 50
Literary Digest 29
logos *141*, *143*
loyalty 220, 221, 222
loyalty programmes 167, *224*
loyalty scores 192

McFadden, Daniel 74
machine learning xi–xii, *13*, 21, 74, 173–74, 236
    see also HB analysis (hierarchical Bayesian analysis)
margin of error 39
market share 11, 33, 84, 86, 125, 136, 165, 191–92, 234
market simulations 10, 23, 34, 126, 234
market simulator programs 63–64, 70, 86–90, 107–17, 124, 126, 133–36, 142–44, 162, 234

marketplace, understanding of 15–16, 84, 94, 106, 121, 122, 160
marketplace scenarios (market scenarios) 60–61, 81, 88, 89, 93–94, 96, 98, 104–05, 120–21
Markov blanket 204, 213
mathematical models 5, 10, 46
MaxDiff (maximum difference scaling) 13, 52, 64–65, 66, 78, 80, 81–82, 84, 163, 230, 231, 232
MD-PREF 230
measurement 8–11, 71–72, 94, 95–96, 98, 99, 103, 104, 122
MECE 183–86
message optimization simulators 142–44, 152–54, 233
message profiles 137
messages 136–47, 152–54
    see also message optimization simulators
Microsoft
    Excel 70, 81, 86–88, 107, 109, 114–17, 136, 152
    Excel Ribbon 87, 88, 114–15, 117, 152
    PowerPoint 70, 133–36
missing values 181, 200
mobile phone towers 5, 110–14
Monty Hall problem 205–10
Morwitz, V. 56
mother logit 166, 199
multinomial logit 166, 199
mutually exclusive and completely exhaustive 185–86

NCSS 20
networks 201, 226
    Bayesian 33, 37, 50, 166, 197, 200–28, 232–35
    neural 166, 228, 230, 235, 236
    simple 204, *214*
newsletters 148, 150
nodes 176, 177, 178, 181, 184, 185, 186, 206–08, 217
non-compensatory theories 118, 120
Nonameo 154–55, 156
'none of these' option 60, 81, 97, 109, 111, 123
NORC 37
normal distribution 103–04
norms 56
null hypothesis 36, 52

Ockham's Razor 94
online interviews 60, 68, 159
    see also web interviews
optimal recoding 100, 172, 189, 191, 192, 195, 200

optimism, of estimation 135–36
optimizers 117
ordinal data 45, 46, 200
orthogonal designs 69, 82, 89–90
outcomes 9–10, 11, 60
overfitting 50, 218, 235, 236

parent variable 203, 217
parents 223–26
partial least squares (PLS) path models 192, 202, 217, 221
partial profile conjoint method 76–77, 156
pen production 132–33
pharmaceutical industry 148–52
    see also drug sales analysis
photos (pictures) 140, *141–42*, *143*
point of inflection (inflection points) 99, *100*
PowerPoint 70, 133–36
pre-teen clothing market 223–24, *225*, 226
precursors (surrogates), for behaviour 9–10, 23
prediction 4, 21, 47, *214*, 215, 217, 222
predictor variables
    Bayes Nets 198–99, 204, 213, 215, 227, 232
    classification trees 173, 176, 181, 192, 211, 231
preferences 9, 11, 23
preset values 117
price elasticity 99
price vs share 98–100
pricing 97–100, 123, 133, 155–56, *214*
print advertisement 140–44, 152–54
privacy issues 11, 14
probabilities, conditional 205, 206, 207, 210, 230
product line synergies 79, 83
product profiles 62, 127–28, 156, 158, 159
products
    awareness of 9, 34–35, 95, 122, 125
    distribution of 34–35, 125
    sensory 119, 125
    see also product line synergies; product profiles; single-product optimization
project planning 27–54
projections 15–18, 25, 29, 31, 84
prospect theory 105–06, 135
psoriasis treatment 193–94, 231

Q-Sort method 13, 52, 60, 65–66, 78, 80, 81–82, 84, 163, 232
    see also Thurstone's Case 5 analysis
qualitative research 94, 95
QUEST 191
questions and answers 10–11, 12, *13*, 14, 23, 24–25, 27, 33, 51–52, 56

see also socially desirable responses (social desirability); straight-line responses (straight lining)
Quiet Financial Services (QFS) case study 91–93, *129*

R (program) 21
R-squared statistic 43, 44, 47
R statistic 43, 44
random forests 173–76, 192, 195, 231, 232
random samples 43
ratings scales (scaled ratings) 9, 12, 33, 46, 55–59, 67, 75, 80, 88–89, 147–48
ratio-level data 46, 65, 77, 80, 149, 231, 232
RCA 154–55
reference case (base case) 96, 106, 109, *110*, *111*, *112*, *113*, 116, 117
reference value 106
regression 43, 44, 47, 50, 166, 191–92, 198–99, 210–11, 212, 221
replication 72
representative (definition) 31
reservation prices 99
results 48–50, 54
revenue neutral 99
   see also gross revenues
Roosevelt, Franklin 29
root-mean-squared error (RMSE) 48, 54

s-curve 105–07, 109, 124, 130, 210–11
sample errors (sampling error) 38–42, 53, 103
sample frames 29–31, 51
sample size 38–41, 42, 53
sampling 148, 150–51
   see also hold-out samples; random samples; sample errors (sampling error); sample size
SAS 20
Savant, Marilyn vos 205
Savvy Sylvia 226
Sawtooth Software 119–20
scaled ratings (ratings scales) 9, 12, 33, 46, 55–59, 67, 75, 80, 88–89, 147–48
scanner data 167
screening 17–18, 203–04
self-effects curve 98–99
sensory products (attributes) 119, 125
service delivery optimization 147–52, 162
share 98–100, 107, 109, 114, 124, 135, 192, 214–15, 221
share of acceptance 52, 63, 64, 84, *134*
share of preference 34, 35, 86, 87, *108*, 120, 125, *135*, 158, 234
significance testing 37–38, 42–43, 52–54
   see also statistical significance
silent donation drives 8

simple networks 204, *214*
single-product optimization 132–36
social media 31
socially desirable responses (social desirability) 12, 58, 128
software programs 20–21, 43, 191, 195, 226, 227
   see also Adaptive Conjoint Analysis (ACA); Choice-Based-Conjoint (CBC); Hadoop; market simulator programs; MaxDiff (maximum difference scaling); message optimization simulators; Sawtooth Software; SPSS
solver, the 117
Sony 35, 119, 154–55
spouse variable 203
SPSS 20, 48
stakeholders 50
Stat 20
Statistica 20
statistical analysis software 20–21
statistical power 36–37, 52
statistical significance 36, 37, 52–53, 171–72, 173, 176–77, 178, 190
   see also significance testing
stimulus items 66
stored data *see* historic data (models)
straight-line responses (straight lining) 12, 57–58, 99, *100*
straight-lines relationships 43, 44, 54, 105, 109, *130*, 198, 211
structural equation models 192, 202
surrogates (precursors), for behaviour 9–10, 23
surveys 17–18, 33, 37, 59, 65, 66, 147
synergistic 170, 195
Systat 20

taglines *141*, *143*
target variables
   Bayes Nets 202, 204, 211, 213, 214, 215, *216*, 217, 222, 227
   classification trees 194, 198–99, 200
telecommunications 22, 84, 147, 161, 162
testing
   A/B 127, 131, 132, 146, 161, 162
   direct-mail 146
   significance 37–38, 42–43, 52–54
   see also statistical significance
text 140, *141*
theoretical models 11, 13, 14, 23, 25
Thurstone's Case 5 method *13*, 60, 65–66, 77, 78, 81, 163, 165, 230, 232
   see also Q-Sort method

Index

TinyCo 99, *100*
toddler clothing market 223–24, *225*
touch points 147, *149*, 162
trade-off methods *see* experimental methods
transaction data 14, 25, 32–33, 51
transportation sector 74, 91
trust, brand 223–26
TwoStep 48
Type I error 36, 52
Type II error 37
typical growth curve 43–44

UK 167
United States (US) 14, 29, 58, 91, 99, 148, 167, 172
user benefits 95, 122
utility 59–60, 86, 88, 105–07, 109, 121, 124, 130, 135, 160

validation 49–50, 54, 217–18
value of information 37
values 106, 117, 181, 200
variables 5, 68–69, 170, *180*, 190, 194–95, 202–04, 210, 212
    categorical 53, 166, 172, 181, 199, 200
    latent 221
    predictor
        Bayes Nets 198–99, 213, 215, 227, 232

        classification trees 173, 176, 181, 192, 211, 231
        random forests *175*, 176
    target
        Bayes Nets 211, 213, 214, 215, *216*, 217, 222, 227
        classification trees 198–99, 200
variance 47, 213
    explained 45, 49, 53
    see also analysis of variance (ANOVA)
variations 59, 70, 71, 94, 122, 144–45
verbatim comments 14–15

wealth index *175*, *180*, 181, *183*
web interviews 64, *65*
    see also online interviews
websites 119–20, 131–32, 136–37, 144–46, *147*, *149*, 161
Weka 20, 21
Wilkinson, Leland 212
William of Ockham 94
win-loss matrix 77

Yudkowsky, Eliezer 210

zero correlation 89, 128, 199